STRONG REPRESENTATIONS

STRONG REPRESENTATIONS

Narrative and Circumstantial Evidence in England

Alexander Welsh

The Johns Hopkins University Press
Baltimore and London

© 1992 The Johns Hopkins University Press
All rights reserved
Printed in the United States of America

The Johns Hopkins University Press
701 West 40th Street
Baltimore, Maryland 21211-2190
The Johns Hopkins Press Ltd., London

The paper used in this book meets the minimum requirements of American National Standard for Information Sciences—Permanence of Paper for Printed Library Materials, ANSI Z39.48-1984.

Library of Congress Cataloging-in-Publication Data

Welsh, Alexander.
    Strong representations : narrative and circumstantial evidence in England / Alexander Welsh.
        p.   cm.
    Includes bibliographical references and index.
    ISBN 0-8018-4271-9
    1. English literature—19th century—History and criticism. 2. Narration (Rhetoric) 3. English literature—18th century—History and criticism. 4. Evidence, Circumstantial, in literature. 5. Evidence, Circumstantial—England. 6. Mimesis in literature. 7. Law and literature. I. Title.
PR468.N29W44   1991
820.9′ 12—dc20   91-30039

FOR RUTH

Contents

Preface

ACCORDING TO A MISCHIEVOUS TALE written by Vol-
taire in 1745, in other times or distant places one could get in
trouble for reaching a conclusion based on circumstantial evidence or
for claiming to know about something one had not directly seen or
been told. Voltaire's hero, Zadig, risks being flogged and sent to Siberia,
merely for describing quite accurately the Babylonian queen's dog and
the king's horse without having set eyes on either. Once Zadig explains
how it is possible to infer the appearance of those animals from some
slight circumstances he has noted, he is let off—but not without being
scolded by his judges and forfeiting his gold for legal expenses.

This book argues that strong representations, which make the facts
speak for themselves as Zadig did, became the single most prominent
form of narrative in the later eighteenth and nineteenth centuries. In
any era a narrative amounts to a way of thinking, a process of sorting
things out temporally, for many purposes. Yet for about a century and
a half, narrative played an especially ambitious and public role in the
West, and this phenomenon really has to do with the dominance of a
particular kind of narrative. In this period, narrative consisting of carefully managed circumstantial evidence, highly conclusive in itself and
often scornful of direct testimony, flourished nearly everywhere—not
only in literature but in criminal jurisprudence, natural science, natural
religion, and history writing itself.

The strong representations examined here are confined to England,
but obviously even the surviving written narratives are pretty much
inexhaustible. At the same time, circumstantial evidence can only be
reviewed in some detail, so a careful selection of texts is necessary. I
have deliberately selected some texts that are well known, but I have
grouped them by field—criminal trials, novels, character criticism that
transforms Shakespeare's plays into narrative, some poetry, natural
science and religion—to give an idea of the wider sampling that is
possible. To preserve a sense of chronology—or to comprise a model
history—each chapter draws on both eighteenth- and nineteenth-cen-

tury texts except the last, which concerns the partial repudiation of circumstances in favor of testimony once again, in three texts that anticipate modernism and thus make their own literary-historical comment on evidence. The track taken by rhetoric at a particular time in history cannot readily be followed without some understanding of the uses to which the rhetoric is put. Were it not for some well-advertised needs of the time—to prosecute crime, to shore up the tenets of Christianity, to discover the hidden motions of matter and the history of living things, or to construe life morally as a trial and thereafter defend against a general guilt—addiction to strong representations probably would never have come about. I try to touch on some of these themes along the way; but one salutary lesson of the project has been that rhetorical and thematic approaches to narrative are inseparable.

The main reason for attaching an intensifier, "strong," to these representations is their endeavor to prove something—to arrive at conviction in a criminal case or acquittal for all heroes and heroines in novels; to demonstrate the existence of a future life or the geological transformation of the earth. Whereas for Cicero and Quintilian the methods of narrative and of proof might seem distinct, for the Enlightenment a narrative arranged from circumstantial evidence became the most favored proof of all. But such representations are also strong in the sense of strenuous, claiming to encompass more than can ever be experienced at first hand. Narratives that feature indirect evidence and play down testimony have surprising rhetorical advantages: they can invite listeners or readers to share in the work of drawing inferences and thus manage to be flatteringly persuasive. They are conclusive, but above all, perhaps, didactic. Because they do describe matters beyond the power of witnessing, however—Zadig's case exactly—their sheer evidentiary flair may win both admiration and distrust. Two recent protestations from scientists come to mind that confirm my sense that strong representations are no longer trusted. Stephen Jay Gould, in *Time's Arrow, Time's Cycle* (1987), protests that a single classic representation of nineteenth-century geology, Charles Lyell's uniformitarian theory, dominated the science for a hundred years largely by force of rhetoric; and J. Allan Hobson, in *The Dreaming Brain* (1988), contends that Freudian theory has effectively blocked or obscured dream research in his field of neurophysiology for much of the twentieth century. These two scientists seem to believe that their hypotheses of punctuated equilibrium and activation synthesis, respectively, can supplant Lyell's and Freud's theories without recourse to any such overbearing rhetoric.

Of immediate concern to students of literature is our own recourse as contemporary thinkers when pondering from day to day (like scientists, lawyers, or divines) the evidence of things not seen. In writing this book, I confess I have been haunted by *Hamlet*—not by the ghost or the hero, but by the play, which lives for me before and after the rhetoric of circumstances I have tried to exhume here. That famous play registers some important differences between unnatural and natural deaths, differences at the intersection of evidence and experience. I mean that *Hamlet* shows we cannot take murder for granted the way we can death. Thus murder always raises the evidentiary question—stridently in a forensic scene, hauntingly perhaps most of the time. But lest this preface give way to Hamlet-like meditation, let me briefly register a few more buoyant forms of indebtedness. What little I know about the common law is due to a Rockefeller Humanities Fellowship that enabled me to spend eight months reading in the British Library and the Institute for Advanced Legal Studies in London, together with more weeks in the Research and Law libraries of the University of California, Los Angeles. The project also owes much to the generosity of the UCLA Research Committee and the College Institute, to regular engagement with students and colleagues at UCLA, and to a sabbatical leave for writing. The Rockefeller Foundation further provided a month's stay at its Study Center in Bellagio: I particularly have to thank Giana Celli and the late Roberto Celli for making that visit as pleasant as it was productive. Portions of the book first appeared in the journals *Representations* ("The Evidence of Things Not Seen: Justice Stephen and Bishop Butler," 22 [Spring 1988]: 60–88) and *New Literary History* ("Burke and Bentham on the Narrative Potential of Circumstantial Evidence," 21 [1990]: 607–27), and I thank the editors for permission to incorporate the revised texts here. John H. Langbein and A. R. Braunmuller reviewed drafts of different chapters and commented very helpfully. Robert Fletcher tracked down some additional materials, and he and Jeanette Gilkison significantly improved the typescript by redoing it entirely. As often before, Ruth Bernard Yeazell's judicious reading of my pages has been a distinct trial but also a kindness for which I am most grateful, and to her I dedicate this modest attempt to get a hold on strong representations.

STRONG REPRESENTATIONS

1

Stories of Things Not Seen

Upon my secure houre thy Uncle stole
With iuyce of cursed Hebona in a viall,
And in the porches of my eares did poure
The leaprous distilment.

— A Ghost, 1604

For the matter of Proofs, you may consider that Impoisonment, of all Offences, is most secret, even so secret, that if in all cases of Impoisonment, you should require Testimony, you should as good as proclaim Impunity.

— Francis Bacon, 1616

WHETHER, ON A SUMMER DAY of 1892 in Massachusetts, Lizzie Borden wielded an ax and slaughtered her father and stepmother could not depend on whether anyone saw her do it, for no one claimed to have seen her. Nor could her innocence be accepted on her word, since the penalty for the crime was great, and since she might easily have wished she had not done it even were there no penalty. Her parents died in their own house, which she shared, and there could be little doubt that they were murdered by someone. Borden, the only suspect, was tried before the Superior Court of Bristol County on the circumstantial evidence. A trial seems an excellent way to determine what at least one person did or did not do on a certain day; many things besides murder occur without being seen, and a trial at common law is one model for finding them out. A criminal trial holds the possibility of conviction—in both senses of the word—and if it fails of conviction, that too has its ritual and psychological value.

For those who believe that verbal representation—a patently important human activity—cannot be fully comprehended without regard to the literary uses it is put to in poems, plays, and novels, the trial of *Commonwealth v. Borden* took an especially gratifying turn in the final arguments of the prosecution. The defense had been unable to show that anyone besides Borden had an opportunity to commit the murder, but the prosecutors did not have a particularly good case either: they were unable to construct the sort of connected narrative that, by gaining consent to a series of events, can make circumstantial evidence entirely convincing; and they had to meet the objection—or rather protest, since the objection had no meaning in law—that the evidence was only circumstantial. In his summing up, Hosea M. Knowlton, a future attorney general of Massachusetts, endeavored to explain the difficulty and the nature of the evidence by citing an incident from a well-known English novel. This was a hundred years ago, and Knowlton would perhaps not have ventured the same comparison today; but so confident was he of the jury's familiarity with the novel that he could introduce it with a couple of easy demonstratives—"that solitary man" and "this island." Quite possibly he waved the book at the jury at this point, as a kind of documentary proof that true inferences can be drawn from very little evidence:

> What is sometimes called circumstantial evidence is nothing in the world but a presumption of circumstances. It may be one or fifty. There is no chain about it. The word "chain" is a misnomer as applied to it. It is the presentation of circumstances from which one is irresistibly driven to the conclusion that crime has been committed. Talk about a chain of circumstances! When that solitary man had lived on this island for twenty years and believed that he was the only human being there, and that the cannibals and savages that lived around him had not found him and had not come to his island, he walked out one day on the beach, and there he saw the fresh print of a naked foot on the sand. He had no lawyer to tell him that was nothing but a circumstance. He had no distinguished counsel to urge upon his fears that there was no chain about the thing which led him to a conclusion. His heart beat fast, his knees shook beneath him, he fell to the ground in a fright, because *Robinson Crusoe knew when he saw that circumstance that a man had been there that was not himself.* It was circumstantial evidence. It was nothing but circumstantial evidence. But it satisfied *him.*[1]

Though the prosecutor's summing up is a fine tribute to the skills of Daniel Defoe, it may seem a little disarming that a work of fiction should be called upon, in a capital case, to show the jury how things not seen might nevertheless be convincingly presented to the mind by evidence. Fact or fiction aside, Knowlton did not feel that his allusion to *Robinson Crusoe* was anachronistic. He obviously assumed that Defoe's novel, first published in 1719, was still a current and classic text; possibly, too, a sense of history moved him, since in early eighteenth-century England lawyers like himself had begun to press openly the advantages of circumstantial evidence in the prosecution of crime. Knowlton sought to attach the familiarity of the novel to his own narrative, the case he had in hand as district attorney. He counted on—without necessarily calculating—the fearful excitement of discovery in the incident from *Robinson Crusoe,* which he paraphrases and then sum-

1. Quoted in John H. Wigmore, "The Borden Case," *American Law Review* 27 (1893): 837.

marizes as conviction: "it satisfied *him*." There can be a spookiness in some evidence of things not seen, in the making present of a frightening truth, and the classic discovery of the footprint in the sand might just prepare the jurors to accept the prosecution's story of what had happened in the Bordens' home. Yet Knowlton could not have been all that smart a district attorney or literary critic, because on 20 June 1893 Lizzie Borden was acquitted. Possibly the jurors appreciated the novel but felt the prosecution had become overly defensive about the evidence.

John H. Wigmore, who would shortly emerge as America's leading authority on evidence at common law, praised Knowlton's argument as "one of the most effective passages in forensic oratory."[2] One might counter that Knowlton was merely wrestling with the defense over a metaphor—"a chain of circumstances"—which had no force in law and that he lost the rhetorical match, though he could certainly have found support for his position. According to one Victorian writer on evidence, for example, "A single circumstance may raise the inference, as well as a long chain of circumstances."[3] The chain most commonly meant circumstances causally connected in a believable narrative. It connoted strong connections, links of iron, but also a story that fell apart if one of the links was broken. As with many overworked metaphors, however, its popularity owed a good deal to its vagueness. In the eighteenth century lawyers used it freely, but after some attempts to analyze what it meant, the chain began to lose its charm. The metaphor, seemingly so useful for narrative, was also said to refer to the inference from an evidentiary fact to the fact to be proved, or to the causal relation of any two events. Even Bentham, who leaned toward the last position, was not very clear about the chain.[4]

Had the jurors in *Commonwealth v. Borden* looked into a copy of *Robinson Crusoe,* they would not literally have read there of a chain of circumstances. They would have found the hero carefully fitting the evidence together with other known facts—what used to be called "natural" and "moral" presumptions, according to whether they pertained to physical or behavioral phenomena. Though the footprint in the sand is the memorable fact, the inferences surrounding it are multiple. The

---

2. Ibid. On Wigmore, see William Twining, *Theories of Evidence: Bentham and Wigmore* (Stanford: Stanford University Press, 1985).

3. J. Pitt Taylor, *A Treatise on the Law of Evidence as Administered in England and Ireland,* 2d ed., 2 vols. (London: Maxwell, 1855), 1:177. Taylor himself adduced two literary instances of judgments based on a single inference, one by Solomon (Kings 3:16–28) and another by Sancho Panza (*Don Quixote,* pt. 2, chap. 45).

4. See note 75 below.

evidentiary fact itself, under Crusoe's searching analysis, breaks into component parts:

> It happen'd one Day about Noon going towards my Boat, I was exceedingly surpriz'd with the Print of a Man's naked Foot on the Shore, which was very plain to be seen in the Sand: I stood like one Thunderstruck, or as if I had seen an Apparition; I listen'd, I look'd round me, I could hear nothing, nor see any Thing; I went up to a rising Ground to look farther; I went up the Shore and down the Shore, but it was all one, I could see no other Impression but that one, I went to it again to see if there were any more, and to observe if it might not be my Fancy; but there was no Room for that, for there was exactly the very Print of a Foot, Toes, Heel, and every Part of a Foot; how it came thither, I knew not, nor could in the least imagine.[5]

Thus Crusoe was a fine detective and a superb witness. He narrates circumstances sufficient to persuade readers of the truth of his account; he gives the place and time of day and does not forget his own first reactions, which tend to verify that he was wide awake and really saw a footprint. But he also tells of a good many inferences, beginning with his silent conclusion that the print was produced by a naked human foot.

The ranging of the narrator's thought shows that Defoe well understood the problems of reasoning from effects to causes. Each inference supposes a possible sequence of events, but not necessarily the right one. The more exhaustive the procedure for ruling out wrong inferences, the stronger will appear a sequence of cause and effect that cannot be ruled out. Despite his fears, Crusoe even returns to the shore some days later to determine whether he could have mistaken the evidence, or if the print could be that of his own foot after all. His most strained alternative hypothesis is that the devil might have made the print on purpose to frighten him, and to dispose of this hypothesis he again weighs probabilities both natural and behavioral—though the agent in question is not human:

> I consider'd that the Devil might have found out abundance of other Ways to have terrify'd me than this of the single Print of a Foot. That as I liv'd quite on the other Side of the Island, he would never have been so simple to leave a Mark in a Place where 'twas Ten Thousand to one whether I should ever see it or not, and in the Sand too, which the first

5. Daniel Defoe, *Robinson Crusoe*, ed. Michael Shinagel (New York: Norton, 1975), 121.

Surge of the Sea upon a high Wind would have defac'd entirely: All this seem'd inconsistent with the Thing it self, and with all the Notions we usually entertain of the Subtilty of the Devil.

Excluding this possibility leaves Crusoe all the more certain that "it must be some more dangerous Creature" than the devil who has left a print in the sand.[6] This conclusion ironically cuts the devil down to size and caps a stirring series of inferences. Defoe might have had his hero stumble directly on the cannibals at any point, but he is far more interested in describing how Robinson Crusoe copes with the sign of their invisible presence on the island.

Seeing is believing, but believing is seldom coterminous with seeing. A footprint stands out from the sand only as evidence of something else, and as evidence it too is subject to doubt, though seen. From its discovery many possible narratives start up, any one of which may be favored and extended for one reason or another. In the present book, I am concerned with longer narratives in roughly the two centuries bounded by the careers of Daniel Defoe and Hosea M. Knowlton; and by stories of things not seen, I mean primarily narratives for which there are no eyewitnesses or narrators in a position to tell what happened at first hand. Instead of acts of seeing and believing that are shared with readers in the form of testimony like Crusoe's, these narratives typically set forth a quantity of circumstantial evidence that is calculated to prove a certain case. Rhetorically they circumscribe testimony where possible and suggest that it is untrustworthy, and historically they for a long time outmanned and outmaneuvered mere authenticity as a criterion of effective narrative.

Robinson Crusoe provides only Crusoe's testimony—not a stroke of evidence that is not from the hero's pen. And of course it is a brilliant performance: as the character's admirer, Knowlton, exclaims, "He had no lawyer to tell him" what was evidence and what not. It was, however, a lawyer, Henry Fielding, who showed off in *The History of Tom Jones* a kind of epitome of narrative for the next 150 years—a narrative much more closely patterned on forensic debate, in which the representation of the facts was carefully managed by a narrator who was not a party to the action. Eyewitnessing and personal recollection have great advantages in narrative, particularly for the interest of the personality seeing and telling; but some aspects of behavior, such as good or bad intentions, cannot be seen, and others, such as unconscious motives, cannot be remembered. It also happens that an impersonal way of

6. Ibid., 122.

6

making representations, far from surrendering all intimacy with character, may claim to penetrate still deeper than confession. The history of narratives founded on circumstantial evidence is multifarious; and neither lawyers nor novelists nor psychologists would have pushed the evidence so far, or forged so many chains, were it not for important precedents in science and natural religion.

In the language of the Authorized Version of the Bible, the apostle Paul declared that faith was "the evidence of things not seen";[7] but from the seventeenth century through the nineteenth century in England, evidences of Christianity were enthusiastically sought in the natural world and treated with scientific respect—or weighed by such everyday reasoning as Crusoe employs, without recourse to prayer or Scripture, to dispose of his devil hypothesis. In this chapter I shall touch on these developments as necessary but stress the role of circumstantial evidence in criminal prosecution.

Making Strong Representations

An impression in the sand does not become evidence, or a sign, or a trace even, without the intervention of some fresh consciousness of it— at a minimum, say, the notice of a dog running along the beach, but certainly including the notice of shipwrecked sailors or of self-conscious savages casting looks behind them. All evidence, in short, has to be read or interpreted as such. Yet it need not be instigated by anyone or originate from a conscious act. On an island somewhere a person not wearing shoes may at any time leave a print in the sand without giving it a thought. Although most signs noticed on an average day by non-solitary persons have been deliberately planted by someone else—in the form of words, whistles, drawings, pokings, and so forth—many things that occur of themselves are only subsequently read as signs. One of the main advantages of circumstantial evidence, often remarked, is precisely this freedom from human deliberation at the origin: the ambiguities are all confined to later interpretation, which looks backward in time without the danger of being misled by anyone other than the interpreter.

As we shall see, "Circumstances cannot lie!" was a brag sometimes heard at the close of the eighteenth century—and no doubt it spoke volumes of the braggers' opinion of other people, who might lie. In

---

7. Hebrews 11:1. "Now faith is the substance of things hoped for, the evidence of things not seen."

earlier times this bias as to the trustworthiness of evidence usually took the opposite direction: unless some upright person was willing to swear to it, no apparent truth should be believed. When Robinson Crusoe entertains the thought that the devil might have planted a footprint, he supposes that circumstances might devilishly lie—and thus Crusoe's sensibility was somewhat archaic for Knowlton's purpose of generally validating circumstantial evidence, as lacking complete confidence in facts that speak for themselves. The facts conveyed by a narrative do not in any event remain in pristine condition. A narrative is a verbal account of things and does not just happen as footprints (most footprints) happen. Narratives, of one fact or many facts, are intended to be read or listened to, and this is so whether the narrative is in the first or third person—the literary type of *Robinson Crusoe* or *Tom Jones*. Persons telling stories—as the idiom commonly suggests—may lie or be mistaken, and verbal representations can be made in such a way as to prove a certain case. It is the last possibility, or narrative strategy, that interests me most. By strong representations, I mean those of the later eighteenth and nineteenth centuries that openly distrust direct testimony, insist on submitting witnesses to the test of corroborating circumstances, and claim to know many things without anyone's having seen them at all. They may be religious or legal or literary representations, as long as no devilish or miraculous interventions are admitted. They are very much of the Enlightenment, representations that mirror without mystery the Pauline evidence of things not seen.

Making strong representations can be reduced to the idea of telling stories, but only stories of a particular kind: the representation purports to be true, for one thing, and therefore in literature the expression is generally appropriate to realism. I offer "strong representations" not as a phrase occurring historically, like "circumstantial evidence," but as summarizing the rhetorical effort of certain narratives that do have a history. Even without the intensifier, the expression "to make a representation" is still current enough that some of its ordinary implications can be mentioned. For example, to make a representation ordinarily means to do so neither casually nor passionately. To remark that I ran into our friend at the corner, or that I think the butcher cheated me, can be regarded as telling a story, but it is not thought of as making a representation. Not even a surprised "I killed her" or an indignant "You cheated me," with ample direct discourse of that kind, is a representation to those effects. Rather, a representation is literally *made*; arguments need to be set forth, evidence marshaled, and words carefully put together. The substance may stir emotions both crude and delicate, but the representation should appear to be dispassionately devoted to the facts. Its colorings must all be concealed, or else of a kind—such as righteousness or heavy irony—conventionally associated with revealing the truth.

To make a representation in practice means to subordinate the facts to a conclusion that makes a difference one way or another. In other words, the representation is conclusive: if it purports to review all the facts that is because, in the opinion of the person making the representation, the facts when considered rightly all point in one direction. If someone should tell the story of an entire life, for example, it would not be a representation in this sense unless the life came to something deserved or undeserved; the particulars would have to amount to something. Next to this subordination of facts, the representation often depends upon an implicit or explicit adversary position. The idea of an opposing representation in theory warrants conclusiveness, since it is imagined that any omissions, distortions, or exaggerations will eventually be canceled out. Indeed, some streamlining of ostensibly true representations is due to the assumption of an adversarial situation that may not effectively exist.

To make a representation usually means representing the facts on someone else's behalf—there can be a slippage in the idiom itself, from representing the facts to representing a client. Representing facts for someone else makes it easier to attack or defend without causing offense; it helps direct attention away from the emotions and toward the dispassionate account of things. People need not go about telling their stories and hoping for the best; instead, the stories should be managed with a careful view to the consequences. This management obviously takes ability and experience and, above all, hard work and therefore can best be left to professionals—and a professional representation is thought to be an impressive performance in its own right. An account of things not personally seen by the maker is admittedly committed to more work than an account of things seen: in making as well as interpreting the representation, things have to be inferred—as the existence of a cow that has passed from sight behind a barn is inferred by philosophers. Most things of a mental order—feelings, memories, intentions—cannot be seen at all, moreover, and others are beyond the immediate experience of professionals representing them. Most of the events of history, as well as truths of religion and laws of nature, have never by any living person been seen. So it is not surprising that representations so hindered—so purely representational—should compensate for this state by strenuous rhetoric and come to be identified with a work ethic.

For all their rhetorical nature, strong representations ought to be placed in historical context. The need for making them, the techniques of uncovering facts, the customs of argument, the vocabulary and audience for them constantly change. In other words, one needs an institutional history or histories to comprehend them; and undoubtedly a most promising model to begin with is the common-law trial. Trials at law try very hard to ensure that facts are represented dispassionately and at the same time conclusively. Upon a true representation of the facts, in this area of human activity, depend sanctions that truly hurt—such as an execution against one's property, an assessment of damages, the inflicting of punishment, or nullification of one's expectations.[8] If the facts represented in a trial are indeed absent and unseen—as of course they must be, as far as the jury is concerned—the persons engaged in telling and reviewing the facts most certainly believe it is possible to make them present and consequential. Yet their customs of representation, which directly affect people's lives, are no more timeless than literary realism and natural religion are timeless. A way of making representations has to be thought of as a human institution like every other, constrained by habit and by history.

For the past two hundred years, irrespective of their differences, Anglo-American and Continental courts of law have put primary emphasis on true representations of the facts. This state of affairs differs markedly from the frank emphasis upon superior rhetoric among ancient authorities; the customs of ordeal, combat, or compurgation known to early medieval Europeans; the finally self-defeating methods of arriving at truth by torture and confession introduced in the twelfth century; or the original uses of the English jury trial.[9] In the history of the common law, rules of evidence and treatises on the subject burgeoned in the later eighteenth century when, for one thing, the sharp increase in the number

---

8. Cf. Paul Vinogradoff, *Common Sense in Law*, 3d ed. (London: Oxford University Press, 1959), 22–23.

9. For overviews of the history of judicial proof, see John H. Langbein, *Torture and the Law of Proof: Europe and England in the Ancient Regime* (Chicago: University of Chicago Press, 1977); and Edward Peters, *Torture* (Oxford: Blackwell, 1985). For the common law, see especially James Bradley Thayer, *A Preliminary Treatise on Evidence at the Common Law* (1898; rpt. New York: Kelley, 1969); and Langbein, "The Criminal Trial before the Lawyers," *University of Chicago Law Review* 45 (1978): 263–316.

of published law reports made modern adjectival law possible.[10] For more than a century thereafter, jurists made much of circumstantial evidence, and the claim was often made, even by those who disputed whether there was any significant difference between direct and indirect testimony, that "a consideration of the degree to which circumstances corroborate each other, and of the intrinsic probability of the matter sworn to, is a far better test of truth than any oath can possibly be."[11] It was an age in which first barristers and then law professors wrote hefty treatises, and *Wigmore on Evidence,* a work that occupies a shelf in most American law libraries today, is essentially a product of the nineteenth century.[12] Most of the tendencies that I associate with strong representations belong to this period, though the law sometimes advanced before and sometimes lagged behind other practices. The novel, for example, may be seen to come to the aid of its subjects a couple of generations before the criminal law afforded much of a defense. In the words of a recent study of the English jury, "the first great watershed in the history of trial practice was the development in Tudor times of a formal prosecution; the second was the increasing recourse to counsel and the development of a true law of evidence in the late eighteenth and early nineteenth centuries."[13]

This development could not occur in a vacuum, and the explanation for why professionals put work into making strong representations and how they theorized about them needs to be carried back at least as far as the general growth of probabilistic thinking in the seventeenth century. Authority, revealed truth, and demonstrative knowledge all came into question in late Renaissance Europe, while probabilistic thinking grew in importance, especially in the "low" sciences touching everyday life. The eclipse of testimony thus reflects the philosophy usually associated with the writings of Locke, though as a practical form of reasoning probabilism was far more multifaceted than is often credited.[14]

10. William Holdsworth, *A History of English Law,* 16 vols. (1903–66; rpt. London: Methuen, 1966), 9:222.

11. James Fitzjames Stephen, *A History of the Criminal Law of England,* 3 vols. (1883; rpt. New York: Franklin, 1964), 1:401.

12. John Henry Wigmore, *A Treatise on the Anglo-American System of Evidence,* 3d ed., 10 vols. (1940; rev. ed. by Peter Tillers, Boston: Little, Brown, 1983). Wigmore was born in 1863; the first edition of his treatise was published in 1904.

13. Thomas Andrew Green, *Verdict according to Conscience: Perspectives on the English Criminal Trial Jury, 1200–1800* (Chicago: University of Chicago Press, 1985), 267.

14. See Barbara J. Shapiro, *Probability and Certainty in Seventeenth-Century England: A*

With physical science chiefly in mind, Ian Hacking has made a case for a watershed in the seventeenth century between medieval appeals to testimony and authority and the modern regard for the evidence of things: "Testimony is supported by witnesses, and authority is conferred by ancient learning. *People* provide the evidence of testimony and authority. What was lacking, was the evidence provided by *things*."[15] A fresh determination to look closely at things, needless to say, could heighten awareness of the problems of representing things not seen—because their existence had to be inferred, because they had occurred at a prior time, or because in the nature of things some were unseeable. Well into the nineteenth century, those who argued from probability in law and religion tended to present their method apologetically, because the sanctions they contemplated—before or after death—continued to bring home the desirability of certainty in both fields of proof. Representations had to be made strong to overcome understandable preferences for proofs that could not be disputed.

Hacking stresses the influence of the Port Royal *Logic*, translated into English in 1717, and there were other important influences on probabilistic thinking from the early Enlightenment in France, particularly in the field of history.[16] Locke himself wrote of history as severely limited by human testimony, in his chapter on the degrees of assent: "What has no other Evidence than the single Testimony of one only Witness must stand or fall by his only Testimony, whether good, bad, or indifferent."[17] If testimony was perforce to be distrusted, then greater reliance had to be placed on circumstantial evidence, even if its proofs stopped short of certainty. In no field of inquiry was this conversion

---

Study of the Relationships between Natural Science, Religion, History, Law, and Literature (Princeton: Princeton University Press, 1983); Lorraine Daston, *Classical Probability in the Enlightenment* (Princeton: Princeton University Press, 1988); and Douglas Lane Patey, *Probability and Literary Form: Philosophic Theory and Literary Practice in the Augustan Age* (Cambridge: Cambridge University Press, 1984), 1–62. Robert Newsom, *A Likely Story: Probability and Play in Fiction* (New Brunswick: Rutgers University Press, 1988), while not a historical study, ranges over some of the same materials.

15. Ian Hacking, *The Emergence of Probability: A Philosophical Study of Early Ideas about Probability, Induction, and Statistical Inference* (1975; rpt. Cambridge: Cambridge University Press, 1984), 32.

16. Ernst Cassirer credited Bayle's *Dictionary* for portraying history as a problem of evidence and exposing the circularity of unexamined appeals to authority: see *The Philosophy of the Enlightenment*, trans. Fritz C. A. Koelln and James P. Pettegrove (Princeton: Princeton University Press, 1951), 201–9.

17. John Locke, *An Essay concerning Human Understanding*, ed. Peter H. Nidditch (Oxford: Clarendon, 1975), 664.

to probability more remarkable than in so-called natural religion, since Christianity values its scriptures and the testimony of its saints so highly and places so much stake in things not seen. Yet natural, as opposed to revealed, religion became perhaps the single most respectable movement for Christian doctrine in England for two centuries. Thus Joseph Butler, in *The Analogy of Religion* of 1736, frames one of the earliest uses of the phrase "circumstantial evidence" itself:

> No one who is serious can possibly think these things to be nothing, if he considers the Importance of collateral things, and even of lesser Circumstances, in the Evidence of Probability, as distinguished, in Nature, from the Evidence of Demonstration. In many Cases indeed it seems to require the truest Judgment, to determine with Exactness the Weight of circumstantial Evidence: but it is very often altogether as convincing, as That, which is the most express and direct.[18]

Butler's earnest didacticism and acceptance of this burden exemplify the force of character with which representations may have to be made, in pursuit of "the truest Judgment" and "Exactness" in dealings of this world. His idiosyncratic voice remained a popular one for serious persons until the end of the Victorian age, and I shall return to his *Analogy* and its argument against death in connection with evidence for murder.

The conclusive nature of strong representations is usually apparent in treatises on natural religion, whether directed to the existence of a future life, as in Butler, or to the design of the created universe, as in many more books. Such treatises were implicitly argued on behalf of others—on behalf of Christians who wished to believe and for doctrines by no means invented by the writers. Some common probabilistic arguments, fully bent on a true representation of the facts, were construed as alternative grounding for religious faith, and these contained advice on the nature of evidence very similar to what would appear in law treatises. Here are examples of the language of two posthumously published works, each among the earliest of the kind in its field. The first, by John Wilkins, bishop of Chester, was published in 1675—and though the argument is based on probability, that date is still well in advance of Locke's *Essay* of 1690. Wilkins's *Natural Religion* was frankly committed to the principle that the existence of God cannot strictly be demonstrated. But no more can any matter of fact be demonstrated:

18. Joseph Butler, *The Analogy of Religion, Natural and Revealed, to the Constitution and Course of Nature* (London: Knapton, 1736), 399; see also 375.

13

From which I infer this. That it is not, ought not to be, any prejudice to the Truth or Certainty of any thing, that it is not to be made out by such kinds of proofs, of which the nature of that thing is not capable, provided it be capable of satisfactory proofs of another kind.

When a thing is capable of a good proof in any kind, men ought to rest satisfy'd in the best evidence for it, which that kind of thing will bear, and beyond which better could not be expected, supposing it were true.[19]

Though this is a work of natural religion, historians of the law may hear in these lines the cadences of the so-called best-evidence rule, as it was formulated in the same era—and not altogether surprisingly, since, though cherished by the common law as its own, the rule actually goes back to Aristotle.[20] The second text is by Geoffrey Gilbert, chief baron of the Exchequer, and was published posthumously in Dublin in 1754. *The Law of Evidence*—the first treatise on the subject in the common law—is a short work at least partly devoted to the principle of probability and acknowledging the authority of Locke on its first page. Here *is* the best-evidence rule, in terms very like those of Wilkins's religious work:

> The first therefore, and most signal Rule, in Relation to Evidence, is this, That a Man must have the utmost Evidence, the Nature of the Fact is capable of; For the Design of the Law is to come to rigid Demonstration in Matters of Right, and there can be no Demonstration of a Fact without the best Evidence that the Nature of the Thing is capable of. . . . For if it be plainly seen in the Nature of the Transaction, that there is some more Evidence that doth not appear, the very not producing of it is a Presumption, that it would have detected something more than appears already, and therefore the Mind does not acquiesce in any thing lower than the utmost Evidence the Fact is capable of.[21]

Once again the strenuousness of making representations is apparent. By sticking with the language of demonstration—a trial must "come to rigid Demonstration"—in an admittedly probabilistic frame of argument, Gilbert registers the stern demand for conclusiveness in a court of law. In one way or another, any sense of the inadequacy of proof must be surmounted if a verdict is to be reached on the best evidence

---

19. John [Wilkins], *Of the Principles and Duties of Natural Religion* (London: Bassett, 1675), 25.

20. Cf. Aristotle, *Nicomachean Ethics*, 1.3.

21. [Geoffrey Gilbert], *The Law of Evidence* (London: Owen, 1756), 4–5.

available. Blackstone praised this "excellent treatise" in his *Commentaries* and followed it closely in his own brief discussion of evidence.[22]

In eighteenth-century law the virtues of circumstantial evidence were first celebrated by the prosecution in criminal cases. In Johnson's *Dictionary* of 1755, the second definition of the word "circumstance" alone reads, "The adjuncts of a fact, which make it more or less criminal; or make an accusation more or less probable"; and it would have to be said that the phrase "circumstantial evidence" has been popularly associated with crime ever since. Prosecution was conducted by barristers appointed by the Crown for the trial, who thus represented the state and indirectly the victims of crime. Also, instruction in the nature of evidence, for the benefit of the jury, could be offered only by the prosecution or the bench. Lawyers were only gradually permitted to represent the prisoner — as the defendant in a criminal trial was invariably called — and only after 1760 were they allowed to cross-examine witnesses on behalf of the prisoner; they were not strictly allowed to address the jury until 1836, when full counsel was ceded to prisoners by statute, over the protests of the sitting judges.[23] Thus circumstances typically told against the individual brought to trial, as Johnson's definition of the word implies. All this while, the advocates of natural religion were studying the circumstantial evidence for the tenets of Christianity, and this scarcely in isolation from the law and criminal prosecution. Many of the formal essays and books on evidence for the next hundred years were written by clergymen, as well as by lawyers and philosophers, and these were frankly of interest to all three kinds of professionals. To cite only the most obvious writer on evidence who influenced opinion in more than one field, William Paley enjoyed a large professional and popular readership for more than half a century, well into the early Victorian years. Paley was mainly known for his books on natural theology — which seem to have inspired nearly as much scientific work as devotional studies in England. But *The Principles of Moral and Political Philosophy*, first published in 1785, also reached many editions, and his chapter on crime and punishment was debated back and forth by lawyers and politicians for three decades. Most especially this chapter was cited for the aphorism, "Circumstances cannot lie," which Paley did not

22. William Blackstone, *Commentaries on the Laws of England,* vol. 3 (Oxford: Clarendon, 1768), 367n.

23. 6 & 7 Will. 4. c. 114. See Glanville Williams, *The Proof of Guilt: A Study of the English Criminal Trial,* 3d ed. (1963; rpt. London: Stevens, 1979), 7–8; and Langbein, "Criminal Trial before the Lawyers," 307–14.

invent. "I do not mean that juries should indulge conjectures, should magnify suspicions into proofs, or even that they should weigh probabilities in *gold scales*," he wrote, with studied moderation,

> but when the preponderance of evidence is so manifest as to persuade every private understanding of the prisoner's guilt; when it furnishes that degree of credibility, upon which men decide and act in all other doubts, and which experience hath shown they may decide and act upon with sufficient safety: to reject such proof, from an insinuation of uncertainty that belongs to all human affairs, and from a general dread lest the charge of innocent blood should lie at their doors, is a conduct which, however natural to a mind studious of its own quiet, is authorized by no considerations of rectitude or utility.

Paley was repeating, at this point, a position that had been stated over and over again about the validity of conclusions that were highly probable though not certain. His trust in providence knew no bounds, and his complacency seems astonishing today, for he praised virtually anything that was common practice or accepted wisdom in his time. Thus he was firmly in favor of capital punishment irregularly administered, because that was what was done in England — "he who falls by a mistaken sentence," he suggested with aplomb, "may be considered as falling for his country." Yet Paley's complacency and his penchant for the verdict of guilty were bolstered by his faith in circumstantial evidence. "A concurrence of well authenticated circumstances composes a stronger ground of assurance," he believed, "than positive testimony, unconfirmed by circumstances, usually affords. Circumstances cannot lie."[24] The aphorism constituted this philosopher's personal verdict in favor of always making strong representations.

Paley was undoubtedly credited with much wisdom in his time because his thoughts were well attuned to what people of influence wanted to hear. Insofar as it is true that circumstances cannot lie, credit for the idea — like that for the best-evidence rule — should probably go to Aristotle.[25] Because circumstances are not human, they never deliberately

---

24. William Paley, *The Principles of Moral and Political Philosophy*, rev. ed. (London: Baldwyn, 1812), 426–28. Leon Radzinowicz confirms my sense of Paley's importance in his day: see *A History of English Criminal Law and Its Administration from 1750*, 4 vols. (1948–68; rpt. London: Stevens, 1974–76), 1:248–49.

25. Aristotle, *Rhetoric*, 1376a; in W. Rhys Roberts's translation, "If you have no witnesses on your side, you will argue that the judges must decide from what is probable . . . that probabilities cannot be bribed to mislead the court; and that probabilities are never convicted of perjury." See *Rhetoric* (New York: Modern Library, 1954), 86.

tell fibs. On the other hand, evidence of every kind has sometimes been faked; and conclusions drawn from the evidence are only probable, as Paley admits, so it is quite possible to err without lying. The aphorism was itself misleading and was repeated by those it comforted most. The best thing that can be said for Paley is that he was abbreviating a slightly different argument, by eighteenth-century prosecutors and judges, that a narrative cannot be shaped from circumstantial evidence without considerably more work than goes into most lies—the argument I shall trace in more detail in the rest of this chapter. "Circumstances cannot lie!" became a rallying cry for enthusiasts of law and order in an era that, among other things, needed to set itself apart from revolutionary Europe; but the promise of strong representations also ran deep in science and natural religion, and "considerations of rectitude or utility" were important for constructing literary narrative too. Novel writers, after all, were free to choose whatever form they pleased to construct their entertainments; yet in practice, from Fielding to James, they usually chose narratives built on carefully managed circumstantial evidence. Geology and evolutionary biology depended directly on the evidentiary projects of natural religion, and these sciences were not as remote as generally supposed from nineteenth-century novel making.[26] In a time of new possibilities, conclusive arguments help to control knowledge and direct it to stable ends.

Yet the excitement about such strong representations eventually passed. After the publication of Bentham's papers on evidence in 1827, a definition of circumstantial evidence was available, but it never became a term of the art, as they say, from which legal consequences followed in a trial. By the mid-Victorian years writers of law treatises no longer expressed much enthusiasm for the subject. Since reasoning in a court of law did not differ from reasoning in other walks of life, as they had said all along, the hope for some sort of breakthrough in systematizing juridical proof was probably in vain—though Bentham and others had certainly felt that much clarification was imminent. J. Pitt Taylor, whose treatise on evidence was dedicated to Lord Brougham and still made reference to books on natural religion, disparaged further attempts by lawyers to gauge "the comparative value of direct and circumstantial evidence" and observed that presumptions of fact "belong equally to any and every subject-matter."[27] Prosecutors and theologians had

26. See George Levine, *Darwin and the Novelists: Patterns of Science in Victorian Fiction* (Cambridge: Harvard University Press, 1988); and Ruth Bernard Yeazell, "Nature's Courtship Plot in Darwin and Ellis," *Yale Journal of Criticism* 2, no. 2 (1989): 33–53.

27. John Pitt Taylor, *A Treatise on the Law of Evidence*, 2 vols. (London: Maxwell,

pressed just this argument about circumstantial evidence, that it worked for the business of everyday life, but now the phrase began to be troublesome. James Fitzjames Stephen, soon to become the foremost Victorian writer on the criminal law, adopted a stance similar to Taylor's and urged that the phrase be dropped altogether. While pointing out the ambiguity of what was meant by "evidence" in the first place, Stephen pretty well ceded that each verdict in a trial was equivalent to accepting a certain narrative, since even the simplest crime was a "transaction" involving several moves and invisible motives. Still, he thought "circumstantial evidence" a misnomer, and one that obscured the painful duty of weighing all the evidence. His antipathy was not entirely consistent: on the one hand, he argued that the phrase led juries to believe they were being scientific when they were only forming conjectures as to the facts; and on the other, that "the only real purpose which the phrase ever serves is that of supplying prisoner's counsel with a convenient sophism"—namely, that all circumstantial evidence was suspect.[28] The reason for the antipathy seems clear. Though Stephen's anxiety was a little premature, now that defendants were fully represented the weaknesses of circumstantial evidence could be advertised to the jury—exactly what disturbed Hosea M. Knowlton thirty years later in Massachusetts. History eventually began to turn full circle on the phrase "circumstantial evidence," and circumstances were no longer so readily identified with conviction. The phrase was wrested from the prosecution by popularizers of the law and fiction writers, by those who viewed circumstances as more of a threat than a blessing, and by the growing sentiment that life was not so much a probation as an occurrence beyond anyone's control.

Two Notorious Poisoning Trials

A specific theory of strong representation can be gleaned from the records of eighteenth-century English criminal trials. Indeed, a number of scholars—John H. Langbein, Thomas Andrew Green, and J. M. Beattie—have lately shown that it is possible to reconstruct in consid-

1848), 1:58–63, 133. Thayer, *Preliminary Treatise on Evidence,* 263–76, takes roughly the same position, but Wigmore, *Treatise on the Anglo-American System of Evidence,* 1:689–93, contends that the law of evidence inevitably includes whatever rules of logic courts have pronounced upon.

28. James Fitzjames Stephen, *A General View of the Criminal Law of England* (London: Macmillan, 1863), 265–75. That Stephen's dislike for the phrase "circumstantial evidence" was pitched at defense counsel appears from an unsigned article of the year before, "Circumstantial Evidence—The Case of Jessie M'Lachan," *Cornhill Magazine* 6 (1862): 699–701.

erable detail how the criminal justice system actually functioned.[29] But for my purposes it is necessary only to call attention to a shift in terminology during the period from "presumptions" to "circumstantial evidence," to note the initial lack of interest in the subject in formal treatises, and then to present the theory articulated in two criminal trials, *R v. Blandy* (1752) and *R v. Donellan* (1781). In comparison with the great sensations caused by the wickedness of the two poisoners, the contention about the powers of circumstantial evidence in these trials created only a small stir; yet because Edmund Burke subsequently gave the argument renewed force and respectability, it passed to the nineteenth century with some authority.

Two general reminders about the history of jury trials are perhaps in order. The role of the jury changed radically but slowly over a period going back to the Norman conquest. Originally, jurors were witnesses and investigators of the fact in issue; by the sixteenth century they had become passive triers of the case, reviewing the testimony before them and reaching a verdict.[30] Only as this newer role developed did they provide a finding of the facts on the basis of one or more representations put to them. A second great change made the criminal trial recognizably modern, as first the prosecution and eventually the defense began to be conducted by lawyers. The prosecution of Mary Blandy and John Donellan was conducted by barristers; professionalization—a move toward expert making of representations—developed rapidly in the eighteenth century.[31] The management of the evidence became nearly as significant as the evidence itself and might be admired or criticized accordingly. As Walter Scott wrote of his most famous fictional trial, "The professional spectators, whom habit and theory had rendered as callous to the distress of the scene as medical men are to those of a surgical operation," readily discussed "the general principle of the statute under which the young woman was condemned, the nature of the evidence, and the arguments of the counsel, without considering even that of the Judge as exempt from their criticism."[32]

29. John H. Langbein, "Shaping the Eighteenth-Century Criminal Trial: A View from the Ryder Sources," *University of Chicago Law Review* 50 (1983): 1–136; Green, *Verdict according to Conscience* (note 13 above); and J. M. Beattie, *Crime and the Courts in England, 1660–1800* (Princeton: Princeton University Press, 1986).

30. Blackstone, *Commentaries*, 3:368–74, still allows that jurors may decide cases "by their own private knowledge," but he gives no modern instance of this; on the contrary, "if a juror knows any thing of the matter in issue, he may be sworn as a witness, and give his evidence publicly in court."

31. Cf. John H. Langbein, "The Origins of Public Prosecution at Common Law," *American Journal of Legal History* 17 (1973): 313–45.

32. Walter Scott, *The Heart of Mid-Lothian* (Edinburgh: Black, 1886), 252.

Before the eighteenth century, the inferences associated with circumstantial evidence were known as presumptions. As often happened, when lawyers needed a technical term, they quietly borrowed one from the civil or canon law, which thrived side by side with the common law in England for longer than is usually recognized.[33] Coke upon Littleton became the favorite authority on this subject right into the nineteenth century, even though his distinction of three degrees of presumption obviously derived from civil law. A so-called violent presumption—the Latinate "violent," preserved in the amber of law language, merely meant strong—is the only degree that Coke illustrated in his *Institutes* and the only degree that counted for anything:

> many times Juries, together with other matter, are much induced by presumptions, whereof there be three sorts, *viz.* violent, probable, and light or temerarie. *Violenta presumptio* is many times *plena probatio,* as if one runne thorow the body with a sword in a house, whereof he instantly dieth, and a man is seene to come out of that house with a bloody sword, and no other man was at that time in the house, *presumptio probabilis* moveth little, but, *Presumptio levis seu temeraria,* moveth not at all.[34]

Not surprisingly this maxim—regularly attributed to Coke, translated as "violent presumption is many times full proof," and accompanied by some version of the same bloody emblem—resonated in courtrooms for two centuries. The ambiguity of "many times," with its multiplier effect, seems calculated to raise high probability to superconviction, while the image of the running man with a bloody sword confirms every ignorant juror's idea of what "violent" means. The true sense of the maxim was buried in scholarly implication, for those who might understand the difference from Continental criminal practice, where a violent presumption amounted to half-proof, or sufficient reason to examine an accused under torture. Coke was simply reiterating the point that the common law, unlike the civil and Mosaic law,[35] did not require two witnesses to find against a defendant directly. The saying

33. See the recent addendum to J. G. A. Pocock, *The Ancient Constitution and the Feudal Law: A Study of English Historical Thought in the Seventeenth Century,* a reissue with a retrospect (Cambridge: Cambridge University Press, 1987), 255–305; and Brian P. Levack, *The Civil Lawyers in England, 1603–1641* (Oxford: Clarendon, 1973).

34. Edward Coke, *The First Part of the Institutes of the Lawes of England: or, A Commentarie upon Littleton* (London: Society of Stationers, 1628), 6b.

35. Cf. Deuteronomy 19:15: "One witness shall not rise up against a man for any iniquity, or for any sin, in any sin that he sinneth: at the mouth of two witnesses, or at the mouth of three witnesses, shall the matter be established"; also Matthew 18:16.

invited conviction; it was not used dismissively of weak presumptions. But it provided no effective guidance, and the single illustration of an inference took much for granted.

The saying thrived, yet presumption in this sense gradually fell out of favor. The term had to be qualified as "presumption of fact" to distinguish it from a presumption of law, a term of the art still very much in use today. A presumption of law is an approved shortcut through otherwise tedious or impassable ways of proof: when evidence of a fact is unavailable, that is, a presumption may allow evidence on a related issue that is easier to prove. Presumptions still touch on fact, it seems, and a few may be thought of as generalizations about human behavior.[36] But in the course of the eighteenth century these fixed presumptions had to be singled out from presumptions in the old sense of Coke's maxim. Lord Mansfield, in a case of 1760, is sometimes cited on the difference of the two: "one, a presumption of law, not to be contradicted; the other, a species of evidence."[37] Meanwhile the word meaning a species of evidence was largely being supplanted by the phrase "circumstantial evidence." Blackstone, in 1768, treats the expressions— "*circumstantial* evidence or the doctrine of *presumptions*"—as synonymous;[38] and eventually, as I have indicated, writers on evidence at common law generally ceased trying to define either presumptions of fact or circumstantial evidence, since a valid inference in one set of circumstances may be nothing of the kind in another. The newer and more popular phrase conveyed a sense of amplitude for gathering and telling of the facts. Whereas "presumption" denotes inference or probability and today connotes arrogance, "circumstantial evidence" scants logic in favor of evidentiary facts, however linked or tied to the point in issue.

A similar tendency can be remarked over the same period in Scotland, within the civil law tradition itself. In his late seventeenth-century book on criminal law, George Mackensie took a very cautious view of presumption, not only because of the revered custom of requiring two witnesses to a crime, but because "presumptions are only founded upon verisimilitude, and what may be, may not be"; because such arguments cannot be held uniform from one trial to another; and because the great civilian writers were also inclined against them—though Mackensie

36. Cf. Charles T. McCormick, *Handbook of the Law of Evidence* (Saint Paul, Minn.: West, 1954), 650: "most presumptions [of law] have a strong footing in probability."
37. *Goodtitle v. Duke of Chandos,* 2 Burr. 1065 at 1072. See Holdsworth, *History of English Law,* 12:505.
38. Blackstone, *Commentaries,* 3:371.

fairly acknowledged a number of recent convictions on the basis of presumption.[39] In the corresponding work of the early nineteenth century, John Burnett first devoted a short chapter to the use of "direct and circumstantial evidence" in conjunction—that is, to prosecuting with only one witness—and then a somewhat longer chapter to the use of "presumptive evidence" by itself—his most modern scenario. The Scottish lawyer mainly stays with the language of presumption, but the possibility he entertains and his reasons for entertaining it reflect the trend in the common law to the south. "It may happen in a particular case," he writes, "that the circumstances are such, as to create in the mind even a stronger degree of faith than direct testimony; and in this, circumstantial evidence (the witnesses being all *credible*) differs from positive, that in the former there is not the same risk of error and falsehood."[40]

The interest in circumstantial evidence was clearly prosecutorial from the start, and it was surely given a boost by the successive movements toward crime prevention in the eighteenth century.[41] Coke's maxim on presumptions itself seems to have emerged from a bitter prosecutorial arena of earlier times. The justice Coke who appears from the pages of Coke upon Littleton is a genial person, wearing his learning lightly, with almost affectionate regard for his fifteenth-century predecessor; but as attorney general prosecuting Walter Raleigh for high treason in 1609 he exhibited a much different temperament—vitriolic and eager for conviction. The charge was plotting in the Spanish interest against James I, and Raleigh turned this charge around by exclaiming, "You try me by the Spanish Inquisition, if you proceed only by the Circumstances, without two Witnesses." He ably defended himself, on precisely the difference in accepted procedures: since "Cannon, Civil Law, and God's Word" all require two witnesses, "bear with me if I desire one." To this defense, however, Justice Warburton parried,

> I marvel, Sir Walter, that you being of such experience and wit, should stand on this point; for so many horse-stealers may escape, if they be not condemned without witnesses. If one should rush into the king's Privy-Chamber, whilst he is alone, and kill the king (which God forbid) and

39. George Mackensie, *Laws and Customs of Scotland in Matters Criminal* (Edinburgh: Glen, 1678), 525–26.

40. John Burnett, *A Treatise on Various Branches of the Criminal Law of Scotland*, ed. Robert Craigie (Edinburgh: Constable, 1811), 523.

41. See Radzinowicz, *English Criminal Law and Its Administration*, 2:1–29; 3:147–207.

this man be met coming with his sword drawn all bloody; shall not he be condemned to death?[42]

Raleigh was duly condemned "by the Circumstances" to be hanged and quartered, though—as the result of this same trial—he was in fact beheaded fifteen years later. Coke won the case, if so highly politicized a trial can be thought of as an adversary proceeding, and in 1628 Warburton's same illustration of *violenta presumptio* reappeared in the *Institutes*.

The law of evidence as first presented in formal treatises on the subject in the eighteenth century generally ignored the whole subject of circumstantial evidence. The earliest and best of the treatises, the posthumous book by Geoffrey Gilbert, though it begins by paying tribute to the probabilistic philosophy of Locke, barely mentions presumptions of fact.[43] Henry Bathurst, in a derivative and shorter book of 1761, stresses mainly matters of written evidence and takes up neither presumptions of fact nor circumstantial evidence.[44] Blackstone, in his chapter on juries, equates these two expressions and repeats Coke's maxim. For once, citing Gilbert as well as Coke, he omits the man with the bloody sword and substitutes two illustrations from landlord–tenant law. But beyond this brief paragraph he has nothing to add.[45] The difference between formal treatises and conventions of the criminal trial in the matter is nicely borne out by the example of Francis Buller, whose charge to the jury in *R v. Donellan* met with Burke's approval and achieved a certain fame. As a young barrister in 1772, nine years before he presided in *Donellan*, Buller composed eighty-two folio pages on the subject of "Evidence in General" without ever mentioning circumstantial evidence.[46] The subsequent pronouncements of Buller from the bench belong to a different tradition, the prosecution of crime, and can be traced in the *State Trials* back to the sixteenth century.[47] Some judges apparently did little more than indicate that, in the evidence they re-

42. The Trial of Sir Walter Raleigh, in *A Complete Collection of State Trials*, ed. T. B. Howell, 34 vols. (London: Longman, 1816–28), 2:15–18. For convenience all citations from the *State Trials* are to this edition, though I have checked passages quoted against the earliest available printings of the trials.

43. [Gilbert], *Law of Evidence*, 159–60.

44. [Henry, Earl Bathurst], *The Theory of Evidence* (London: Bathurst, 1761).

45. Blackstone, *Commentaries*, 3:371–72.

46. Francis Buller, *An Introduction to the Law relative to Trials at Nisi Prius* (London: Bathurst, 1772), 217–97.

47. See the arguments following the verdict in the Trial of John Udall, 1590, *State Trials*, 1:1302–4.

viewed for the jury, there was "some positive, some circumstantial," or there might be a desultory effort to register the law's preference of the former: "though there be no direct proof, you are to consider what is circumstantial."[48] But in the eighteenth century juries began to hear, together with the judge's summation, actual advice about the advantages of circumstantial evidence such as did not yet appear in treatises. "Witnesses, gentlemen, may either be mistaken themselves, or wickedly intend to deceive others. God knows, we have seen too much of this in the present cause on both sides! But circumstances, gentlemen, and presumptions, naturally and necessarily arising out of a given fact, cannot lie."[49] Such instructions were the immediate source of Paley's aphorism about circumstances—no more original, obviously, than Coke's maxim about presumption 150 years earlier. For all the slipperiness of both sayings, there was a significant progression—significant for English narrative in and out of the courtroom, that is—from "Violent presumption is many times full proof" to "Circumstances cannot lie."

A transcription of an entire trial, such as those collected in the *State Trials,* was rarely drawn upon to establish legal precedent. The common law is most authoritatively reflected in the so-called reports compiled by barristers, usually on rather narrow points of law within cases that might originally have been short or long, relatively simple or formidably complicated. The earliest such compilation devoted to evidence alone dates from 1717, and it too registers no particular interest in circumstantial evidence.[50] Full transcriptions of criminal trials owed their existence to mere stenographers and a commercial sense of which trials were remarkable enough to sell in published form. Hence they have a rather awkward and even extraneous bearing on the more sanctified records of the law, though because of their detailed evidence and coherent narrative, they have been of much use to historians.[51] The transcriptions consist mostly of testimony, of course, and in that respect are more like dramatic literature than narrative—certainly moments in any trial, criminal or otherwise, can be highly dramatic by any standard. But in two places the record of a criminal trial has already taken on

48. The Trial of Henry Harrison, 1692, *State Trials,* 12:865; the Trial of Spencer Cowper and Others, 1699, *State Trials,* 13:1188.

49. Trial in Ejectment between James Annesley and Richard Earl of Anglesea, 1743, *State Trials,* 17:1430.

50. [William Nelson], *The Law of Evidence* (London: Gosling, 1717).

51. Langbein, "Criminal Trial before the Lawyers," 264–67, cautions against relying on the *State Trials* as a history of practice in the courts. I am using them here primarily for the language they contain about circumstantial evidence.

narrative form: in the prosecution's introduction of the case and in a judge's summary of it before the jury is asked to give a verdict (the judge's version being somewhat inferior as a story in that it contains more cross-reference to the testimony and because it ought to be less conclusive). Journalistic summaries and fictionalized accounts of a trial freely reordered the evidence as a sequential narrative of events, usually of a biographical cast.

A plausible narrative is often persuasive by itself. In the absence of eyewitness testimony, however, a representation of the facts had to be pieced together, from a handful of circumstances or a hundred. To show that this could be done, and to overcome the idea that it took one or more witnesses, or the prisoner's confession, to prove a capital crime, prosecutors and judges began to theorize for the jury about probability and drawing inferences. This was the case for closely related arguments in *R v. Blandy* and *R v. Donellan*: poisoning trials are bound to depend on the evidence of things not seen. In the Middle Ages, Henry Bracton defined all murder as secret killing, to distinguish the crime from killing in self-defense or killing and paying compensation.[52] The act of poisoning is not inherently more secret than stabbing or battering, though it may be less obvious or more easily disguised. Because poison takes effect from the inside out, the evidence of the cause of death is hidden, and proving that death has not resulted from natural causes may be as difficult as proving who administered a poison. Accordingly, juries were tutored about inferences in these cases, and especially about the value of attending to the full story.

Mary Blandy was convicted at the Oxford Assizes in 1752 of poisoning Francis Blandy, an attorney and her father. The trial was taken down in shorthand and published in full,[53] as well as in several partial versions. The motive established was love for another man, with a doubtful past, who fled England and escaped punishment. Cranstoun, the accomplice, provided the arsenic with a curious present of pebbles from Scotland—where he was already married, only a little ambig-

52. "Murder is the secret killing of a Man, when none besides the killer, and his companions saw, or knew it; so that it was not known who did it, nor fresh-suit could be made after the doer." Bracton is thus cited by Thomas Hobbes, in *A Dialogue between a Philosopher and a Student of the Common Laws of England*, ed. Joseph Cropsey (Chicago: University of Chicago Press, 1971), 112.

53. *The Tryal of Mary Blandy, Spinster; for the Murder of her Father, Francis Blandy, Gent. at the Assizes held at Oxford for the County of Oxford, on Saturday the 29th of February, 1752* (London: Rivington, 1752). No reporter is named, but this appears to be the source of the record in the *State Trials*, which adds a report of the hanging and the tears shed by the students of Oxford.

uously, to another woman. Blandy fed the powder to her father but claimed she did not know it was poison. Both she and Cranstoun inspired a number of instant biographies, including her own supposed history that read like a novel and was protested as being self-serving.[54] On the whole, because of the love interest and parricide, the following for *R v. Blandy* was more literary than legal, and the prosecution itself indulged in much pathos and moralism at the trial. The tale of Mary Blandy stirred both tragic and comic spirits, as if the case was finally absurd and the countryside on holiday.[55] "If only she had been the creature of some great novelist's fancy," mused the editor of *Mary Blandy* for the Notable Trials series as late as 1914: "imagine her made visible for us through the exquisite medium of Mr. Henry James's incomparable art—the subtle individual threads all cunningly combined, the pattern wondrously wrought, the colours delicately and exactly shaded, until, in the rich texture of the finished tapestry, the figure of the woman as she lived stood perfectly revealed."[56]

John Donellan was convicted at the Warwick Assizes in 1781 of poisoning his young brother-in-law, Sir Theodosius Boughton, before the latter came of age. A motive was never proved very clearly, but supposedly Donellan's wife would inherit if Sir Theodosius died a minor. Within the family, the deceased's mother, Lady Boughton, became most suspicious. There was the clumsy business of Donellan's washing out a medicine bottle, with other awkwardnesses, to account for. Yet the crime only gradually unraveled: a dissection of the body, heavily corrupted after eleven days, provided some highly odoriferous testimony from the doctors, who were divided at the trial, four for poison and one—the most expert—noncommittal. Another military man like

54. See *Miss Mary Blandy's own Account of the Affair between her and Mr. Cranstoun, from the Commencement of their Acquaintance, in the Year 1746, to the Death of her Father, in August 1751, With all the Circumstances leading to that unhappy Event* (London: Millar, 1752); and *A Candid Appeal to the Publick, Concerning the Case of the late Miss Mary Blandy: wherein, All the ridiculous and false Assertions contained in a Pamphlet, entitled Miss Mary Blandy's Own Account . . . are exploded, and the Whole of that Mysterious Affair set in a True Light* (London: Gifford, 1752), which explains that Blandy's mother was also in love with Cranstoun.

55. Cf. *The Fair Parricide: A Tragedy of three Acts, founded on a late melancholy Event* (London: Waller, n.d.); and *The ★★★★ Pocket Broke-open; or, A Letter from Miss Blandy, in the Shades Below, to Capt. Cranstoun, in his Exile Above* (London: Cooper, 1752). For others, see British Library shelf listings G 14288 and 1493.r.2.

56. William Roughead, ed., *The Trial of Mary Blandy* (Edinburgh: Hodge, 1914), 55. Though James's interest may be doubted, in 1855 Dickens apparently thought of using Blandy's story somehow: see *Charles Dickens' Book of Memoranda*, ed. Fred Kaplan (New York: New York Public Library, 1981), 90–91.

Blandy's Cranstoun, Captain Donellan had been in trouble before.[57] He was dismissed from the army in 1759 after a court-martial convicted him of extortion in India. In 1777 he eloped with Miss Boughton, hence had been married about four years when Sir Theodosius became ill. The trial for murder produced a sensation and the usual biographies, including one "As Written by Himself" that makes rather good sense of the bottle-washing business but casts blame in so many directions that it recalls the pamphlet explaining away his court-martial: Sir Theodosius had venereal disease and was fond of playing with poison, the apothecary Powell behaved inexplicably, Lady Boughton was greedy and possibly dangerous, and so forth.[58] The proceedings of the trial were taken down in shorthand by Joseph Gurney and by W. Blanchard and thereupon published in two independent and nearly complete transcripts.[59] Though *R v. Donellan* was not included in T. B. Howell's edition of the *State Trials,* it was often cited, excerpted, or summarized in nineteenth-century works on evidence and popular histories of crime.

Such trials were remarked, retold, and sold because of their patent human interest and moralized pornography of violence, and they were indeed colorful stories.[60] On the present occasion, nevertheless, I am to frustrate the reader by focusing on the theory of circumstantial evidence articulated by the prosecution and the bench for the instruction of the jury. One consequence of *Donellan* was the publication in 1815 of a little book called *The Theory of Presumptive Proof,* almost certainly the work of Samuel March Phillipps, the writer of a contemporary

57. *The Case of Captain John Donnellan* (London, 1772). British Library shelf listing T.77*(9)—not to be confused with his later murder trial.

58. *The Genuine Case of John Donellan, Esquire, (At Large) As Written by Himself; And in Pursuance of his Dying Request, Now Published by Mr. Thos. Webb, his Solicitor* (London: Wenman [1781]). A much longer pamphlet identified with the same source, *A Defense and Substance of the Trial of John Donellan . . . published at the Request of his Solicitors, Messrs Inge and Webb* (London: Bell, 1781), sought to "vindicate" his character and also demonstrate "the defect of circumstantial evidence in general" (iv).

59. Joseph Gurney, *The Trial of John Donellan, Esq. for the Wilful Murder of Sir Theodosius Edward Allesley Boughton, Bart. at the Assize at Warwick, On Friday, March 30th 1781* (London: Kearsley and Gurney, 1781); and W[illiam Isaac?] Blanchard, *The Proceedings at large on the Trial of John Donellan, Esq. . . .* (London, n.d.). The transcripts differ just enough to suggest that they are two independent trial records.

60. In poisoning cases the postmortem had to substitute for the scene of violence. Unlike the horrors of *Donellan,* the postmortem in *Blandy* took place the day after death, and the spectacle was still colorful, as a single paragraph of testimony on the hitherto unseen side of Francis Blandy shows: *livid, pale, yellower, brownish, purple, blotted, pale, black, discoloured, boiled, dark, dirty yellow, inclining to red, livid, bloody,* and *inflamed.* See the Trial of Mary Blandy, *State Trials,* 18:1138–39.

treatise on evidence; and to this skeptical account I am indebted for pointing out the relation between *Blandy* and *Donellan*. By then the use made of the latter trial by Edmund Burke was well known, and the argument therefore had greater interest: Burke to the contrary notwithstanding, Phillipps declared the theory pronounced by Justice Buller in *R v. Donellan* "new to the practice of English law," and the earliest notice of this theory he could find was Baron Legge's charge to the jury in *R v. Blandy*.[61] As soon as one studies the didactic burden of those charges, it becomes evident that they fall within the convention of circumstances' not lying. But they also advanced two additional reasons for gravely respecting circumstances.

It is easier to study Buller's charge to the jury first, because here the argument is fully stated, and these were the words approvingly cited by Burke. The following is from Joseph Gurney's record of *R v. Donellan*:

> On the part of the prosecution a great deal of evidence has been laid before you. —It is all circumstantial evidence, and in its nature it must be so, for in cases of this sort, no man is weak enough to commit the act in the presence of other persons, or to suffer them to see what he does at the time; and therefore it can only be made out by circumstances, either before the committing of the act, —at the time it was committed, —or subsequent to it. —And a presumption, which necessarily arises from circumstances, is often more convincing and more satisfactory than any other kind of evidence, because it is not within the reach and compass of human abilities to invent a train of circumstances which shall be so connected together as to amount to a proof of guilt, without affording opportunities of contradicting a great part, if not all of those circumstances. But if the circumstances are such, as when laid together bring conviction to your minds, it is then fully equal, if not, as I told you before, more convincing than positive evidence.[62]

61. *The Theory of Presumptive Proof; or, An Inquiry into the Nature of Circumstantial Evidence, including an Examination of the Evidence in the Trial of Captain Donnellan* (London: Clarke, 1815), 25–29. The copy in the British Library, shelf listing 509.c.6, is bound with S. M. Phillipps, *A Treatise of the Law of Evidence*, 2d ed. (London: Butterworth, 1815). Cf. also Phillipps's *Famous Cases of Circumstantial Evidence* (New York: Cockcroft, 1873), xiv–xxix.

62. Gurney, *Trial of John Donellan*, 52. Comparison with Blanchard's *Proceedings*, 141, shows that Burke (see notes 68 and 69 below) definitely used Gurney's version, with minor changes in punctuation and added emphasis on "*all*" in the second sentence and "*more*" in the last.

Mainly Buller's language is of circumstances, which he classifies as falling before, during, and after the fact in issue; but presumptions also come into play, as the speaker seeks to touch all bases. It is probable that at least some of the jurors knew what a "presumption" was and that "positive evidence" meant eyewitness testimony. Buller's special application of circumstantial evidence to persons with something to hide, who do things unseen, is all very much to the purpose. But far from protesting that circumstances can be simple, he features "a train of circumstances." Connectedness and persistence over time, the very intricacy of the story that emerges, help to secure a true representation, "because it is not within the reach and compass of human abilities to invent a train of circumstances . . . without affording opportunities of contradicting a great part, if not all." Science and natural religion stand not far from this theory, which when pushed to an extreme appears to say that circumstances are both more to be trusted and more ingenious than humanity.

The notions of connectedness and inimitability of circumstantial evidence are both to be found in *R v. Blandy,* which Buller had probably read.[63] Baron Legge's charge to the jury, however—thirty years earlier—is somewhat more old-fashioned and comes down more heavily on the language of presumption:

> In the present case, which is to be made out by circumstances, great part of the evidence must rest upon presumption, in which the law makes a distinction: a light or probable presumption only has little or no weight: but a violent presumption amounts in law to full proof, that is, where circumstances speak so strongly, that to suppose the contrary would be absurd: I mention this to you, that you may fix attention on the several circumstances that have been laid before you, and consider whether you can collect from them such a presumption, as the law calls a violent presumption, and from which you must conclude the prisoner to be guilty: I would observe further, that where that presumption necessarily arises from circumstances, they are more convincing and satisfactory, than any other kind of evidence, because facts cannot lie.

Legge did not urge the virtues of circumstantial evidence from the bench in the way Buller was to do, but the prosecution in *Blandy* had made those same arguments. Thus Serjeant Hayward, in his opening speech

---

63. Mary Blandy did find her way into the *State Trials,* initially in vol. 10 (1779) of Francis Hargrave's edition, or two years before Donellan was tried at Warwick.

for the crown, directed attention to the "train of circumstances" that would satisfy the jury of the prisoner's guilt:

> Experience has taught us, that in many cases a single fact may be supported by false testimony; but where it is attended by a train of circumstances that cannot be invented (had they never happened), such a fact will always be made out to the satisfaction of a jury, by the concurring assistance of circumstantial evidence. Because circumstances that tally one with another are above human contrivance. And especially, such as naturally arise in their order, from the first contrivance of a scheme to the fatal execution of it.[64]

Circumstantial evidence, in the eighteenth century, was a prosecutorial property. In the little refrain or tripping of this prosecutor's tongue, circumstances are "above human contrivance," which indeed is more suited to the "contrivance of a scheme" of wickedness. In a sentence immediately before this, Hayward remarks that "it is absolutely necessary for me to make some observations upon that chain of circumstances, that attended this bloody contrivance and detested murder"— a good reminder that "chain" and "train" are virtually interchangeable in this context. These metaphors imply linear connectedness, as do references to "their order" and classifying circumstances before, during, and after the event in an explicit temporal sense. The trial, which must end in conviction or acquittal, confers the idea of completeness upon that of connectedness. All these claims express conditions for narrative, conditions endowed with greater spatial and temporal range by the tendency to move from talk of "presumption" to "circumstantial evidence."

Besides the literary interest of Mary Blandy's unhappiness and its manifest production of pathos and carnival spirits at the time, the prosecution's theory of circumstantial evidence had some immediate impact on legal history. Within the following year, in Scotland and the West Indies, two trials occurred in which similar arguments were tendered (in Francis Hargrave's edition of *State Trials* they were printed next to *R v. Blandy*). The first was the infamous and storied trial of James Stewart of Appin as accessory to the murder of Colin Campbell, in which eleven of the fifteen jurors were named Campbell. Both prosecution and defense discussed the nature of circumstantial evidence at length in terms similar to those heard at the Oxford Assizes that spring.[65]

---

64. The Trial of Mary Blandy, *State Trials*, 18:1186–87, 1130.
65. The Trial of James Stewart, *State Trials*, 19:33–34, 73–80.

In the second, the trial of John Barbot for murder on the island of Saint Christopher in early 1753, the prosecutor came prepared with a copy of the original printing of *Blandy* in his hand. He brandished it—"I have here two printed trials of persons indicted for murder"—first to contend that the prisoner was not entitled to counsel any more than Blandy had been. He stole from it, for his opening statement, the argument about circumstances "which the wit of man could never forge" and facts that "will never lie." Most surprising, after giving due weight to Coke's maxim, in his summary he elevated the authority of Baron Legge in *Blandy* above that of Coke:

> But, Gentlemen, I have another authority in my hand still more explicit of this matter, and which may enable you still more clearly to judge of it; and that is from a trial which I had occasion to mention this morning to another purpose; which is of Miss Blandy, who (as I make no doubt you have all heard) was tried at Oxford no longer ago than the month of March last, for the murder of her own father.

And he went on to use the words from Baron Legge's charge to the jury already quoted above.[66] In a certain sense, Barbot was tried by the journalism of the law. Just possibly the said copy of *The Tryal of Mary Blandy, Spinster* found its way to the West Indies through the good offices of the shorthand reporter who was present on 5 January 1753 in the trial on Saint Christopher. It is not as if a great many people were likely to be traveling that distance with the latest trials in their pockets.

Burke and Bentham on Narrative

In the course of the long impeachment of Warren Hastings, Edmund Burke clashed with the law judges advising the Lords on the admissibility of evidence. One of the managers of the prosecution brought by the Commons, Burke was not a lawyer himself; such were his powers and the fame of the trial, however, that in the century that followed his definition of circumstantial evidence was as often quoted as any other. In this public forum he found himself contending against the

---

66. The Trial of John Barbot, *State Trials,* 18:1232, 1243–44, 1299. The judge, who was president of council for the island, supported the prosecution's view of circumstantial evidence in his charge to the jury and added his opinion "that in cases of murder, and the like atrocious crimes, the law has relaxed much of its severity and scrupulousness in the proofs, and does not so absolutely require such positive proof as in matters of *meum* and *tuum,* where they may be had, but in these cannot" (1314).

same rules of evidence that were attracting Jeremy Bentham's ire at the time, and the historical conjunction of two such opposed thinkers as Burke (1729–97) and Bentham (1748–1832) merits notice on its own account. The law of evidence that both men sharply criticized—what Edward Christian, the editor of Blackstone's *Commentaries,* called "perhaps the most beautiful and philosophical branch of English jurisprudence"[67]—was largely an eighteenth-century compilation. It consisted, as it does today, of precedents for introducing and proving documents, the qualifications of witnesses, and the exclusion of certain evidence. The rules were restrictive, in other words, though they were hedged with exceptions—the rule against hearsay, for example, had a number of exceptions. Thus the law of evidence was basically a negative approach to the subject, founded in the law reports and almost opposite in spirit to the expansive idea of circumstantial evidence in criminal prosecution. Bentham, who wanted trials at law to be systematic and completely rational, attacked the rules as obtuse and unnecessary constraints on efficient proof. Burke, the prosecutor in a hugely complicated case in which he was eagerly involved, was frustrated by the rules and wanted to get on with it.

Burke's contribution to the subject of evidence was for him a digression from the trial of Hastings. The digression, in his report for the House of Commons dated 30 April 1794, was nevertheless equivalent to a substantial essay, reviewing civilian authorities, common-law reports, and the criminal case of *Donellan.*[68] His recourse to the last, and especially to the charge to the jury by "the learned judge who presided," was perhaps a little disingenuous, for Francis Buller does not seem to have had an outstanding reputation as a judge, and the conviction of Donellan for poisoning his brother-in-law was controversial. As for the question of how the brilliant commoner who had mastered the arcane details of Indian affairs and thrown himself into the philosophical and rhetorical resistance to the French Revolution in the same decade came across the sensational murder trial, I suspect the hand of a reporter again, and this time one who can be identified. Joseph Gurney, who transcribed *The Trial of John Donellan* that Burke consulted, was then working for the managers—that is, for Burke—in reporting all the

---

67. Edward Christian, *A Dissertation shewing that the House of Lords in cases of judicature are bound by precisely the same rules of evidence as observed by all other courts* (Cambridge: Archdeacon, 1792), 13.

68. *Report from the Committee of the House of Commons,* 30 April 1794, in *The Works and Correspondence of the Right Honourable Edmund Burke,* 8 vols. (London: Rivington, 1852), 8:67–100. Hereafter referred to as *Report,* with page references to this edition.

proceedings against Hastings.[69] If lowly clerks have sometimes drafted learned opinions in the law, this expert shorthand writer could well have called the prosecution's notice to the trial he had published a dozen years earlier.

Personal frustration aside, Burke's opposition to the rules of evidence was deeply, if not wholly, consonant with his empiricism. "As human affairs and human actions are not of a metaphysical nature, but the subject is concrete, complex, and moral," he wrote, "they cannot be subjected (without exceptions which reduce it almost to nothing) to any certain rule" (*Report,* 79). Without much difficulty he found in the law reports praise of the best-evidence rule, sometimes said to be the foundation of all the rules. He cited Lord Hardwicke to the effect that there is only one "general rule of evidence—the best that the nature of the case will admit."[70] In practical terms, the best-evidence rule says that a brief implying the existence of evidence stronger than what is actually introduced has something wrong with it; as a bit of logic it is generous enough, since it depends on the nature of the case. But this accords well with Burke's philosophy: "such is the genius of the law of England, that these two principles of the general moral necessities of things, and the nature of the case, overrule every other principle, even those rules which seem the very strongest" (*Report,* 87). And having disposed of the rules by subordinating them to necessity and the nature of the case, he turns to the requirements of narrative—to the wholeness, connectedness, and linearity of an arrangement that will render the nature of the case plain. It is just here that he invokes *R v. Donellan* for the argument of Buller about circumstances "connected together" in reality and their representation "laid together" at trial. In Hastings's trial, Burke protests, "The lords compelled the managers to declare for what purpose they produced each separate member of their circumstantial evidence; a thing, as we conceive, not usual, and particularly not observed in the trial of Donellan." Thus *Donellan* emerges as a model of strong representation. "We have observed in that trial, and in most others to which we have had occasion to resort, that the prosecutor is suffered to proceed narratively and historically, without interruption" (*Report,* 97).

69. See the *Dictionary of National Biography* under Thomas Gurney (1705–70), the father of Joseph Gurney (1744–1815). On the Gurneys, see also Langbein, "Shaping the Eighteenth-Century Criminal Trial" (note 29 above), 12–18.

70. *Report,* 84. Cf. *Omychund v. Barker* (1744), 1 Akt. 21 at 29: "there is no general rule without exception that we know of but this, that the best evidence shall be admitted, which the nature of the case will afford."

Obviously Burke will never explicitly argue that, since Donellan was guilty so must Hastings be guilty; but in turning from reasoning and sayings taken from the law reports to the narrative materials typical of the *State Trials* he invokes a certain story, and clearly a story of acquittal on the basis of circumstantial evidence would not do. Burke's protest is against having the construction of his narrative unduly interrupted; and since a murder trial like that of Donellan occupied a matter of hours and the impeachment of Hastings was then in its sixth year, one can sympathize with his impatience. He could find no precedent for attempts

> by any court to call on the prosecutor for an account of the purpose for which he means to introduce each particle of this circumstantial evidence, to take up the circumstances one by one, to prejudge the efficacy of each matter separately, in proving the point; and thus to break to pieces and to garble those facts, upon the multitude of which, their combination, and the relation of all their component parts to each other, and to the culprit, the whole force and virtue of this evidence depends. To do anything which can destroy this collective effect, is to deny circumstantial evidence.

He thereby advocates a sweeping but closed narrative, a narrative both inclusive and conclusive. From the "multitude," "combination," and "relation" of facts something follows. The narrative or "collective effect" confirms the fact in issue *and* the facts brought in evidence. This narrative ending—a conviction, he feels sure—awaits the telling of the whole story, whereas his opponents in *Hastings* demand "that every several circumstance should in itself be conclusive, or at least should afford a violent presumption; it must, we were told, without question, be material to the charge depending: but, as we conceive, its materiality, more or less, is not in the first instance to be established" (*Report*, 95, 99). Burke's treatment of narrative shows the importance of closure to a strong representation: a story without a theme or verdict fails to represent fully in all its parts. Full conviction—or credence—in the facts always awaits conviction or acquittal at the end; a strong representation takes for granted that sanctions are to follow and quite naturally begins, in a criminal case, with accusations. But it cannot always cohere about a single question or fact in issue, and Burke usefully suggests why poisoning trials such as *Donellan* serve as prime illustrations of this. Precisely because expert testimony on the cause of death was extremely uncertain in such cases, proof that murder had occurred awaited to some extent proof that some culprit—to use Burke's term—was the murderer. Buller was criticized, in fact, for failing to discriminate for the jury the two questions: Was there a murder? And who was the murderer?[71] Burke is saying, in effect, that one cannot always separate these questions.

The idea of waiting for the whole story, of getting the full picture, of not ruling anything out did not depend on criminal prosecution alone for its currency. The rise of science played a part in the general respect for narrative, as did logic and natural theology; and these fields of inquiry were not as sharply distinguished as they are today. According to the English translation of the Port Royal *Logic,*

> Circumstances are to be compar'd and consider'd together, not consider'd apart. For it often happens, that a Fact, which is not very probable in one Circumstance, ought to be esteem'd and taken for certain according to other Circumstances: and on the other side, a Fact which appears to us true, according to one Circumstance which is usually join'd with Truth, ought to be deem'd false, according to other weakening Circumstances.[72]

And according to Butler's *Analogy of Religion,*

> though each of these direct and circumstantial things, is indeed to be considered separately, yet they are afterwards to be joined together; for that the proper Force of the Evidence consists in the Result of those several things, considered in their Respects to each other, and united into one View.[73]

Thus the law had no monopoly on circumstances "not consider'd apart" and "united into one View," and Burke's arguments have many parallels outside the law. Yet—and this is a point quite separate from the substantive interest of cases like *Blandy* and *Donellan*—criminal prosecution was helping to focus attention on a shift from direct to indirect testimony as a species of narrative; in trials at law the advance of circumstantial evidence occurs within a limited scene, concentrates on the fact or facts in issue, and anticipates a decision—hence is already committed to a closed narrative of human affairs. Meanwhile trials were changing from a scene dominated by witnesses to one dominated by lawyers, and from the cautious admission of anything other than direct testimony to the professional management of a mixture of evidence. Just as Burke urged that the prosecution should be free "to proceed narratively and historically" in *Hastings,* such developments in law were common to the management of narrative in history and novels of the period.

71. *Defense and Substance of the Trial of John Donnellan* (note 58 above), 69–72.
72. *Logic; or, The Art of Thinking,* trans. John Ozell (London: Taylor, 1717), 442–43.
73. Butler, *Analogy of Religion,* 256–57.

As can well be imagined, Bentham's *Rationale of Judicial Evidence,* a compilation by the young John Stuart Mill of papers written between 1802 and 1812, resembles in style and argument nothing ever writ or spoke by Edmund Burke.[74] On the subject of the rules, to be sure, the two think alike: "as on every other part of the field of evidence, rules capable of rendering right decisions secure, are what the nature of things denies." Bentham's very next sentence, however, shows his irreverence toward tradition: "to the establishment of rules by which misdecision is rendered more probable than it would otherwise be, the nature of man is prone" (*Rationale,* 3:219). Among other things—many other things—the *Rationale* is a satire on the law; at least half of the long work is an attack on what he likes to call "the technical system" of "Judge and Co." While Burke rhetorically makes it difficult to deny his case for circumstantial evidence, Bentham is more persistently analytical than any other writer on the subject. He does not forget that, since all evidence is introduced in court through testimony, the distinction between direct and indirect evidence cannot be a true dichotomy. His definition of these types runs as follows:

> The evidence afforded by any given mass of testimony is either direct or circumstantial, according to the relation it bears to the fact to which it is considered as applying. It is direct, in respect of any and every fact expressly narrated by it; and, in particular, every fact of which the witness represents himself as having been a percipient witness. It is circumstantial, in respect of any and every fact not thus expressly narrated by it; in particular, every fact of which the witness does *not* represent himself as having been a percipient witness, and the existence of which, therefore, is matter of inference, being left to be concluded from its supposed connexion with the facts spoken to by the testimony in its character of direct evidence. (*Rationale,* 3:7–8)

At this point he has already located the inference upon which circumstantial evidence depends in the relation of two facts: "1. the *factum probandum,* or say, the *principal* fact, —the fact the existence of which is supposed or proposed to be proved, —the fact evidenced to, —the fact which is the subject of proof"; and "2. the *factum probans,* —the evidentiary fact, —the fact from the existence of which that of the *factum*

74. Jeremy Bentham, *Rationale of Judicial Evidence,* 5 vols. (London: Hunt and Clarke, 1827), preface, v; hereafter cited by volume and page as *Rationale.* William Twining, *Theories of Evidence,* 19–108, offers a partial summary and commentary on the work. See also Mill's account in his *Autobiography,* in *Collected Works of John Stuart Mill,* ed. J. M. Robson, vol. 1 (Toronto: University of Toronto Press, 1981), 116–19.

probandum is inferred" (*Rationale*, 3:2–3). These facts differ not in kind, note, but in their position in the argument.

With this distinction in hand, Bentham tries to define what is meant by a chain of circumstances. "In this way, a chain of facts, of any length, may be easily conceived, and chains of different lengths will be frequently exemplified: each such link being, at the same time, with reference to the preceding link, a principal fact, and with reference to a succeeding one, an evidentiary fact."[75] The metaphor of a chain, thus expounded, is that of a series of linked inferences. The order denoted is temporal rather than spatial and constitutes a narrative, but one that seems in Bentham's analysis to abandon the notion of the principal fact at issue by multiplying it endlessly. A footnote implies that a representation imputing cause and effect has the best chance of being believed. Bentham's mention of causality seems to promise more precision than Burke's discussion of the "relation" or "combination" of events, but it still remains vague. Even his treatment of "*real* evidence"—"evidence of which any object belonging to the class of *things* is the source"— invokes the authority of science only very obliquely. "The properties of things are the subject-matter of the different branches of physical science. A work having for its subject any such branch of science, is, as to a great part of its contents, a treatise on circumstantial evidence."[76] Such remarks, however, are typical of the tendency in the early nineteenth century to hold up science as a model for inference in the law. Ubiquitous cause and effect—"the grand principle of the uniformity of causation," as one writer puts it[77]—promise an inexhaustible supply of evidence such as no criminal or would-be criminal can hope to elude.

The question of criminal intent falls within this program. Bentham makes the important point that intention is essential to the definition of crime and that in a trial, short of confession, circumstantial evidence is necessary to prove intention:

> to constitute a criminal act, one or more facts of the psychological kind are indispensably requisite: in most instances, the sentiment of *consciousness*, with relation to the existence of divers exterior facts; in all cases,

75. *Rationale*, 3:3. See also 3:222, on the weakness to which a long chain is liable.

76. Ibid., 3:26. For measuring degrees of persuasion in evidence, in opposition to Coke's maxim, Bentham envisioned some instrument of gradation like a thermometer: "the electrometer, the calorimeter, the photometer, the eudiometer, not to mention so many others, are all of them so many productions of this age. Has not justice its use as well as gas?" (1:80).

77. [Samuel Bailey], *Essays on the Pursuit of Truth, on the Progress of Knowledge, and on the Fundamental Principle of All Evidence and Expectation* (London: Hunter, 1829), 299.

intentionality, viz. the intention of bringing about the obnoxious event, or at least of doing the physical act by which it is produced or endeavoured to be produced. . . . Unless stated by the individual himself in whose mind the fact is considered as having place, the existence of any such psychological fact can only be matter of inference.[78]

Both the necessity of proving intent and the observation that, absent confession, intention could only be proved indirectly were accepted principles at this time. Bentham is restating, in his characteristic style, principles enunciated much earlier. In a trial for assault in 1721, for example, both the prosecution and the bench linked intent to circumstantial evidence. In an argument with one of the defendants after the verdict, the prosecutor avers, "These are all facts which the jury only could determine, either by positive, presumptive, or circumstantial evidence: for no man's thoughts or intentions can be otherwise proved than by his actions."[79] Even one of the tracts capitalizing on the notoriety of Mary Blandy's fate makes the point:

Whatever is done by a *moral* Agent, as such, is consequent to some *Intention* of the Mind, which excites to, which circumstantiates and characterizes the Action. But our Judgment concerning the *Intention* of an Agent, must follow a Survey of the *Action.* This must be carefully sifted, and the ingredient Circumstances thereof nicely and impartially examined, and clear Ideas of all these must precede that of the *Intention* or *Motive* of the Agent, in our Understanding; as a Judgment of the *Intention* must be the Result of a Proof of those Circumstances, or of the Fact, in judicial Proceedings.[80]

These are commonplaces, then, of criminal practice. But Bentham's distinct relegation of confession to a minor and frequently unavailable path to intention reflects the tendency of the time, while his use of the word "psychological" indicates another dimension of the role of science in evidence. The process of ascertaining motive or intent from the outside held new implications for the way individuals were perceived and perceived themselves.

Burke also states that crime "consists rather in the intention than the action," and that intention can be proved in two ways: either by con-

---

78. *Rationale,* 3:5–6; see also 3:100–30.

79. The Trial of John Woodburne and Arundel Coke, *State Trials,* 16:85.

80. *The Secret History of Miss Blandy, from her first Appearance at Bath, to her Execution at Oxford, April 6, 1752* (London: Williams, n.d.), 67–68. The writer proceeds to draw up four sets of circumstances that prove Blandy's intention.

fession, which "is rare but simple," or by circumstantial evidence, which "is difficult, and requires care and pains." It is just here, in fact, that Burke launches the most familiar passage of his words on evidence. So often were the final clauses of this passage quoted in the nineteenth century that one forgets they grow out of a discussion of intention:

> The connexion of the intention and the circumstances is plainly of such a nature, as more to depend on the sagacity of the observer, than on the excellence of any rule. The pains taken by the civilians on that subject have not been very fruitful; and the English law writers have, perhaps, as wisely, in a manner abandoned the pursuit. In truth, it seems a wild attempt to lay down any rule for the proof of intention by circumstantial evidence; all the acts of the party; all things that explain or throw light on these acts; all the acts of others relative to the affair, that come to his knowledge, and may influence him; his friendships and enmities, his promises, his threats, the truth of his discourses, the falsehood of his apologies, pretences, and explanations; his looks, his speech; his silence where he was called to speak; every thing which tends to establish the connexion between all these particulars;—every circumstance, precedent, concomitant and subsequent, become parts of circumstantial evidence. (*Report,* 95)

The passage is eloquent of the demands of a fully managed narrative replete with incident, characters, and things, with speech and silence, and the connection of all the circumstances over time. But it is important to note this far-reaching narrative bears, precisely, on someone's state of mind.

The great triumph of circumstantial evidence over direct testimony— including confession—is that it can turn even false testimony to account. Thus in the trial of someone like Hastings, the very "falsehood of his apologies, pretences, and explanations" will betray him when the full story is told. Similarly, Bentham posits that circumstantial evidence has the important capacity to assimilate "a mixture of truth and falsehood" from direct testimony or partial confession. "Not only when the whole narrative is viewed together, in a general point of view, falsehood is, to the apprehension of every rational mind, a strong indication and symptom of delinquency." And even "in respect of the details of the transaction, this or that particular falsehood" can serve to establish a "particular truth" (*Rationale,* 3:9–10). Thus motive and intent can be wrested away from both defendant and witness and reconstructed from circumstances over which neither had anything like complete control, just as, in the larger eighteenth-century scene, confessions, memoirs, letters, and eyewitness history are giving way to more complex but connected narratives, in which even states of mind can be described from the outside. Not altogether surprisingly, Burke's trust in "the sagacity of the observer" and Bentham's more intricate review of particulars will one day be turned around by Michel Foucault to proclaim a narrative based in "surveillance."[81] The movement in the English novel from first-person to third-person narratives should not be seen as an isolated literary development, and in novels as elsewhere, circumstantial evidence might emerge as a threat to private being.[82] One of the designs co-opted from Defoe and Richardson by strong representations was the privilege of narrating a character's own thoughts.

A particular virtue claimed for circumstantial evidence by the prosecution in *R v. Blandy* and the bench in *R v. Donellan* is not especially regarded by either Bentham or Burke: namely, the thesis that such evidence cannot easily be fabricated. Though Burke cites precisely this portion of Buller's charge to the jury—"It is not within the reach and compass of human abilities to invent a train of circumstances which shall be so connected together"—he fails to exploit the argument for the prosecution of Hastings: he was constrained, perhaps, by not having achieved this state of connectedness in his narrative. Though Bentham remarks that either direct or indirect evidence may lie, he too recites a version of the argument by noting that, with circumstantial evidence, "the aggregate mass on either side is, if mendacious, the more exposed to be disproved" (*Rationale,* 3:249–52). The thesis goes well beyond Aristotle's point that circumstances do not offer bribes or deliberately lie; it depends upon extensive narrative, whose internal consistency can be checked and whose many facets, as Bentham notes, are exposed to refutation. Such an elaborate account of events, *if* invented, the argument goes, would fall of its own inconsistency or vulnerable part.

Because the thesis depended partly on the extent of the evidence, it was distinctly popular with philosophers and natural theologians, who had the entire universe before them to contemplate. Thomas Reid, for example, writes in 1785, "If the testimony be circumstantial, we consider how far the circumstances agree together, and with things that are

81. See especially Michel Foucault, *Discipline and Punish,* trans. Alan Sheridan (1977; rpt. New York: Random House, 1979); John Bender, *Imagining the Penitentiary: Fiction and the Architecture of the Mind in Eighteenth-Century England* (Chicago: University of Chicago Press, 1987); and D. A. Miller, *The Novel and the Police* (Berkeley: University of California Press, 1988).

82. For some nineteenth-century implications of circumstantial evidence, see Alexander Welsh, *George Eliot and Blackmail* (Cambridge: Harvard University Press, 1985), esp. 85–109.

known. It is so very difficult to fabricate a story, which cannot be detected by a judicious examination of the circumstances, that it acquires evidence, by being able to bear such a trial."[83] Paley regularly embarks upon the same argument, whether in defense of the criminal law or of the Bible narrative. Of the Acts of the Apostles and the Epistles of Paul, he remarks how the "*undesignedness* of the agreements, which undesignedness is gathered from their latency, their minuteness, their obliquity, the suitableness of the circumstances . . . and the circuitous references by which they are traced out, demonstrates that they have not been produced by meditation, or by any fraudulent contrivance."[84] For trials at law, practically limited in aim and duration, any notion of evidence implying that the more the better may overshoot the mark. For a natural theology, obviously, the more of the created universe is brought into evidence, the better the case for creation. Still, the argument was something of a dare and not without risk, for as more and more regions were exposed to view the narrative could become strained. A wholly different explanation of the same universe in 1859 made this intellectual trial, between natural theology and natural selection, the most dramatic of Victorian England.

Paradoxically, the thesis that circumstantial evidence could not be falsified was of the most lasting use to inveterate falsifiers. As Maximillian E. Novak reminds us, "Just as the courts of law came to focus more and more on facts and evidence, so fiction came to function in a world of secondary causes and events."[85] The most designing of designers, novelists rose to the challenge of the prosecution in *Blandy* to invent "a train of circumstances that cannot be invented"; novelists, contrary to the opinion of the bench in *Donellan,* demonstrated that a narrative so connected was "within the reach and compass of human abilities."

> If the Reader will please to refresh his Memory, by turning to the Scene at *Upton* in the Ninth Book, he will be apt to admire the many strange Accidents which unfortunately prevented any Interview between *Partridge* and Mrs. *Waters,* when she spent a whole day there with Mr. *Jones.*

---

83. Thomas Reid, *Essays on the Intellectual Powers of Man* (Edinburgh: Bell, 1785), 692. See also James Edward Gambier, *An Introduction to the Study of Moral Evidence* (London: Rivington, 1806), 22–25.

84. William Paley, *A View of the Evidences of Christianity* (Dublin: Milliben, 1794), 476–77. See also his *Horae Paulinae; or, The Truths of the Scripture History of St. Paul* (London: Faulder, 1790), 12–13.

85. Maximillian E. Novak, *Realism, Myth, and History in Defoe's Fiction* (Lincoln: University of Nebraska Press, 1983), 125.

Instances of this Kind we may frequently observe in Life, where the
greatest Events are produced by a nice Train of little Circumstances; and
more than one Example of this may be discovered by the accurate Eye,
in this our History.

A few chapters later, Fielding a little impertinently puts in the mouth
of the character in *Tom Jones* with whom he most identifies a version
of the thesis that he boasts of violating here. "I need not, Madam,"
Allworthy says to Mrs. Waters, "express my Astonishment at what
you have told me; and yet surely you would not, and could not, have
put together so many Circumstances to evidence an Untruth."[86]

Precisely in the decades when the "probative force" of circumstantial
evidence was most seriously sought after by theorists and practitioners
of the law, the attitude of English novelists toward fictionality itself
underwent a change. Before the nineteenth century, novels were typically surrounded by a false frame of pretended documentation—letters,
memoirs, lost papers, and so forth that purported to account for the
real-life existence of the narrative they contained. But increasingly,
through the conscious practice of Fielding and others, the claim to
represent reality in novels was expressed by their internal connectedness
of circumstances, their deliberate response to the challenge of making
representations, until by the time of James novelists scorned either to
pretend truth or to concede falsehood in their work. It became the
professional thing to let the completeness and closure, the probing of
the states of mind of the actors themselves, present their own claim to
the truth. On the other hand, quick as they were to *forge* chains of
circumstances, novelists soon made it known that they were not to be
counted on always to write for the prosecution, as Burke and Bentham
seem to have imagined competent managers of evidence always would.

86. Henry Fielding, *Tom Jones,* ed. Martin C. Battestin and Fredson Bowers (Middletown, Conn.: Wesleyan University Press, 1975), 916, 942.

2

The Evidence in Two Novels

That which makes me believe, is something extraneous to the thing I
believe; something not evidently joined on both sides to, and so not
manifestly shewing the Agreement, or Disagreement of those *Ideas,*
that are under consideration.

—John Locke, 1690

Witnesses to the fact may be mistaken, or may falsify; —"they may
err," as Lord Stair says, "through inadvertence or precipitancy, and
through the secret insinuations of favour and hatred, which they themselves do not perceive"; but circumstances, which are clearly proved,
if apt and coherent in themselves, and established by witnesses uncon-
nected with each other, are not liable to such objections; but carry with
them, in some instances, a safer and more satisfactory conclusion than
direct testimony.

—John Burnett, 1811

M ARY BLANDY WAS FOUND GUILTY of murdering her father on 3 March 1752, three years after the publication, on 10 February 1749, of *The History of Tom Jones, a Foundling*. Thus Fielding knew nothing of Blandy when he wrote the novel, though her trial partly inspired a little work called *Examples of the Interposition of Providence in the Detection and Punishment of Murder,* compiled by the novelist, or at least published under his auspices, on 13 April 1752.[1] By that year Fielding had also written and published *Amelia.*

Before reviewing the trials of Tom Jones one may still profitably reflect on the nearly contemporaneous *R v. Blandy.* Such trials—whether playful and partial as in the novel or for life and death as in *Blandy*— did not merely teach the use of circumstantial evidence in constructing a narrative. They empowered evidence with real or imagined, always fittingly administered, consequences. They shared certain assumptions about individual fate and providential design, and even a common didactic purpose. More especially, they treated a lifetime as a trial, or series of trials, in which the main actor's intention played a significant part. His or her intention could be known, was spoken to by the evidence, and was registered in the ensuing narrative. Although co-operation to the extent of enduring trial was required of the protagonist, confession was not. What produced a satisfying outcome was management of the evidence throughout.

Not surprisingly, in *Blandy* the prosecutors flourished before the jury the idea of providential discovery. They professed sorrow for the prisoner and wished that the evidence were not so strong against her yet could not resist triumphing a little because she had been caught. Thus Henry Bathurst (who would become Lord Chancellor in 1771) brought

1. Henry Fielding, *Examples of the Interposition of Providence in the Detection and Punishment of Murder* (London: Millar, 1752), in which Blandy's story supplies the thirty-third and final example. Providential discovery and conviction are explicitly linked to "circumstantial evidence" (11). See F. Homes Dudden, *Henry Fielding: His Life, Works, and Times,* 2 vols. (Oxford: Clarendon, 1952), 2:956–59.

to a close his contribution to the prosecution's opening case with happy
reflections on the providential and didactic value of Blandy's example.
Her story proves "how evidently the hand of Providence has inter-
posed"—compare the title of Fielding's book of such examples, published a month later—"to bring her to this day's trial, that she may
suffer the consequence." Bathurst continues, exalting the evidence and
its story:

> For what, but the hand of Providence, could have preserved the paper
> thrown by her into the fire, and have snatched it unburnt from the
> devouring flame? —Good God! how wonderful are all thy ways! and
> how miraculously hast thou preserved this paper, to be this day produced
> in evidence against the prisoner, in order that she may suffer the pun-
> ishment due to her crime; and be a dreadful example to all others who
> may be tempted in like manner to offend thy divine majesty![2]

Not vengeance or justice, then, but didactic narrative is uppermost in
the prosecutorial mind, or foremost on the prosecutorial lips.

The myriad extensions of this didactic impulse were left to Serjeant
Hayward, also appointed for the crown. Hayward, whose personal
inclination would be "to cast a veil over the guilty scene," goes so far
as to imagine the victim of the crime witnessing his daughter's trial, a
rhetorical flight that lofts the full story of Miss Blandy beyond the pain
of death: "Oh! Were he now living, and to see his daughter there, the
severest tortures that poison could give, would be nothing to what he
would suffer from such a sight." Luckily the trial had a live audience
of Oxford students to be instructed and admonished, and Hayward
could convey the didactic theme directly to the "young gentlemen of
this university."

> Who could have thought that Miss Blandy, a young lady virtuously
> brought up, distinguished for her good behaviour and prudent conduct
> in life, till her unfortunate acquaintance with the wicked Cranstoun,
> should ever be brought to a trial for her life; and that for the most desperate
> and bloodiest kind of murder, committed by her own hand, upon her
> own father? Had she listened to his admonitions, this calamity never had
> befallen her. Learn hence the dreadful consequences of disobedience to
> parents: and know also, that the same mischief, in all probability, may
> happen to such who obstinately disregard, neglect, and despise the advice
> of those persons who have the charge and care of their education; of

2. The Trial of Mary Blandy, in *A Complete Collection of State Trials,* ed. T. B. Howell,
34 vols. (London: Longman, 1816–28), 18:1129.

governors likewise, and of magistrates, and of all others who are put in authority over them. . . . Let us defend ourselves against the first temptations to sin, and guard our innocency as we would our lives; for if we once yield, though but a little, in whose power is it to say, Hitherto will I go, and no further?

Begin by disobeying parents or despising authority, and proceed to murdering fathers; murder a father, and end by hanging. In this generalized narrative Serjeant Hayward has not entirely forgotten the task of the jury: this indeed is Mary Blandy's story, he implies. But the didactic spirit predominates as he goes on to distinguish love from lust and to personify innocence and guilt:

> Innocence, celestial virgin, always has her guard about her; she dares look the frowns, the resentments, and the persecutions of the world in the face; is able to stand the test of their strictest inquiry; and the more we behold her, still the more shall we be in love with her charms. But it is not so with Guilt: The baneful fiend makes use of unjustifiable means to conceal her wicked designs, and prevent discovery. Artifice and cunning are her supporters, bribery and corruption the defenders of her cause; she flies before the face of law and justice, and shuns the probation of a candid and impartial enquiry.[3]

Without question the prosecution intends to please by instruction, to instruct by pleasing—Hayward could easily have borrowed the apostrophe to Innocence and Guilt in *Amelia*.[4] Paramount to the argument, as in Fielding's novel, is the assumption that life itself is a trial. One cannot fail to hear the speaker shifting down from third, to second, to first person: "Who would have thought that Miss Blandy . . . Learn hence the dreadful consequences . . . Let us defend ourselves." The very vocabulary of these paragraphs tells of life as a trial: *behaviour, conduct, trial, admonitions, consequences, disobedience, probability, advice, education, authority, temptations, persecutions, inquiry, probation.* Young gentlemen of the university in one paragraph, gentlemen of the jury in the next, all are on trial here.

The verdict in *R v. Blandy,* as in other criminal trials, hinged upon intention. Since Blandy's administering of "the powder" to her father was never in doubt, the issue turned on whether she knew it was poison. Baron Legge so directed the jury:

3. Ibid., 18:1130–34.
4. Henry Fielding, *Amelia,* ed. Martin C. Battestin (Middletown, Conn.: Wesleyan University Press, 1983), 171–72; see also 347.

If you believe, that she knew it to be poison, the other part, viz. that she knew the effect, is consequential, and you must find her guilty: On the other hand, if you are satisfied, from her general character, from what has been said by the evidence on her part, and from what she has said herself, that she did not know it to be poison, nor had any malicious intention against her father, you ought to acquit her. But if you think she knowingly gave poison to her father, you can do no other than find her guilty.[5]

Up to the time of her execution, and in a written declaration that she left to be read after her death, Blandy denied knowing that it was poison. The jury, in finding her guilty, decided her intention on the circumstances and against her solemn word. The story they accepted—the prosecution's story initially—was that she knew all along and intended death. Thus in this trial, a narrative founded on circumstantial evidence overrode the prisoner's word. Though she prayed for the forgiveness of her sins, neither before nor after sentencing did Blandy confess to the fact in issue. Her state of mind during her father's illness and death had to be established objectively by the jury.

As we have seen, the whole project and promise of circumstantial evidence in the eighteenth century acquired a prosecutorial bent. The potential of this evidence for narrating, fixing intention, and bringing conviction was worked out by prosecutors and judges in criminal trials like *Blandy*, then further articulated and theorized by such as Burke and Bentham. Meanwhile Henry Fielding (1707–54), while writing *Tom Jones*, was appointed a magistrate in London and took a leading role in the campaign against crime. If anything, like those of other judges at the time, Fielding's services have to be regarded as mainly prosecutorial.[6] Yet the founder of the Bow Street runners and entertainer of social reforms that barely distinguished the poor from criminals, when he composed his classic novel, redirected virtually the whole enterprise of circumstantial evidence on behalf of the defense. Few works in the language can have referred so persistently, both explicitly and implicitly, to the trials of a hero "born to be hanged";[7] yet these same references

5. The Trial of Mary Blandy, *State Trials*, 18:1187.
6. See Wilbur L. Cross, *The History of Henry Fielding*, 3 vols. (New Haven: Yale University Press, 1918), 2:223–44, 250–300; Dudden, *Henry Fielding*, 2:740–96; and John H. Langbein, "Shaping the Eighteenth-Century Criminal Trial: A View from the Ryder Sources," *University of Chicago Law Review* 50 (1983): 60–76.
7. Henry Fielding, *The History of Tom Jones, a Foundling*, ed. Martin C. Battestin and Fredson Bowers (Middletown, Conn.: Wesleyan University Press, 1975), 3.2.118. Subsequent references to book, chapter, and page are given in parentheses.

and the plot itself are ironic, Jones is finally acquitted—at least by the author and most readers—and Fielding acknowledges the sufferings of the poor and other unfortunates. In *Tom Jones* he manages the evidence imaginatively, wittily, and triumphantly for the defense, in a pattern that I take to be prototypical of novels of circumstance: first various representations of the facts are marshaled against the protagonists, then a fuller representation exonerates them.[8]

False Testimony about Jones

Ample authority for prefacing a reading of *Tom Jones* with observations on a murder trial was provided thirty years ago by Ian Watt. In elaborating the parallel between eighteenth-century epistemology and formal realism in the novel, Watt suggested comparing a novel's readers to a jury:

> The novel's mode of imitating reality may . . . be equally well summarized in terms of the procedures of another group of specialists in epistemology, the jury in a court of law. Their expectations, and those of the novel reader coincide in many ways: both want to know "all the particulars" of a given case—the time and place of the occurrence; both must be satisfied as to the identities of the parties concerned . . . and they also expect the witnesses to tell the story "in his own words." The jury, in fact, takes the "circumstantial view of life," which T. H. Green found to be the characteristic outlook of the novel.[9]

The comparison is fully warranted, more especially since both of its terms can be historicized. Not only were novelists, as Watt demonstrated, adopting a circumstantial view of life, but jurists were becoming sharply conscious of circumstantial evidence in this period. Such a novelist and lawyer was Fielding, though as novelist he was far more

---

8. Cf. John Bender, *Imagining the Penitentiary: Fiction and the Architecture of the Mind in Eighteenth-Century England* (Chicago: University of Chicago Press, 1987). Very roughly, Bender locates an advanced model of punishment within eighteenth-century narratives and treats mainly *Jonathan Wild* and *Amelia* among Fielding's novels. I try to engage *Tom Jones* at the level of its overt representations to the reader and single out the model of a trial.

9. Ian Watt, *The Rise of the Novel: Studies in Defoe, Richardson, and Fielding* (Berkeley: University of California Press, 1957), 31. It might be noted that T. H. Green is one of those Victorians who stubbornly resist the circumstantial view in novels: see his 1862 prize essay, "An Estimate of the Value and Influence of Works of Fiction in Modern Times," in *Works of Thomas Hill Green,* ed. R. L. Nettleship, 3 vols. (London: Longmans, 1911), 3:20–45.

skeptical than Defoe or Richardson about witnesses telling their own stories.

At about the same time that Watt offered this comparison, William Empson suggested that Fielding, apparently even before he was appointed to the bench, combined the careers of novelist and judge: "Fielding . . . is always ready to consider what he would do if one of his characters came before him when he was on the bench." Empson then extended this idea of judgment to the act of reading the novels, to make a point not unlike Watt's comparison of readers to the jury, but specific to readers of Fielding: "as to the reader of the novel, Fielding cannot be bothered with him unless he, too, is fit to sit on a magistrate's bench, prepared, in literature as in life, to handle and judge any situation."[10] This line of thinking has since prompted important studies of the role of the reader of fiction, notably by John Preston and Wolfgang Iser, and it is no accident that these studies feature large the novel *Tom Jones*. "The book is *about* judgment," according to Preston. "It focuses attention, not only on events, but on the mind which perceives and judges them."[11] What I have to say about the novel is harmonious with this reader-oriented criticism — which Fielding, for all his vaunted superiority to the reader, obviously invited. But my purpose in reviewing the trials of Jones and his friends is to uncover the evidentiary basis of Fielding's realism.

The manifest ironies of *Tom Jones* complicate this review but do not render it impossible. When the hero was about fourteen, "he had been already convicted of three Robberies, *viz.* of robbing an Orchard, of stealing a Duck out of a Farmer's Yard, and of picking Master *Blifil's* Pocket of a Ball" (3.2.118). Those convictions — three of the very few that are not narrated in some detail — are told ironically, the reader can be sure. *All* of the hero's convictions turn out to bear a different aspect than first supposed by somebody, whether a character or reader of the novel — a turn not difficult to repeat indefinitely when the model action

10. William Empson, *"Tom Jones," Kenyon Review* 20 (1958), reprinted in *Fielding: A Collection of Critical Essays,* ed. Ronald Paulson (Englewood Cliffs, N.J.: Prentice-Hall, 1962), 145.

11. John Preston, *The Created Self: The Reader's Role in Eighteenth-Century Fiction* (London: Heinemann, 1970), 117; cf. Wolfgang Iser, *The Implied Reader: Patterns of Communication in Prose Fiction from Bunyan to Beckett* (Baltimore: Johns Hopkins University Press, 1974), 55. Both writers were influenced by Wayne Booth, whose star "implied author" is Fielding: see *The Rhetoric of Fiction,* 2d ed. (Chicago: University of Chicago Press, 1983), esp. 215–21. The congruity between these critical approaches and my stress on managed evidence in the narrative is also borne out to some degree by Iser's chapter on *Waverley* (81–100).

is a trial at common law. In reading *Tom Jones,* we cannot afford to ignore the irony and would scarcely enjoy the novel if we did. But ironic treatment is not the same as a refutation of a principle or obliteration of the model. Fielding's irony serves his didactic view of "HUMAN NATURE" (1.1.32) by repeatedly calling on the reader to take a second look. Before Jones's banishment from Allworthy's house in book 6, his offenses are especially varied; thereafter, the irony of incidental and minor misapprehensions broadens out, in longer stretches of suspense and ironies of fate; but the condition of trial is constant.

As our hero comes of age, with three robberies against him, the trials thicken. In rapid succession we hear of a partridge shot on Mr. Western's land, for which "*Tom* was presently convened before Mr. *Allworthy*" (3.2.121); a horse sold for the benefit of Black George's family, for which "the Criminal" received "a Reprieve" because of his generosity (3.8.142); and a Bible met with the same fate, which aggravates a debate over justice between the parson Thwackum and the philosopher Square—"*Thwackum* was resolved, a Crime of this Kind, which he called Sacrilege, should not go unpunished" (3.9.145). Needless to say, in these successive trials, which take place also before a jury of readers, the accused is not the only participant to be judged, and often the foremost witness is exposed more thoroughly than the hero. An excellent example is the trial of Jones for giving Blifil a bloody nose, after the latter has called him "a *Beggarly Bastard.*" Note how Fielding typically exaggerates the forensic language (a giveaway to the irony) and at the same time quite plausibly characterizes the situation as a trial (his model representation):

> Master *Blifil* now, with his Blood running from his Nose, and the Tears galloping after from his Eyes, appeared before his Uncle, and the tremendous *Thwackum.* In which Court an Indictment of Assault, Battery, and Wounding, was instantly preferred against *Tom*; who in his Excuse only pleaded the Provocation, which was indeed all the Matter that Master *Blifil* had omitted.
>
> It is indeed possible, that this Circumstance might have escaped his Memory; for, in his Reply, he positively insisted, that he had made Use of no such Appellation; adding, "Heaven forbid such naughty Words should ever come out of his Mouth."
>
> *Tom,* though against all Form of Law, rejoined in Affirmance of the Words. Upon which Master *Blifil* said, "It is no Wonder. Those who will tell one Fib, will hardly stick at another. If I had told my Master

such a wicked Fib as you have done, I should be ashamed to shew my Face." (3.4.130)

And so Blifil unravels Jones's concealment of the gamekeeper George's role in the affair of the partridge. The witness's attempt to detract from his silences by betraying Jones's, the narrator relates in the following chapter, probably saved the hero "from a good Lashing: For the Offence of the bloody Nose would have been of itself sufficient Cause for *Thwackum* to have proceeded to Correction," and that outcome is now checked by "a general Pardon" from Allworthy. A dispute with Square rages briefly on "the Punishment of such Crimes" and "the Correction of Children," but Allworthy "could not be prevailed upon to sign the Warrant for the Execution of *Jones*" (3.5.131–32). Not as yet will the hero be hanged.

Allworthy stands both as benefactor to the bastard hero and as judge. The deliberate exaggerations in Fielding's language construct a series of mock trials, yet Allworthy, Western, and others of the squirearchy also function in the society of the novel as justices of the peace, so that the line between mock trial and represented trial is indistinct. Jones's accumulated convictions begin to spell trouble with the law after his seduction of Molly, the gamekeeper's daughter (or her seduction of him). The narrator, or author of all, supposes that Allworthy may have "exceeded his Authority a little" in arresting the woman, and when Jones offers to take the blame, she is discharged—but not before the justice delivers his harangue. "Are you then so profligate and abandoned a Libertine, to doubt whether breaking the Laws of God and Man, the corrupting and ruining a poor Girl, be Guilt? I own, indeed, it doth lie principally upon you, and so heavy it is, that you ought to expect it should crush you." Subsequently Square compounds the hero's offense by suggesting to Allworthy that "he supported the Father in order to corrupt the Daughter" (4.11.192, 193, 195). The reader still distrusts the validity of the charges, but the novelist resorts to a little suspense and is careful not to supply enough evidence to resolve all doubt. This state of affairs—and the carefully designed game between novelist and reader—persists through the end of book 6, when the hero's tampering with the affections of Sophia Western, his behavior during Allworthy's illness, and a beating he has given to Thwackum culminate in another trial and his dismissal. Fielding always supplies just enough incident and commentary to sustain the reader's belief in Jones, while he widens the distance between the hero and his judges within the novel and draws out the suspense in preparation for the action on the road and in London.

"It was Mr. *Allworthy's* Custom never to punish any one, not even to turn away a Servant, in a Passion. He resolved, therefore, to delay passing Sentence on *Jones* till the Afternoon." The aside, "not even to turn away a Servant," gives some idea of the power of the squirearchy, for the class relations implicit in this proviso are no more called in question than the authority of the same character, similarly tempered, as justice of the peace. "When Dinner was over, and the Servants departed," on this occasion, Allworthy turns to the matter at hand with powers of patriarch and magistrate combined (the novel provides a different comic version of these powers in Squire Western):

> He set forth, in a long Speech, the many Iniquities of which *Jones* had been guilty . . . and concluded by telling him, "that unless he could clear himself of the Charge, he was resolved to banish him from his Sight for ever."
>
> Many Disadvantages attended poor *Jones* in making his Defence; nay, indeed, he hardly knew his Accusation: For as Mr. *Allworthy*, in recounting the Drunkenness, &c. while he lay ill, out of Modesty sunk every thing that related particularly to himself, which indeed principally constituted the Crime, *Jones* could not deny the Charge. His Heart was, besides, almost broken already, and his Spirits were so sunk, that he could say nothing for himself; but acknowledged the whole, and, like a Criminal in Despair, threw himself upon Mercy.

But Allworthy reproves himself for previous acts of forgiveness and prates on about the "audacious Attempt to steal away the young Lady" reserved for Blifil. "There is scarce any Punishment equal to your Crimes," he exclaims at last and banishes the young man from home (6.11.309–10). This patriarchal move mitigates the legal threat, even as banishment often conveys some residual forgiveness.

Once separated from Allworthy, the hero experiences fewer trials for day-to-day behavior, though his innocence or guilt is still subject to similar, incidental irony. At Upton, after Miss Western has departed but Squire Western has caught up with him, Jones is tried by "a grave Gentleman" who happens to be present and has "the Honour to be in the Commission of the Peace for the County of *Worcester*," for the supposed theft of Sophia's muff. This trial, which occupies four or five paragraphs, is recounted as lightly as the early trials before Allworthy, though the institution of the justice of the peace and the absence of any other relation between Jones and the unnamed gentleman make it a perfectly common episode of the social life represented in the novel.

The chambermaid whom Sophia directed to place the muff in the hero's room luckily testifies on his behalf:

> Whether a natural Love of Justice, or the extraordinary Comeliness of *Jones,* had wrought on *Susan* to make the Discovery, I will not determine; but such were the Effects of her Evidence, that the Magistrate, throwing himself back in his Chair, declared that the Matter was now altogether as clear on the Side of the Prisoner, as it had before been against him; with which the Parson concurred, saying, The Lord forbid he should be instrumental in committing an innocent Person to Durance. The Justice then arose, acquitted the Prisoner, and broke up the Court. (10.7.552–53)

Trials at law are never very far away in *Tom Jones,* and ultimately, as threatened all along, the hero is taken for murder in London. On this last occasion irony still hovers around the business, because he is innocent of drawing his weapon first and the witnesses are suborned agents of Lord Fellamar, but it is scarcely light or amusing irony anymore, unless to Squire Western, who capers and chortles, "Murder, hath he committed a Murder, and is there any Hopes of seeing him hanged? —Tol de rol, tol lol de rol" (17.3.885). The main actions at the end—discovery of the hero's identity, reconciliation with Allworthy, and marriage to Sophia—are not incidental trials of the same order, but all can be thought of as acquittals in a trial of longer duration, coterminous with the novel itself.

More persons than the hero find themselves incidentally on trial. In the early books of *Tom Jones,* Jenny Jones, Partridge, and Black George are formally tried before Allworthy in his seat of justice. Even Sophia's maid, Honour, is brought before Squire Western in this capacity. Of course, since all four are associated with Jones, they are like accomplices undergoing trial. Curiously, the very characters with whom the reader is invited to sympathize are the ones to endure trials. Even the Man of the Hill expected to be tried at the Oxford Assizes but was discharged when no one appeared against him; and other trials in the novel are metaphorical, as when "Sentence of Water-Gruel was passed upon" Jones, after he has injured himself in rescuing the heroine (4.14.204). More significantly, trials become analogues for inward debate and decision on the part of some characters. In a famous passage, Conscience and Avarice litigate the question, in the mind of George, whether to return five hundred pounds to Jones; and shortly thereafter, Honour the maid ponders the question of betraying Sophia:

She was, however, too upright a Judge to decree on one Side before she had heard the other. And here, first, a Journey to *London* appeared very strongly in Support of *Sophia*. . . . She then cross-examined all the Articles which had raised her Fears on the other Side, and found, on fairly sifting the Matter, that there was very little in them. And now both Scales being reduced to a pretty even Ballance, her Love to her Mistress being thrown into the Scale of her Integrity, made that rather preponderate, when a Circumstance struck upon her Imagination, which might have had a dangerous Effect . . . But while she was pursuing this Thought, the good Genius of *Sophia*, or that which presided over the Integrity of Mrs. *Honour*, or perhaps mere Chance, sent an Accident in her Way, which at once preserved her Fidelity, and even facilitated the intended Business. (7.8.353–54)

Thus a little sketch of the mind of a servant almost parodies the plot of the novel itself, or the judgment the reader is to reach about its hero.

Reasons for the trials that pervade *Tom Jones* can be sought not only in the author's legal calling and the prosecution of crime but in his religion and in the emergence of a strong doctrine of works in his day.[12] In a popular construction, life itself was to be viewed as a trial, and not merely in the sense that life in this world is preparation for the next. Butler's *Analogy of Religion*, for example, in the main an argument for the existence of a future life, cited the common experience of life as a trial as a kind of proof, in chapters entitled "Of a State of Probation, as implying Trial, Difficulties, and Danger," and "Of a State of Probation, as intended for moral Discipline and Improvement." As I have noted, one can read this underlying theme in Mary Blandy's criminal trial for her life, just as one can read it nearly everywhere in *Tom Jones*— in the constant judgments of behavior on the part of narrator and characters both, or in the kind supposition of its heroine at the close: "I think, Mr. *Jones* . . . I may almost depend on your own Justice, and leave it to yourself to pass Sentence on your own Conduct" (18.12.971). Besides countless verdicts of guilt or innocence in the many incidental trials, and the implied judgment of providence in Jones's good fortune, there are always more issues for inward and outward appeal—for there

12. See James A. Work, "Henry Fielding, Christian Censor," in *The Age of Johnson: Essays Presented to Chauncey Brewster Tinker*, ed. Frederick W. Hilles (New Haven: Yale University Press, 1949), 139–48; Martin C. Battestin, *The Moral Basis of Fielding's Art: A Study of "Joseph Andrews"* (Middletown, Conn.: Wesleyan University Press, 1959); and Michael McKeon, *The Origins of the English Novel, 1600–1740* (Baltimore: Johns Hopkins University Press, 1987), 398–409.

is still "a wide Difference," in the words of the Man of the Hill, "between the Case of a Man who is barely acquitted of a Crime in a Court of Justice, and of him who is acquitted in his own Heart, and in the Opinion of the People" (8.12.460–61). Such an acquittal, beyond that of the law, Fielding works hard for in the novel, on behalf of his hero and indirectly for himself and some fortunate ones among his readers.

The theme of probation in the novel has long been appreciated, even by readers not particularly sympathetic to Fielding and his hero. Jones is spirited and good-natured but must learn to be prudent: on this point the critics are more insistent than the novelist. Even a critic such as Empson, who leads one to believe that the novel concerns judgment, sees that as a moral rather than a cognitive theme. He is led to his conclusion, after all, by defining Fielding's idea of a *gentleman* as "a person fit to sit on the bench as a magistrate."[13] Fielding is undeniably a great moralist—the rival of Richardson, but also of Thackeray and George Eliot among novelists who set up as moralists—and that makes it especially difficult to hold his conclusions in abeyance while studying his methods. The purpose of the present review of the trials in *Tom Jones,* however, is to study their representation of reality, and hence their evidentiary aspect.[14] It was obviously important for Fielding to distinguish correct inferences from incorrect, and one kind of evidence from another in his novel. In truth, only the long-term trials of the hero and the comic irony of his fate are trustworthy; the ironies expended along the way, in metaphorical and incidental trials, are mainly told at the expense of supposed evidence. The very concentration of the trials on the novel's protagonist and his friends is one indirect measure of the attack, but there are others as well: those who are formally tried—if they are not pardoned by Allworthy—are usually wrongfully convicted; some of their trials are distorted by false witness or false inference, others by testimony that is little better than gossip; above all, the trials take place when the facts are only partly known and the evidence is incomplete.

In this novel of many recurring trials Fielding goes over a great deal of evidence in detail, and he never tires of showing that much of it is

13. Empson, "*Tom Jones,*" 145.

14. A move in this direction is made by Malinda Snow, "The Judgement of the Evidence in *Tom Jones,*" *South Atlantic Review* 48 (May 1983): 37–51, though Snow concludes, somewhat like Empson, by deferring to the reader's training for life: "If anyone learns to judge better, the reader learns" (48). For the novel's teaching of probable judgment, see also Douglas Lane Patey, *Probability and Literary Form: Philosophic and Literary Practice in the Augustan Age* (Cambridge: Cambridge University Press, 1984), 197–212.

false.[15] For example, in a mock trial early in the novel, Mrs. Partridge becomes "convinced of her Husband's Guilt"—guilt of adultery, that is, with his pupil Jenny Jones. The narrative shows how the inference arises, by carefully going over the evidence as it appears to the wife:

> It occurred instantly to her, that *Jenny* had scarce ever been out of her own House, while she lived with her. The leaning over the Chair, the sudden starting up, the Latin, the Smile, and many other Things rushed upon her all at once. The Satisfaction her Husband expressed in the Departure of *Jenny,* appeared now to be only dissembled; again, in the same Instant, to be real; but yet to confirm her Jealousy, proceeding from Satiety, and a hundred other bad Causes. (2.4.88)

Similarly, though in direct discourse with her brother the squire, Mrs. Western argues that Sophia is in love with Blifil by rapidly running over the evidence:

> Did she not faint away on seeing him lie breathless on the Ground? Did she not, after he was recovered, turn pale again the Moment we came up to that Part of the Field where he stood? And pray what else should be the Occasion of all her Melancholy that Night at Supper, the next Morning, and indeed ever since? (6.2.276)

Or Blifil, for that matter, has reasons for believing that Jones is not in love with Sophia, delivered in a series of speculations by the narrator: "He fancied that he knew *Jones* to the Bottom, and had in reality a great Contempt for his Understanding, for not being more attached to his own Interest" (6.7.295). Such false inferences usually tell more about the character who renders them than about their object, and Fielding makes regular sport of the reasoning of Thwackum and Square in the early books of the novel, for the way their conclusions can easily be predicted from their mind-sets. One of the author's purposes, obviously, in displaying so much misapprehension of reality, is not moral at all but to promote by contrast his own history of Tom Jones.

For it is not only narrow-minded, self-serving, hypocritical, or hostile inference that must give way to the more comprehensive narrative. Squire Allworthy, whose standing in the novel is pretty well expressed by his name and genesis,[16] can also be deceived. Though he is a model of goodness, neither his scrupulousness nor his love can always penetrate

15. Cf. Leo Braudy, *Narrative Form in History and Fiction: Hume, Fielding, and Gibbon* (Princeton: Princeton University Press, 1970), 158.

16. Allworthy has traditionally been identified with Fielding's patrons George Lyttleton and Ralph Allen. See the dedication of *Tom Jones* and Battestin's note to 1.4.42.

to the truth. As justice of the peace and moral judge of the other characters, he cannot reach true verdicts without knowing all the facts. Quite early in the novel, Fielding draws attention to the limited perspective of even this most far-seeing character:

> For the Reader is greatly mistaken, if he conceives that *Thwackum* appeared to Mr. *Allworthy* in the same Light as he doth to him in this History; and he is as much deceived, if he imagines, that the most intimate Acquaintance which he himself could have with that Divine, would have informed him of those Things which we, from our Inspiration, are enabled to open and discover. Of Readers who from such Conceits as these, condemn the Wisdom or Penetration of Mr. *Allworthy,* I shall not scruple to say, that they make a very bad and ungrateful Use of that Knowledge which we have communicated to them. (3.5.135)

In this tease, the reader is first thrust into Allworthy's shoes, then hectored for being critical. Of course, the author has not revealed to the reader *all* "those Things which we, from our Inspiration, are enabled to open and discover," or the case would be complete and the novel over. Thus both the reader and the judge within the story are obliged to await the inspiration of the narrator, who marshals all the evidence and presents it in the order most likely to bring conviction. From book 6 until nearly the end of *Tom Jones,* Allworthy labors under the impression that he is in possession of all the relevant facts. He defends his conclusions to Mrs. Miller in strong terms: "I promise you, it was upon the fullest and plainest Evidence that I resolved to take the Measures I have taken." But Mrs. Miller trusts to a longer view: "I make not the least doubt, but Time will shew all Matters in their true and natural Colours, and that you will be convinced this poor young Man deserves better of you than some other Folks that shall be nameless" (17.7.899). Her proverbial appeal to time and truth is another reminder that Allworthy is not in possession of the full story, which can be known only from a complicated and nearly exhaustive mixture of evidence.

The main thrust, in the strong representation called *Tom Jones,* is against testimony of one form or another. The novel itself stands over against narratives that supposedly flow from the pen of one or more participants in the action—against memoir and confession and analogous forms of direct testimony—while scene after scene described in the novel devolves into erroneous or partial testimony. In terms of a distinction such as Bentham's, between two kinds of evidence presented in a court of law, the evidence that holds up in *Tom Jones* is nearly all indirect, and the evidence that misleads is mostly direct. The narrator is famously involved with the reader rather than the actors, and his narrative should be thought of in evidentiary terms as *indirect*. He is not an eyewitness but a manager of the evidence, analogous to a prosecutor or a judge and to later defense attorneys in a trial. Fielding swiftly subordinates Allworthy as judge in the case and revels in showing up characters who serve as witnesses—so much so that misrepresentation can be thought of as a principal countertheme in the novel.

This demolishing of witnesses occurs on page after page, but occasionally an incident is elaborated in such a way as to spell out the weakness of testimony in general. When the hero tells his story to the barber Benjamin—who turns out to be Partridge—his listener exclaims that he must have been traduced by enemies or Allworthy would never have dismissed him. Now the reader has some grounds for agreeing with this position and will be supplied with more evidence of its truth by the end. But at this point Fielding abruptly challenges Partridge's conclusion, because the character judges from his former knowledge of the young man's relation to Allworthy and what Jones has just told him. Fielding further analyzes Jones's account of the matter, testimony that notably excludes "those injurious Lights" in which his earlier actions "had been misrepresented to Allworthy," which he could not know about. The hero's account of the matter omits "many material Facts."

> Not that *Jones* desired to conceal or to disguise the Truth . . . but, in Reality, so it happened, and so it always will happen: For a Man be never so honest, the Account of his own Conduct will, in Spite of himself, be so very favourable, that his Vices will come purified through his Lips, and, like foul Liquors well strained, will leave all their Foulness behind. For tho' the Facts themselves may appear, yet so different will be the Motives, Circumstances, and Consequences, when a Man tells his own Story, and when his Enemy tells it, that we can scarce recognize the Facts to be one and the same. (8.5.420)

This is not a moral point, for the narrator has ceded the moral point to Jones; rather, it is a point about making representations. Neither an honest account by a party to the action nor an enemy's account can be relied upon, because neither takes in all the relevant "Motives, Circumstances, and Consequences." Fielding allots many pages of the novel to explaining the shortcomings and worse of testimony against Jones; here he explains Jones's unreliability as a witness.

A slightly different reading of the novel would present the narrative's countertheme as slander perhaps. Wherever the hero goes he makes his personal impression, usually favorable, on others; when his back is turned, slander and mere gossip rapidly undo this impression.[17] But given the repeated trials of the hero and the implicit analogy of life to a trial, gossip and slander can be classed with other testimony, most of which can be traced, amended, contraverted, or scorned outright. Thus Fielding treats one gossiper, at Gloucester, with special contempt: "This fellow, I say, stiled himself a Lawyer, but was indeed a most vile Petty-fogger, without Sense or Knowledge of any Kind." No sooner is Jones quit of the room than the fellow begins disputing his reputation with Dowling and the landlady of the Bell. Abruptly, the narrative assimilates his gossip to one of the metaphorical trials that abound in *Tom Jones*: "Petty-fogger calling to mind that he had not been sworn, as he usually was, before he gave his Evidence, now bound what he had declared with so many Oaths and Imprecations, that the Landlady's Ears were shocked, and she put a Stop to his swearing, by assuring him of her Belief" (8.8.431, 433). The deliberately skewed comparison of barroom oaths to the swearing of witnesses in a trial both makes the point and attacks the need for making it. Most novelists of the eighteenth and nineteenth centuries take gossip very seriously,[18] and Fielding examines the subject repeatedly in *Tom Jones*. Gossip is another form, obviously, of competing representation. It can be a form of testimony on oath, as in the instance of the pettifogger; or by a person clever and selfish enough, it can be systematically directed to particular ends. Such a person, of course, is Blifil, the villain of the novel and rival of the novelist as a manipulator of evidence.

While Blifil's talebearing may be put down to his innate nastiness, his scheming against Jones affords the novel's chief instance of false testimony. It is Blifil who orchestrates the hero's dismissal in book 6. Carefully couching his testimony in expressions of sorrow and pretending to be a reluctant witness, he proceeds to tell of Jones's carousing when Allworthy was sick, of discovering him with a woman, and of his beating Thwackum. Of the first of these tales, Coleridge observed in an essay on truth telling, "Blifil related accurately Tom Jones's riotous joy during his benefactor's illness, only omitting that this joy was occasioned by the physician's having pronounced him out of danger."[19] The hypocrite's manner is perfect and compels Allworthy to apologize even for calling a second witness: "Not that I want any Confirmation

---

17. Cf. Braudy, *Narrative Form in History and Fiction*, 152: "Gossip is the normal mode of perception in the early stages of [*Tom Jones*]."

18. See Patricia Meyer Spacks, *Gossip* (New York: Knopf, 1985), esp. 147–228.

19. Samuel Taylor Coleridge, *The Friend*, ed. Barbara E. Rooke, 2 vols. (Princeton: Princeton University Press, 1969), 1:49.

of what you say; but I will examine all the Evidence of this Matter, to justify to the World the Example I am resolved to make of such a Monster." In the event, Thwackum "corroborated every Circumstance which the other had deposed; nay, he produced the Record upon his Breast, where the Handwriting of Mr. *Jones* remained very legible in black and blue." The handwriting evidence, of course, is another of Fielding's special touches: like the terrific swearing of the pettifogger, it both confirms the trial aspect of the whole episode and exposes its outrageousness. The parson also usefully testifies that Blifil begged him not to inform on Jones earlier: the timing of this trial as well as the doctoring of the facts have been Blifil's doing, and he emerges temporarily as one who can manipulate indirect as well as direct evidence.

> In reality, *Blifil* had taken some Pains to prevail with the Parson, and to prevent the Discovery at that Time; for which he had many Reasons. He knew that the Minds of Men are apt to be softened and relaxed from their usual Severity by Sickness. Besides, he imagined that if the Story was told when the Fact was so recent, and the Physician about the House, who might have unravelled the real Truth, he should never be able to give it the malicious Turn which he intended. Again, he resolved to hoard up this Business, till the Indiscretion of *Jones* should afford some additional Complaints; for he thought the joint Weight of many Facts falling upon him together, would be the most likely to crush him. (6.10.308–9)

That Fielding can unravel this truth shows that he only bides his time, that the novel is hoarding up the business of crushing Blifil. Yet that he narrates the villain's plan without bothering to cite evidence for it betrays some impatience to assert his dominance. Much later, when Allworthy has begun to share Mrs. Miller's suspicion and the novel is drawing to a close, Blifil is compared to those "whose Business it is to conceal Truth, or to defend Falsehood," at the Old Bailey but who may be surprised by cross-examination despite their careful preparation. Some answers even "the most fertile Invention cannot supply in an Instant," and so it proves with Blifil. On this last occasion his face betrays him, and he is thus "obliged to give Evidence against himself" (18.5.932).

Suborned witnesses were not uncommon at the Old Bailey, and because of two such witnesses Jones, awaiting trial for the murder of Fitzpatrick, falls in danger of being hanged in earnest. His friend Nightingale warns him that precisely because witnesses for hire have no connection with the accused and apparently no motive to lie, they are likely to be believed: "What Reason will an indifferent Court of Justice be able to assign why they should not believe them?" Nightingale has interviewed the two witnesses, and they have answered that they "would abide by their Evidence upon Oath" (17.9.908). This is a practice that Fielding caustically refers to in *Amelia* by having the lawyer Murphy dismiss the need for any knowledge of the law but evidence: "The Chapter of Evidence is the main Business; that is the Sheet-Anchor: that is the Rudder, which brings the Vessel safe in Portum. Evidence is indeed the Whole, the *Summa totidis,* for *de non apparentibus et non insistentibus eandem est ratio."*[20] But in *Tom Jones* as well, the lawyer Dowling reaches the witnesses against the hero and, to Allworthy's indignant surprise, has offered to pay them. "There are two Ways of delivering Evidence," he explains—meaning for or against the prisoner. "I told them therefore, that if any Offers should be made them on the other Side, they should refuse them, and that they might be assured they should lose nothing by being honest Men, and telling the Truth" (18.8.948–49). Fortunately, since Fitzpatrick lives, these efforts are unnecessary; but it is typical of the novel that direct evidence should be put in such a bad light, and typical that most evidence should point to the hero's guilt until it is masterfully arranged for his acquittal.

Important witnesses alter their testimony at the end of *Tom Jones,* once a preponderance of evidence has made their positions untenable. Jenny Jones, the most likable of false witnesses, confesses that she is not the hero's mother. A letter from a repentant philosopher speaks to "the principal Fact, upon the Misrepresentation of which" Allworthy dismissed Jones, and Square thus becomes a faithful character witness after all, "serving the Cause of Truth, of doing Right to the Innocent, and making all the Amends in my Power for a past Offence" (18.4.927). The villain Blifil, whose evidence stands most in need of correction, seizes the chance to confess directly to his brother, as the person most likely to forgive him. "*Blifil* was at first sullen and silent, balancing in his Mind whether he should yet deny all: But finding at last the Evidence too strong against him, he betook himself at last to Confession." Thus he is subdued in the end only by the sum of evidence arrayed against him; otherwise, given this novel's onslaught upon testimony, his confession would be worth no more than his previous lies. Indeed it still is a lie, as Fielding portrays it. It is another performance on Blifil's part, and an unseemly one at that: "He then asked Pardon of his Brother in

---

20. Fielding, *Amelia,* 61. As Battestin demonstrates in his note, Murphy has quite altered the meaning of the maxim by substituting *insistentibus* for *existentibus* in the original. Thus "things not seen are treated as if they did not exist" becomes something like "things neither seen *nor insisted upon* are not evidence," a sly invitation to perjury.

the most vehement Manner, prostrated himself on the Ground, and kissed his Feet: In short, he was now as remarkably mean, as he had been before remarkably wicked" (18.11.968).

Such are the negative means by which Fielding directs his narrative and asserts his claim to a superior representation of the facts. He exposes false and partial inferences, false and partial testimony as he can. In frequent invented or metaphorical trials, he teaches the reader to distrust the witnesses and await more facts. The numerous forensic failures, in their variety, merely prepare for the aggrandizement of all the evidence by the narrative of *Tom Jones*. While the incidental trials are typically shorn of their capacity to establish the facts—and this despite Fielding's commitment to the moral idea of probation—the narrative as a whole subsumes all the powers of representation and claims to serve as a better trial in the end, with the readers of the novel still as jurors, if you like. The many misrepresentations of Jones and his friends, through a pleasing comedy and overturning of judgments, give way to a true representation won by superior management of the evidence.

The tactics of this grand strategy were roughly those of Fielding's first venture in prose fiction, *An Apology for the Life of Mrs. Shamela Andrews*. In that burlesque, he purported to show that Richardson's Pamela was a false witness who wrote under a false name. His anonymous pamphlet challenged "the many notorious Falsehoods and Misrepresentations" of the epistolary novel and held out other evidence, "exact Copies of authentick Papers" by Sham.[21] In *Joseph Andrews* he rapidly diverted parody to a fiction with different aims and reclothed Don Quixote in the garb of an English parson. Then, after experimenting with thoroughly corrupt witnessing in *Jonathan Wild*, he worked with a persistent organization commensurate with epic and a concentration on evidence studied from trials at common law to create *The History of Tom Jones*. The resulting classic could not be replicated, to be sure, yet four or five generations of novelists would commonly adopt the same narrative strategy—the management of evidence in the book.

Fielding's Management of the Evidence

Again I would return to Ian Watt's account of the novel, with undiminished admiration and a minor corrective. Watt's argument, wide-ranging as it is, made Defoe and Richardson exemplary for realism.

21. [Henry Fielding], *An Apology for the Life of Mrs. Shamela Andrews* (London: Dodd, 1741). Quotations are from the title page.

They are prosers justly celebrated for their "closeness" to the events described and their "concrete particularity," whereas Fielding's very literary ambitions compromised the novel form and sometimes diverted attention "from the content of the report to the skill of the reporter." Yet diversion is not a bad idea for a defense lawyer, one might retort, and in the trial of *Tom Jones* there is also an evidentiary difference to be marked from these novels by other hands. Very accurately, Watt states of the novel, "Reading *Tom Jones* we do not imagine that we are eavesdropping on a new exploration of reality; the prose immediately informs us that exploratory operations have long since been accomplished, that we are to be spared that labour, and presented instead with a sifted and clarified report of the findings."[22] Fielding, in other words, specializes in the management of evidence. Watt's implicit comparison between Defoe's or Richardson's realism and Fielding's applies equally well to distinctions between direct and indirect evidence, between testimony and circumstantial evidence, or between evidentiary facts and facts arranged, in Burke's terms, "narratively and historically." In a given trial, each kind of evidence may have its virtues, as the nature of the case or personality of the witnesses will determine. The same is true of the novel, but it is managed evidence—Fielding's specialty—that generally invigorates the English novel for the next hundred years, even for admirers, like Jane Austen, of *Sir Charles Grandison.*

In another remark, following this observation, Watt writes, "Formal realism is, of course, like the rules of evidence, only a convention."[23] True, many of the rules of evidence, which were increasingly enforced as conventions at this time, concern witnesses and testifying and hence correspond to the conventions governing characters who tell their stories in a novel. Thus the *rules* of evidence provide an interesting gloss on the realism of Defoe and Richardson. But Fielding's narrator in *Tom Jones* (or the author of *Tom Jones*—it makes little difference to my argument) follows a different convention, that of presenting and summarizing and evaluating the evidence. He should be compared not to a witness constrained by the rules of evidence but to a prosecutor or judge—or later the counsel for the defense—in a criminal trial. Quite apart from his writing of novels, as a lawyer Fielding opposed rules of evidence that interfered with the prosecution of criminals. In his most substantial contribution to the literature of crime prevention, *An Enquiry into the Causes of the Late Increase of Robbers* (1751), he wrote as follows:

22. Watt, *Rise of the Novel,* 29–30.
23. Ibid., 32.

> I shall not enter here into a Disquisition concerning the Nature of Evidence in general; this being much too large a Field; nor shall I examine the Utility of those Rules which our Law prescribes on this Head. Some of these Rules might perhaps be opened a little wider than they are, without either Mischief or Inconvenience; and I am the bolder in the Assertion, as I know a very learned Judge who concurs with this Opinion. There is no Branch of the Law more bulky, more full of Confusion and Contradiction, I had almost said of Absurdity, than the Law of Evidence as it now stands.

This is a familiar prosecutorial stance. Specifically, Fielding goes on to criticize the exclusion of interested parties as witnesses: that is, "to keep more closely to the Point—Why shall not any Credit be given to the Evidence of an Accomplice?"[24] His mild questioning of the "Utility" of the rules of evidence should put us in mind of Bentham. Fielding's protest is hardly a ripple compared with the waves Bentham set in motion on this same subject fifty years later, though neither writer was able to effect any immediate change in the law.[25] Their objections to the exclusion for interest stem not merely from the inconvenience to prosecutors but positively from the belief that juries can weigh the evidence for themselves. A comprehensive narrative, which will bring conviction one way or the other, relies on a mixture of evidence.

Even as the use of circumstantial evidence was advertised by eighteenth-century prosecutors and by judges echoing the prosecutors in their charges to the jury, prosecution might be said to be Fielding's normal mode in his brief career as a magistrate. This is not to say he was an unfair judge, of course, but to recall that he was elevated to the bench on a wave of anticrime sentiment. While completing *Tom Jones* he was appointed justice of the peace for Westminster and shortly thereafter for the county of Middlesex.[26] On 29 June 1749 he delivered his first charge to the grand jury, which was well received by the other

24. Henry Fielding, *An Enquiry into the Causes of the late Increase of Robbers and Related Works,* ed. Malvin R. Zirker (Middletown, Conn.: Wesleyan University Press, 1988), 161.

25. Jeremy Bentham, *Rationale of Judicial Evidence,* ed. John Stuart Mill, 5 vols. (London: Hunt and Clarke, 1827), 5:34–77. "Absurdity," the word pronounced and withdrawn by Fielding, is sounded repeatedly by Bentham. The exclusion of interested witnesses seems to have originated with Coke for civil cases and somewhat later in criminal law; it was not reformed until Victorian times, by legislation of 1843 (6 & 7 Victoria 85). See William Holdsworth, *A History of English Law,* 16 vols. (1903–66; rpt. London: Methuen, 1966), 9:190–96.

26. For the chronology, see W. B. Coley, "Fielding's Two Appointments to the Magistracy," *Modern Philology* 63 (1965): 144–49.

justices and subsequently published. Though Fielding said the usual complimentary things about the jury system and the liberty of Englishmen, he mainly focused on the constraining and punitive functions of the common law.[27] A similar prosecutorial bent is well documented by his *Enquiry* of 1751 and *A Proposal for Making an Effectual Provision for the Poor* of 1753. And of course it is more than evident in his fiction, in the satirical thrust of all four novels (but especially *Jonathan Wild*) and in the numerous subordinate and tentative actions of *Tom Jones*. Indeed a tentative marshaling of evidence against the protagonist, I am suggesting, is characteristic of this mode of representation. Only on the basis of a strong indictment can Fielding conduct his long, adroit, and masterly, rather *un*magisterial, defense of Jones.

Fielding's most strenuous literary ambition was the emulation of Cervantes, and in *Joseph Andrews* he succeeded memorably in domesticating Don Quixote as Parson Adams. His very invention of that novel, in that it was parodic, was Cervantine in a sense now widely accepted.[28] Though it is harder to locate a Cervantine principle in *Tom Jones,* the process of exposing false inference and false testimony provides, in a sense, a forensic version of the same model for realism: in sum, not only is Jones to be tried and acquitted, but the superiority of this form of narrative to others will be established once and for all; and the forensic model that Fielding thereby creates will have the special merit of opposing an extraliterary means of representation in daily use and fraught with sanctions of the law. The strategy belongs to a long rhetorical tradition, honed by the adversary practice of the common law. (In contrast, Cervantes opposed the narrative of *Don Quixote* to romance, a form with fewer pretensions to reality in the first place.)[29] Though the positive strengths of the method of representation in *Tom*

27. Henry Fielding, *A Charge Delivered to the Grand Jury, at the Sessions of Peace Held for the City and Liberty of Westminster,* in *An Enquiry . . . and Related Works,* 1–30.

28. The notion of Cervantine realism, "passing from the imitation of art through parody to the imitation of nature," has been championed by Harry Levin. This phrase is from his essay "The Example of Cervantes," in *Contexts of Criticism* (Cambridge: Harvard University Press, 1957), 96; the principle appears elsewhere in Levin's writings and most notably in *The Gates of Horn: A Study of Five French Realists* (New York: Oxford University Press, 1963). For the role of parody in nineteenth-century English novels, see George Levine, *The Realistic Imagination: English Fiction from Frankenstein to Lady Chatterley* (Chicago: University of Chicago Press, 1981).

29. For other modifications of Cervantes by Fielding, see Walter L. Reed, *An Exemplary History of the Novel: The Quixotic versus the Picaresque* (Chicago: University of Chicago Press, 1981), 117–36; and my *Reflections on the Hero as Quixote* (Princeton: Princeton University Press, 1981), 40–43, 81, 190. I try to reserve the word "Cervantine" for the method and "quixotic" for the heroic tradition begun by Cervantes.

Jones may be harder to describe than its opposition to false inference and testimony, we can expect to find claims analogous to those made for circumstantial evidence in eighteenth-century criminal prosecutions: claims to minuteness of circumstances and probability, to comprehensiveness and closure, and to the correct estimate of character.

In regard to the first of these claims, Fielding certainly discourses effectively on minuteness of circumstances and probability, even though he may not provide as many concrete particulars as Defoe or Richardson. The same narrative that exposes Mrs. Partridge's false inference as to her husband's adultery, or Mrs. Western's mistaken belief that her niece is in love with Blifil, keeps a close eye on Sophia's muff, so as to prepare its own carefully laid train of circumstances. Whereas in the inferior narratives of this novel minutiae tend to mislead, in the master narrative they tend to confirm the truth—at least such is the claim. After Sophia's snatching the muff from the fire signals her love to Jones, Fielding discourses on the danger of omitting the smallest facts. "In reality, there are many little Circumstances too often omitted by injudicious Historians, from which Events of the utmost Importance arise. The World may indeed be considered as a vast Machine, in which the great Wheels are originally set in Motion by those which are very minute, and almost imperceptible to any but the strongest Eyes" (5.4.225). If anything, this clockwork motion of circumstances gained in popularity over the next hundred years, and though we may think of Sterne as its progenitor in novel writing, Thackeray and George Eliot founded their idea of it directly on Fielding. Thus an excursus on the fateful difference made in life by walking down one side of Regent Street or the other, in *A Shabby Genteel Story*, recalls very nearly Fielding's manner. Then Thackeray examines the train of circumstances his own story comprises and comments, "When Fate wills that something should come to pass, she sends forth a million of little circumstances to clear and prepare the way."[30] Even the slight snobbishness about circumstances is like Fielding's. Only superior observation—capable of detecting signs "almost imperceptible"—and greater coherence of evidence finally warrant the superiority of the master narrative.

Cultivating the reader's respect for the narrator's forensic powers (compare the "*in*judicious Historians" glanced at in the same passage) may be tempered with ostensible sharing of these powers. Just as a

---

30. *A Shabby Genteel Story*, in *The Works of William Makepeace Thackeray*, Biographical Edition, 13 vols. (Toronto: Morang, 1899), 11:51–53.

good lawyer may sometimes claim merely to present the facts, from which the jury can draw conclusions as to some principal fact in issue, Fielding the novelist may pretend to stop short of making any inferences. Early in *Tom Jones* he pronounces, "It is our Province to relate Facts, and we shall leave Causes to Persons of much higher Genius" (2.4.87). Of course he does not adhere to this stance very long, for one of the ways he can establish his authority and make strong representations is, precisely, to trace causes. So perhaps, at another juncture, he will "oblige" the reader with reasons for Mr. Western's abrupt appearance in London (15.6.803). Much of the admiration expressed for the novel, over the years since it was written, has finally to do with the way Fielding seemingly lets the reader have the facts and only later helps with the inference (as in subsequent detective stories). Thus he may be said to have invited the praise of Henry James Pye in his *Commentary on Aristotle* in 1792:

> No reader I believe ever guessed that the hero of the piece would turn out to be the nephew of Allworthy and the son of Mrs. Bridget, till the moment before the discovery takes place, and yet how natural is the behaviour of those who know the circumstance, when the incidents are examined afterwards. With what nice touches is the conduct of the mother expressed, and especially her partiality to Jones; and Dowling, when he accidentally meets Jones on the road, actually calls Allworthy his uncle without giving the reader the least suspicion of the truth; so inimitable is the art of the poet.[31]

This aesthetic judgment simply turns on its head—"so inimitable is the art of the poet"—the judicial thesis of the time on the nonfalsifiability of a chain of circumstantial evidence. That thesis celebrated as inimitable any series of closely connected evidentiary facts; Fielding demonstrated that a long and very carefully arranged fiction can do the trick.

It is with a mixture of evidence in *Tom Jones* that Fielding achieves his triumphant representation of supposed fact. His general berating of testimony, including lies and deliberate concealments, does not prevent him from using both true and false testimony to advantage in the end. At the same time, and with the same strategy, that he solicits admiration for his plotting, he might be said to anticipate Bentham on the effective admixture of several kinds of evidence:

31. Henry James Pye, *A Commentary Illustrating the Poetic of Aristotle* (London: Stockdale, 1792), 357. A comparison to the discovery in Sophocles' *Oedipus* became commonplace. Pye thought Fielding's plot superior to Sophocles' (358). See also 181–82.

Now it is, that the testimony, not being, in respect of such part of it as is true, full enough to operate of itself with a conclusive force in the character of direct evidence, is consulted (as it were), and made to operate further, in the character of circumstantial evidence; in which character it may be full enough to operate, and even conclusively; affording full satisfaction—generating a full persuasion, —although, in the character of direct evidence, it was deficient.

And as we have seen, Bentham thus accounts for the inclusion in a narrative not only of testimony that is inadequate in itself but of testimony that is false. The latter, when recognized as false, may "contribute in support of the conclusion, just as much as facts that are true." Both "when the whole narrative is viewed together, in a general point of view," and for a single apprehension, falsehood is "a strong indication and symptom of delinquency."[32] Bentham is really only summarizing and laying out the logic of commonplace inferences, and as usual in regarding falsehood and delinquency, he has the culprit in mind—the defendant in a criminal trial. But the novel *Tom Jones* takes a similar purview of evidence in nearly all of its pages. Through most of it, the bastard Jones is assumed to be the culprit. In the end, the burden of proof and of guilt has shifted to the legitimate Blifil, a false witness. Thus Mrs. Miller cannot help exclaiming, not of the original defendant but of the witness, "Guilty, upon my Honour! Guilty, upon my Soul!"

Fielding's aesthetic purpose and his consciousness of evidence are therefore closely allied. Not surprisingly, the famous introductory chapters to each book of *Tom Jones*—their fame pertinaciously asserted in the course of writing—apply to both concerns: his literary meditations on probability and completeness cohere with the principles of circumstantial evidence. The self-pronounced "longest" of such chapters mounts a careful argument against "that Species of Writing which is called the Marvellous." For the Christian and modern writer, Fielding explains, the supernatural is doubly ruled out: the doings of pagan deities have to be regarded as false, and the objects of Christian faith are off-limits. "Man therefore is the highest Subject" for history and novel writing, and "great Care is to be taken, that we do not exceed the Capacity of the Agent we describe." This turn introduces the test of probability, and here Fielding follows Aristotle on the difference between history and fiction—though "to say the Truth, if the Historian will confine himself to what really happened, and utterly reject any Circumstance, which, tho' never so well attested, he must be well

32. Bentham, *Rationale of Judicial Evidence,* 3:9–10.

assured is false, he will sometimes fall into the Marvellous, but never into the Incredible," and there he follows Locke. In one of the few places in *Tom Jones* where he openly discusses the fictionality of the work, he draws a further distinction between narratives of public and of private lives, in order to argue the special onus of probability on the latter. Again the issue is evidence, including testimony, which actually exists for narratives of public lives to draw upon but has to be manufactured for narratives of private lives such as novels pretend to. "But we who deal in private Character, who search into the most retired Recesses, and draw forth Examples of Virtue and Vice, from Holes and Corners of the World, are in a more dangerous Situation. As we have no publick Notoriety, no concurrent Testimony, no Records to support and corroborate what we deliver, it becomes us to keep within the Limits not only of Possibility, but of Probability too" (8.1.395–402). That is to say, at a certain level of apprehension, a faked narrative that is circumstantial is less offensive than faked notoriety, testimony, or records. Probability is the most important ground shared by fictional and nonfictional representations. It is also the chief test of "Conservation of Character," or consistency of behavior over time, the final point raised in this chapter.

Opposition to the marvelous advertises the quotidian virtues of a true representation. The Cervantine principle at work here is not unknown to philosophy, for Hume's chapter on miracles similarly celebrates experience and probability.[33] Beliefs tend to define themselves against earlier beliefs, and in this era the idea of probability was thus enhanced in philosophy, theology, and novel writing. Though Fielding, trained in the law, theorized about narrative more openly than his rival Richardson, the latter also, in a postscript to *Clarissa,* claimed "that there was frequently a necessity to be very circumstantial and minute, in order to preserve and maintain that Air of Probability, which is necessary to be maintained in a Story designed to represent real Life."[34] Surviving manuscript notes for this postscript, which was written after the publication of *Tom Jones,* show Richardson contrasting his epistolary method to "the dry Narrative" of Fielding and, still more interesting, connecting his own use of evidence with trials at common law. "Attentive Readers have found, and will find," he writes, "that the Prob-

33. See David Hume, *Enquiry concerning the Human Understanding,* in *Enquiries concerning the Human Understanding and concerning the Principles of Morals,* ed. L. A. Selby-Bigge, 2d ed. (Oxford: Clarendon, 1902), 109–31.

34. [Samuel Richardson], *Clarissa; or, The History of a Young Lady,* 4th ed., 7 vols. (London: Richardson, 1751), 7:368.

ability of all Stories told, or of Narrations given, depends upon small Circumstances; as may be observed, that in all Tryals for Life and Property, the Merits of the Cause are more determinable by such, than by the greater Facts; which usually are so laid, and taken care of, as to seem to authenticate themselves."[35] Though it is not certain what Richardson means by "the greater Facts" set forth in trials, presumably he too contrasts the impression received from inclusive and detailed circumstantial evidence to direct testimony on the fact at issue. Quite apart from defending the sheer length of his novel, he could hardly have failed to associate multiple observations and "small Circumstances" with the probability of his representation.[36]

Fielding renews his argument for probabilistic narrative as *Tom Jones* draws to a close. If generic form is allowed to take over the representation, the denouement of the novel will most likely shake the reader's credulity. In the introductory chapter to book 17, therefore, he attempts to forestall this possibility by contrasting his method with both tragedy and comedy. Precisely in the denouement, writers are likely to violate probability: "When a Comic Writer hath made his principal Characters as happy as he can; or when a Tragic Writer hath brought them to the highest Pitch of human Misery, they both conclude their Business to be done, and that their Work is come to a Period." Since Fielding has every intention of bringing his novel to a thumping comic ending, this chapter functions a little like a stage magician's invitation to watch his performance carefully. First he feints with tragedy, offering to bring about "a Murder or two, and a few moral Sentences," and then, fending against comedy, threatens to sacrifice "this Rogue, whom we have unfortunately made our Heroe"—if the latter cannot extricate himself by "some natural Means," without doing violence to "the Truth and Dignity of History" or the author's "Integrity."[37] The referral of the matter of truthfulness to a supposed question of honor is sufficient hint that a compromise with comedy is in the making. Fielding feels the need to recapitulate his stance against the marvelous at this point, as if the supernatural summed up all imaginable improbabilities:

35. Samuel Richardson, *Clarissa: Preface, Hints of Prefaces, and Postscript,* Augustan Reprints 103 (Los Angeles: Clark Library, 1964), 13, 5. All these remarks, including the postscript reprinted here, seem to have been written after the publication of *Tom Jones.* Cf. Lennard J. Davis, *Factual Fictions: The Origins of the English Novel* (New York: Columbia University Press, 1983), 181–83.

36. Cf. Patey, *Probability and Literary Form,* 102, 175–76.

37. Battestin's note to this passage compares *Jonathan Wild* bk. 4, chap. 6, where Fielding protests that he "would rather have suffered half Mankind to be hang'd, than have saved one contrary to the strictest Rules of Writing and Probability."

In this the Antients had great Advantage over the Moderns. Their Mythology, which was at that Time more firmly believed by the Vulgar than any Religion is at Present, gave them always an Opportunity of delivering a favourite Heroe. Their Deities were always at the Writer's Elbow, to execute any of his Purposes; and the more extraordinary the Intervention was, the greater was the Surprize and Delight of the credulous Reader. Those Writers could with greater Ease have conveyed a Friend from one Country to another, nay from one World to another, and have brought him back again, than a poor circumscribed Modern can deliver him from a Gaol.

Nevertheless, like a hardworking lawyer at gaol-delivery time, the modern writer turns to his task: "To natural Means alone are we confined; let us try therefore what by these Means may be done for poor *Jones*" (17.1.875–76).

Having deliberately associated the demands of comedy with the marvelous once again—the competing representation that always puts the best light on his realism—Fielding presents two last books of *Tom Jones* in which the action, though satisfyingly comic, can all be circumstantially defended as probable. In accounting for Allworthy's altered judgment of Jones, for example, he cautions that "Revolutions of this Kind . . . do frequently occur in Histories and dramatic Writers, for no other Reason than because the History or Play draws to a Conclusion." The writers justify themselves by "Authority of Authors," he supposes, as if to stake out room for his own operations in the camp of science. Then he hovers smilingly in the territory of arbitrary fiction himself, as he partially withdraws his promise: "though we insist upon as much Authority as any Author whatever, we shall use this Power very sparingly, and never but when driven to it by Necessity, which we do not at present foresee will happen in this Work" (18.3.924). By inviting readers to watch him exercise his power only sparingly, he means to win their agreement to the supposed facts of the story. Besides the commitment to circumstances and probability, however, Fielding promises completeness, or the convergence of two further criteria for narrative—comprehensiveness and closure—that are not very scientific. The two criteria are complementary: the narrative should leave out no relevant circumstances but at the same time should enable readers to reach a conclusion. The model is very much a trial based on circumstantial evidence such as *Blandy* or *Donellan*, for unlike a general scientific inquiry into the natural or social world, the trial requires a verdict. A generic narrative, comedy or tragedy, may force a verdict also, as

Fielding suggests, but the open-ended model of a trial at once anticipates a conclusion and bases it upon a true representation; and the model is just as much a real-life model as any other actual, as opposed to fictitious, inquiry—history as opposed to poetry. The history of a Miss Blandy or a Captain Donellan is nothing short of conclusive; yet as Burke argued in extending this model to the trial of Hastings, judgment should be suspended until "all the acts of the party; all things that explain or throw light on these acts; all the acts of others relative to the affair . . . every thing which tends to establish the connexion between all these particulars; —every circumstance, precedent, concomitant and subsequent, become parts of circumstantial evidence."

Fielding insists, for the novel, on a corresponding privilege in the hero's defense. Though "it is our Province to relate Facts" (2.4.87), he will brook no arrangement of the facts but his own, since the arrangement more than anything else induces a satisfying conclusion. The reader must simply await all the needful evidence like a juryman, and no one meanwhile must judge the case.

> We warn thee not too hastily to condemn any of the Incidents in this our History, as impertinent and foreign to our main Design, because thou dost not immediately conceive in what Manner such Incident may conduce to that Design. This Work may, indeed, be considered as a great Creation of our own; and for a little Reptile of a Critic to presume to find Fault with any of its Parts, without knowing the Manner in which the Whole is connected, and before he comes to the final Catastrophe, is a most presumptuous Absurdity. (10.1.524–25)

The author then apologizes for the reptile metaphor, but without abandoning the divine idea of creation that has assigned the critic so low a rank in the chain of being. Far from being an arbitrary deity, moreover, he will provide a circumstantial accounting of each turn of fate.[38] In the next introductory chapter, he remarks that most critics imagine themselves to be lawyers lately and apparently intend "Judgment in the legal Sense, in which it is frequently used as equivalent to Condemnation." Again he cautions against passing "a severe Sentence upon the Whole, merely on account of some vicious Part" (11.1.566, 570). Fielding proposes to reverse that tendency to equate judgment with condemnation. His readers are not necessarily disposed to criticize either the presentation of the case or the defendant, but he continues to insist that they are in order to forestall them. Thus after producing some evidence favorable

---

38. Battestin's note to 10.1.524 gives some theological parallels to this authorial claim.

to Jones's character—his behavior to Nightingale—he pretends to divide the jury, in order to win them:

> Those Readers who are of the same Complexion with him will perhaps think this short Chapter contains abundance of Matter; while others may probably wish, short as it is, that it had been totally spared as impertinent to the main Design, which I suppose they conclude is to bring Mr. *Jones* to the Gallows, or if possible, to a more deplorable Catastrophe. (15.8.816)

Upon character the trial of Tom Jones ultimately turns. The hero's good nature, his spontaneous sympathy, friendship, and goodwill, his loyalty and truth telling, high spirits and courage—even his imprudence, insofar as it signifies disregard of his own interests—are qualities amply instanced in the narrative. His sexual escapades, delineated as gallantry and shielded by the double standard for men and women, turn out to be his main crimes; the rest consists largely of misapprehension and misrepresentation. As in "An Essay on the Knowledge of the Characters of Men," written six years earlier, character is something fixed, "some unacquired, original distinction, in the nature or soul of one man from that of another," that can be penetrated only by study and observation of actions. And though Fielding obviously qualified his central tenet on the good-natured man when he came to write *Amelia,* in *Tom Jones* he was still working well within the definition set forth in that essay: "Good-Nature is that benevolent and amiable Temper of Mind which disposes us to feel the Misfortunes, and enjoy the Happiness, of others; and consequently pushes us on to promote the latter, and prevent the former; and that without any abstract Contemplation on the Beauty of Virtue, and without the Allurements and Terrors of Religion."[39] This original propensity is in Jones, and precisely because the novel's action is construed as a trial, or series of trials, he can be acquitted by uncovering it. He never intends any wrong, hence cannot be criminally guilty: as Nightingale conveniently relates to Allworthy near the end, Jones has "often protested in the most solemn Manner" that he has "never been intentionally guilty of any Offence towards you" (18.3.923). The proof of this lack of intent, however, and the proof of his inherent good nature, rests not with Tom Jones but with Fielding. The hero's defense is managed for him.

---

39. Henry Fielding, "An Essay on the Knowledge of the Characters of Men," in *Miscellanies by Henry Fielding, Esq: Volume One,* ed. Henry Knight Miller (Oxford: Clarendon, 1972), 158. See also Battestin, *Moral Basis of Fielding's Art,* 52–81; and Martin Price, *To the Palace of Wisdom: Studies in Order and Energy from Dryden to Blake* (New York: Doubleday, 1964), 285–304.

The novelist himself thus inaugurated a classic criticism of his book and its hero. Coleridge, one of his great admirers, admitted that as much as the character of Jones spoke for itself, it was "wholly incongruous and without any psychological truth"; this truth was otherwise supplied, by the author's observation.[40] In another tortured compliment, Henry James wrote of Fielding's hero as "a young man of great health and spirits" without "a grain of imagination." Jones "has so much 'life' that it amounts . . . almost to his having a mind, that is to his having reactions and a full consciousness." It scarcely matters, because "his author—*he* handsomely possessed of a mind—has such an amplitude of reflexion for him and round him."[41] James, too, accounted for the greatness of the novel largely on Fielding's own terms; and so with Empson and others.[42] For my purposes, these aesthetic judgments should be placed side by side with the literature of legal intent. The mind of Tom Jones, more especially the way it is known, can be compared to the mind of Titius—a character whom only Bentham has ever heard of, since the name arises merely to illustrate the role of circumstantial evidence in drawing psychological conclusions:

> Because, unless stated by the individual himself in whose mind the fact is considered as having place, the existence of any such psychological fact [as would prove intent] can only be a matter of inference. What passes or has passed in my own mind, I know by my own internal consciousness, and without any interference: concerning what passes or has passed in the mind of Titius, I cannot know but by one or other of two means, viz. either from what he himself declares (so far as I credit what he says), or from the observations I have had the opportunity of making on the subject of his exterior deportment.[43]

That the second of these two means is Fielding's in the novel, we have already understood from his contentions with testimony. He employs this means for the acquittal of Jones and affirms it as his method.

Fielding addresses inferences to and from character as the final point

40. Samuel Taylor Coleridge, *Lectures 1808–1819 on Literature*, ed. R. A. Foakes, 2 vols. (Princeton: Princeton University Press, 1987), 1:309.

41. Henry James, Preface to *The Princess Casamassima*, in *Literary Criticism: French Writers, Other European Writers, the Prefaces to the New York Edition*, ed. Leon Edel (New York: Library of America, 1984), 1094.

42. "I take it [Fielding] refused to believe that the 'inside' of a person's mind (as given by Richardson in a letter, perhaps) is much use for telling you the real source of his motives," says Empson ("*Tom Jones*," 135). Cf. Watt, *Rise of the Novel*, 272; and Irvin Ehrenpreis, *Fielding: Tom Jones* (London: Arnold, 1964), passim.

43. Bentham, *Rationale of Judicial Evidence*, 3:6.

in his chapter on probability—the chapter, that is, countering the marvelous. So-called conservation of character demands not only temporal consistency from moment to moment but agreement of character and action that is implicitly causal and called for by the rhetorical tradition.[44] "The Actions should be . . . likely for the very Actors and Characters to have performed: For what may be only wonderful and surprizing in one Man, may become improbable, or indeed impossible, when related of another" (8.1.405). Such likelihood can be studied only from experience, which also teaches the difference that character produces in the actions of different persons. Fielding repeatedly scans the motives for actions in *Tom Jones*: determining a motive, or beginning, sometimes completes the proof of what has occurred.[45] Before Blifil, for example, there were two brothers of the same name, a doctor and a captain. Dr. Blifil was first to enjoy Allworthy's hospitality and the company of Miss Bridget Allworthy; but he was married, and "what was worse, known to be so by Mr. *Allworthy.*" As for seducing the gentleman's sister, he never thought of it: "This was owing either to his Religion, as is most probable, or to the Purity of his Passion, which was fixed on those Things, which Matrimony only, and not criminal Correspondence, could put him in Possession of, or give him any Title to." (Of course, when Fielding remarks that a religious motive was most probable, he means the opposite; and when he mentions the purity of a competing motive, it turns out to be pure greed. Though irony risks the reader's misunderstanding, it flatters understanding as it would the understanding of a juror. Successful irony encourages the reader to join in the inferences and to believe them all the more eagerly.) The novelist has thus far merely begun his representation of the mind of Dr. Blifil, the evidence for which is solely his actions. When the doctor manages to introduce his brother the captain to Allworthy's house, this deed requires more understanding of motive before it can be believed: "why the Doctor, who certainly had no great Friendship for his Brother, should for his Sake think of making so ill a Return to the Hospitality of *Allworthy,* is a Matter not so easy to be accounted for." Since motive is so important to the representation, the novelist suggests three pos-

44. Battestin's note cites Aristotle, *Poetics* (15.4), and Horace, *Ars Poetica* (119–27).
45. Cf. Sheldon Sacks, *Fiction and the Shape of Belief* (1964; rpt. Chicago: University of Chicago Press, 1980), 115; and Ronald Paulson, *Satire and the Novel in Eighteenth-Century England* (New Haven: Yale University Press, 1967), 141–50. But Paulson further states, "In *Tom Jones* Fielding has reached a conclusion that is essentially alien to the classical, and so to the satiric tradition—that judgment is only possible when made of a whole being and not of an individual action" (149).

sibilities—none very flattering to the character—before withdrawing with the words, "Whether any of these Motives operated on the Doctor we will not determine; but so the Fact was"—that is, Dr. Blifil "sent for his Brother" (1.10.62–64). (The stopping short of inference, like the irony, is another way of securing the reader's participation in reconstructing the mind from the outside in, from "the Fact" in evidence to the motive.) Much later in the novel, in representing the behavior of another dubious character, Lady Bellaston, Fielding will refer to this procedure as his method. "It may be proper, according to our Method, to return a little back, and to account for so great an Alteration of Behaviour in this Lady" (16.9.867). The novelist has no particular brief for narrating the thoughts of Dr. Blifil or Lady Bellaston. He gains a satiric edge in both cases, but the "Method" is mainly for representation. A persuasive narrative accounts for itself by tracing motives and remarking the consistency of character and action.

In the longer view of literary history, *Tom Jones* is a very model of the management of evidence. But why novels importing the argument from circumstantial evidence should be basically defensive remains a significant question. Of course most novels are comedies, in which prosecution may be one more mishap for heroes and heroines to outlive. Novels are also frequently products of Cervantine realism, which thrives by giving the lie to other conceivable narratives: since circumstantial evidence gained preeminence in criminal prosecution, novels conceivably aspired to a true representation of fact by opposing the prosecutorial use of the evidence. That answer is a little too neat, but indeed it is probably not possible to explain fully the triumphant showing for the defense in *Tom Jones* and other novels except retrospectively, through the glass of subsequent literary history. Fortunately a second novel, called *Waverley; or, 'Tis Sixty Years Since* and describing the same moment in history as *Tom Jones,* can help place this inclination to the defense in perspective and explain its hold on the imagination of the nineteenth century.

The Arrest of Waverley

Walter Scott (1771–1832) was already famous as a poet and man of letters when his first novel appeared anonymously in 1814 and began the series known as the Waverley Novels. In an introduction to Fielding, for Ballantyne's Novelists Library in 1821, Scott noted that the earlier novelist "considered his works as an experiment in British literature"—

and so was he experimenting.[46] But whereas *Tom Jones,* with its express commitment to epic design, became an instant classic, *Waverley* was more like a world historical literary event.[47] Its author could recognize it as such by the end of his life—hence his musing over sources and analogues in his general preface to the novels. In *Waverley* he described the same historical moment that Fielding touched upon in *Tom Jones*— the Jacobite uprising of 1745—and crucially developed the earlier novel's trial of its hero. In so doing he notably contributed *to* the era of historicism that is still with us.[48]

To remark the generic difference between a comic epic in prose and a historical novel tells only part of the story. In ways that Defoe had pioneered but that did not much interest Fielding, Scott was bent on "illustrating the existing state of the Highlands"—so much so that he apologizes somewhat for the geography lesson.[49] The phrase is from a

46. Walter Scott, "Henry Fielding," in *Sir Walter Scott on Novelists and Fiction,* ed. Ioan Williams (London: Routledge, 1968), 55. For analysis of Scott's turn from poetry and editing to novel writing, see Jane Millgate, *Walter Scott: The Making of the Novelist* (Toronto: University of Toronto Press, 1984), 3–57.

47. Georg Lukács, *The Historical Novel,* trans. Hannah and Stanley Mitchell (London: Merlin, 1962), makes the strongest claims for Scott in twentieth-century criticism. The most convincing evidence, of course, remains in well-known works by Stendhal, Balzac, Hugo, Cooper, Pushkin, Tolstoy, Manzoni, Galdós, and Fontane, as well as the English novelists of the nineteenth century (on whom Scott's influence may be less well understood).

48. Michael McKeon, in *Origins of the English Novel,* esp. 39–64, writes of a much earlier development of historicism. In his sense, *Tom Jones* is indeed a "history" of the foundling. But history of course is as old as language itself, even if McKeon has sensible grounds for associating it with the invention of printing. The modern idea that individuals are subject to history is a more recent development still, and one for which not even Fielding was quite prepared. McKeon writes, "Fielding's entanglement of the micronarrative of *Tom Jones* with the macronarrative of the '45 Rising provides the most intricate vindication in his work of the view that novelistic 'invention' is consistent with a painstaking truth to 'history' " (418). In the abstract this statement is true and worth making, but at the level of concrete representation it can be misleading. Fielding's use of the forty-five provides his action with not much more than a chronological reference point. As history it is entirely inconsequential. One has only to compare the apparent inconsequentiality of Waterloo in *La Chartreuse de Parme* or *Vanity Fair,* which then is made consequential by Stendhal and Thackeray in the private lives of their characters. By their time, after the Waverley Novels and above all after the discovery of geological time, the age of modern historicism has truly arrived. I would argue that even where Fielding *was* fully engaged with the forty-five, in his journalism, it was without much sense of the present as subject to history. See his dream vision of a Jacobite takeover in the *True Patriot* for 19 November 1745 (*The True Patriot,* ed. Miriam Austin Locke [University: University of Alabama Press, 1964], 53–54) and compare Waverley's dreamlike experience of history.

49. Walter Scott, *Waverley; or, 'Tis Sixty Years Since,* ed. Claire Lamont (Oxford:

chapter entitled "Waverley proceeds on his Journey," and this hero perambulates even more readily than Jones; but Waverley is additionally an observer of the customs of the country, its economic livelihood and political bearings.[50] The characters he observes are not types of humanity, or if so, they are associated with a specific environment, which is also temporal. The larger journey of the novel, its historical thesis, looks not only backward but forward in time.[51] In one of *Waverley*'s overt statements about history, "Had Fergus Mac-Ivor lived sixty years sooner than he did, he would, in all probability, have wanted the polished manner and knowledge of the world which he now possessed; and had he lived sixty years later [the time of writing], his ambition and love of rule would have lacked the fuel which his situation now afforded" (19.91–92). Here Scott places Mac-Ivor, a creature of rebellion, more specifically in time than he would place Waverley, his hero of civil society; yet for this novel nothing is more thoroughly historicized than the present, which constantly asserts itself as an achievement of time and civilization irrespective of sixty-year intervals, in the implicit *now* of the repeated invitation to compare then and now. A nice example is Waverley's unspoken praise of England in peaceable present times — that is, unspoken by him within hearing of readers of the novel, but mediated and returned to him by Rose Bradwardine, who will one day become the young Englishman's Scottish wife: "I hope God will protect you, and that you will get safe home to England, where you used to tell me there was no military violence nor fighting among clans permitted, but every thing was done according to an equal law that protected all who were harmless and innocent" (28.139–40). Needless to say, this gently mediated promise harks not to the past but to the future of the two nations. Once the hero's dreamlike experience with the Stuart rebellion is behind him, he can reflect that "the romance of his life was ended, and that its real history had now commenced" (60.283).

Scott was also a formidable literary historian. In the study of drama and romance, ballad and folktale, as well as political and military history, he can have had few equals among creative writers. He produced weighty editions of border ballads, the works of Dryden and Swift,

---

Clarendon, 1981), 18.88. Subsequent references to chapter and page are given in parentheses.

50. Cf. David Daiches, "Scott's Achievement as a Novelist," in *Literary Essays* (Edinburgh: Oliver and Boyd, 1956), 93. For the idea that the hero is an observer, see also Scott's own review of his early novels, *Quarterly Review* 16 (1817): 432.

51. See Alexander Welsh, *The Hero of the Waverley Novels* (New Haven: Yale University Press, 1963), 55–57, 85–92, 234–35; and Robert C. Gordon, *Under Which King? A Study of the Scottish Waverley Novels* (Edinburgh: Oliver and Boyd, 1969).

and plays of the English Renaissance. Though he cites the classics less often than Fielding does, he can be credited with being a true comparativist, and the early chapters of *Waverley* allude to more than one tradition of the novel.[52] Though his informality belies it, he is as much a theorist of the novel as Fielding and generally stands with his predecessor against the epistolary mode of writing.[53] But unlike Fielding, from the very outset Scott distinguished his practice from that of Cervantes.[54] After detailing Waverley's reading habits and fondness for vicarious adventure, he begins a chapter called "Choice of a Profession" as follows:

> From the minuteness with which I have traced Waverley's pursuits, and the bias which they unavoidably communicated to his imagination, the reader may perhaps anticipate, in the following tale, an imitation of the romance of Cervantes. But he will do my prudence injustice in the supposition. My intention is not to follow the steps of that inimitable author, in describing such total perversion of intellect as misconstrues the objects actually presented to the senses, but that more common aberration from sound judgment, which apprehends occurrences indeed in their reality, but communicates to them a tincture of its own romantic tone and colouring. (5.18)

As Mark Twain knew and Hegel had already in effect confirmed, this un-Cervantine stance was prophetic of the century ahead.[55] The confidence that objects and events can finally be perceived "in their reality"

52. Alexander Welsh, "Contrast of Styles in the Waverley Novels," *Novel* 6 (1973): 218–28.

53. Scott experimented with the epistolary method in *Redgauntlet* (1824) but broke off about a third of the way through. "A genuine correspondence of this kind (and Heaven forbid it should be in any respect sophisticated by interpolations of our own!) can seldom be found to contain all in which it is necessary to instruct the reader for his full comprehension of the story." After two paragraphs of apology, in effect, he announces that he will "proceed to narrate some circumstances which Alan Fairford did not, and could not, write to his correspondent" and returns to his usual method (though later he also employs a journal by Darsie Latimer for some chapters). See *Redgauntlet* (Edinburgh: Black, 1887), 157, 179. In this "Tale of the Eighteenth Century" (the subtitle of the novel) the young heroes are acquainted with both *Tom Jones* and *Clarissa* (22, 28), which Waverley of course could not know. Fairford's father, the Edinburgh lawyer, has himself met Henry Fielding's brother John (94).

54. Welsh, *Hero of the Waverley Novels,* 8–18.

55. Mark Twain, *Life on the Mississippi* (New York: Heritage, 1944), 271–73; G. W. F. Hegel, *The Philosophy of Fine Art,* trans. F. P. B. Osmaston, 4 vols. (London: Bell, 1920), 2:372–76. Cf. Judith Wilt, *Secret Leaves: The Novels of Walter Scott* (Chicago: University of Chicago Press, 1985), 1–18; and her "Steamboat Surfacing: Scott and the English Novelists," *Nineteenth-Century Fiction* 35 (1981): 459–86.

prepares for an age of positivism, while allowance for the hero's "bias" and "aberration" is strictly to be confined to his growing up. The romance of life is coterminous with youth, and after that its real history shall begin (and not the middle-aged foolishness of Don Quixote). Scott surely distanced himself also from Fielding's interpretation of Cervantes, and nineteenth-century bildungsromans could be said to pay tribute to this firm declaration of purpose.

At the same time, Waverley's mind is more interesting than Jones's, if only because it has room for so much more uncertainty of direction. His strictly moral behavior is never an issue, but the political influences upon him are. Fergus Mac-Ivor, Scott's Jacobite chieftain, is said to attain "a considerable ascendancy over the mind of Waverley" (25.126): such an idiom could not be used of Square or Thwackum, who, as Jones's tutors after all, ought to affect his education. Fergus's ascendency grows and wanes in the course of the novel, only less rapidly than the hero's love for Flora Mac-Ivor flares and subsides. Flora directly advises the young Englishman of her needs and his own: "Consult your own good sense and reason rather than a prepossession hastily adopted, probably only because you have met a young woman possessed of the usual accomplishments, in a sequestered and romantic situation" (27.136). The very idea of a hero thus instructed opens a vein of feeling that has little to do with morality or good nature. Consider the unlikely thought of Jones's being rejected by a woman: the difference is due not merely to individual character but to the refinement of manners, of which Scott and his contemporaries were highly conscious. Even the word "masculine" at this time signified above all constraint rather than prowess of any sort.[56] These are some of the fixed conditions governing a hero to whom "the question indeed occurred, where he was to direct his course," and for whom "fortune had settled that he was not to be left to his option" (37.181).

The young Waverley advances far enough from his preoccupations in the library at Waverley-Honour, his uncle's estate, to take up a commission with a regiment stationed in Scotland in 1745. Being unused to discipline and curious about his relations in Perthshire, he soon requests a leave of absence and rides off to visit the Baron Bradwardine at Tully-Veolan. From there he gets the chance to trek into the High-

56. Welsh, *Hero of the Waverley Novels*, 25. The values and contradictions studied by Mary Poovey, *The Proper Lady and the Woman Writer* (Chicago: University of Chicago Press, 1984), especially in Jane Austen's novels (172–240), are not ideologically very distant from the Waverley Novels.

lands, in pursuit of the baron's rustled cows, while he remains largely oblivious to the political rising on behalf of that most romantic of lost causes, the return of the Stuarts to the throne. It is only after he has become the guest of Fergus Mac-Ivor, well into the novel, that he is apprised by the letter from Rose Bradwardine that sojourning in the Highlands has brought him under suspicion.

> How *he* should have been involved in such suspicions, conscious that until yesterday he had been free from harbouring a thought against the prosperity of the reigning family, seemed inexplicable. . . . Still he was aware that unless he meant at once to embrace the proposal of Fergus Mac-Ivor, it would deeply concern him to leave this suspicious neighbourhood without delay, and repair where his conduct might undergo a satisfactory examination. (28.140)

Actually both young women of Waverley's acquaintance have suggested that he depart, and he now adopts that course of action. Even were he inclined—as invited by Fergus Mac-Ivor the day before—to join the Stuart cause, it would not be while he holds the Hanoverian king's commission. Assuring his host that "my innocence, my rank, my father's intimacy with Lord M——, General C——, &c. will be a sufficient protection" (28.141), he makes the best of his way from the Highlands to a town called Cairnvreckan, where he stops to find a blacksmith.

The action that ensues with the blacksmith finally has no bearing on Waverley's arrest, though its comic ferocity may signal the underlying terror of the calm formalities in the chapters that follow. Scott probably did not plan for the scene but drew it instinctively in nightmarish colors, to defuse the tension of the hero's arrest. It is a scene in the low style, most of it in dialect, as so often in the Scottish novels. Waverley unfortunately stumbles into a violent quarrel between the Vulcan of Cairnvreckan and his virago Venus, she more than usually inflamed by Jacobite passions and he charged with the opposite persuasion. A narrator's quotation from "the sapient Partridge" tells us, in fact, that *Tom Jones* is one inspiration for the explosive action in this chapter. The hero, threatened by the rabble and madly surmised to be "the Chevalier himsel," actually draws a pocket pistol to ward them off, when the blacksmith, one John Mucklewrath, decides to discharge his domestic fury upon Waverley and rushes upon him with a "red-hot bar of iron" (30.152–53). The hero fells the man with a shot from his pistol and is immediately seized by the crowd; he is saved from further violence only by the arrival of the village pastor. The smith, it seems, was merely grazed by the ball and, afterward, even makes peace with his wife. No harm comes to Mucklewrath, or immediately to Waverley.[57]

The pastor, named Morton, leads Waverley before the laird of Cairn-vreckan, an elderly major named Melville. And though the recovery of Mucklewrath, like the recovery of Fitzpatrick in *Tom Jones,* puts an end to charges on his account, Waverley is promptly arrested on other grounds. Now comes the formal sequence of three chapters for which the farcical scene in the low style has prepared the way. The first, entitled "An Examination," begins coolly: "Major Melville of Cairnvreckan . . . received Mr Morton with great kindness, and our hero with civility, which the equivocal circumstances in which Edward was placed rendered constrained and distant" (31.154); and if the civility of Melville's house and the high style strike the reader as possibly more ominous than a hot poker and dialect in the village, that response is warranted. When Major Melville's examination of him is over, Waverley will exclaim, "I hope he and I shall never meet more: he had neither sympathy with my innocence nor with my wretchedness; and the petrifying accuracy with which he attended to every form of civility, while he tortured me by his questions, his suspicions, and his inferences, was as tormenting as the racks of the Inquisition" (33.168). The comparison to Continental practices is a barbed one: kindness, civility, and restraint may be British tortures.

One question posed by the examination of this hero is whether his own civility torments him, in ways that do not affect Fielding's characters sixty years earlier because they had hardly been discovered yet. The room is cleared of people, and Waverley is asked his name:

> "Edward Waverley."
>
> "I thought so; late of the ——— dragoons, and nephew of Sir Everard Waverley of Waverley-Honour?"
>
> "The same."
>
> "Young gentleman, I am extremely sorry that this painful duty has fallen to my lot."
>
> "Duty, Major Melville, renders apologies superfluous."

Despite his lofty sense of position and imposition, much of the strain of the hero's examination results from his own accession to the pro-

---

57. As in Shakespeare's plays, actions in the low style in Scott's novels resound to the themes of the high style. The entire history of the forty-five is resolved between the smith and his quarrelsome wife in a matter of minutes. Just so, the role of the hero of society as bystander is figured here. The episode, brief as it is, is prototypical of many actions in the Waverley Novels, in two other respects: the hero does not inflict death upon anyone, and he regularly submits his conduct to some constituted authority for judgment. See Welsh, *Hero of the Waverley Novels,* 207–29.

cedure. Though his arrest catches him by surprise, it should not have, since he already proposed to himself, while still in the Highlands, "to repair where his conduct might undergo a satisfactory examination." Now he is participating in such an examination as preliminary to a criminal trial, however, and requests "to know what [the] charge is, and upon what authority I am forcibly detained to reply to it." The charges are both military—desertion and inciting mutiny—and civilian—"high-treason, and leveling war against the king, the highest delinquency of which a subject can be guilty."

> "And by what authority am I detained to reply to such heinous calumnies?"
>
> "By one which you must not dispute, nor I disobey."
>
> He handed to Waverley a warrant from the supreme criminal court of Scotland, in full form, for apprehending and securing the person of Edward Waverley, Esq. suspected of treasonable practices and other high crimes and misdemeanours.
>
> The astonishment which Waverley expressed at this communication was imputed by Major Melville to conscious guilt, while Mr Morton was rather disposed to construe it into the surprise of innocence unjustly suspected. There was something true in both conjectures; for although Edward's mind acquitted him of the crimes with which he was charged, yet a hasty review of his own conduct convinced him he might have great difficulty in establishing his innocence to the satisfaction of others. (31.155–56)

Thus Waverley not only accedes to the formalities of his arrest but inwardly weighs the evidence against him. He knows his innocence, because he has not held any wicked or criminal intention in what he has done. At the same time, he realizes that his intentions will be judged by the circumstances, whatever he says. Before the episode is over, he conceives of his situation as hopeless, the more so because he thoroughly acknowledges the rule of law.

The hero who has been handed a warrant for his arrest is immediately obliged to disgorge any papers he may have about him. " 'You shall [see them], sir, without reserve,' said Edward, throwing his pocketbook and memorandums upon the table; 'there is but one with which I wish you would dispense.' " That one, which with dreamlike anxiety he vainly tries to withhold from the major, consists of verses by Flora Mac-Ivor on the grave of Captain Wogan, conveyed to Waverley at his departure that morning. The surrender of these verses is triply or quadruply embarrassing to him. First, verses are a poor thing compared with "a warrant from the supreme criminal court of Scotland, in full form." Second, though our hero has treasured them as if they were a love poem, they were undoubtedly given him by Flora as a reminder that her heart belongs solely to the Stuart cause. Third, Captain Wogan's name was also Edward, and the parallel to one who deserted the Puritans for the Royalist side in 1648 will not be lost on his captors. And fourth (if you will), verses are simply not very satisfying evidence one way or the other. A hero wrongly accused would almost rather be caught with more serious proof of rebellion in his pockets. Eventually this is what happens: the accusations of the government help drive Waverley to serve briefly with Prince Charles, a hundred years after his namesake went over to Charles II.[58]

The prisoner—"for such our hero must now be considered"—defends himself ably enough at first, though he scarcely needs an accuser. The remainder of the examination covers pretty much all of the circumstantial evidence against Waverley, and he firmly denies or curtails as many damaging inferences from the evidence as he can. A point comes, however, when Melville speaks of an incident at Tully-Veolan (the baron defended the hero's honor while he slept) that "cannot be charged against you in a court of justice" but ought nevertheless to be answered to, and the scene takes a turn reminiscent of Tom Jones's despair under Allworthy's accusations ("like a Criminal in Despair"), only more fraught with anxiety and concluding in silence:

> This was too much. Beset and pressed on every hand by accusations, in which gross falsehoods were blended with such circumstances of truth as could not fail to procure them credit, —alone, unfriended, and in a strange land, Waverley almost gave up his life and honour for lost, and, leaning his head upon his hand, resolutely refused to answer any further questions, since the fair and candid statement he had already made had only served to furnish arms against him.

Though Melville has reminded Waverley that this is not a trial ("your examination will be transmitted elsewhere"), so much rehearsing of his faults exhausts the hero's spirit of cooperation. The major makes one attempt to circumvent his silence by asking about his friends in the Highlands, and Waverley gives the civil libertarian reply that he will not incriminate others or abridge their "unsuspecting hospitality." But this reply affirms that, where he himself is concerned, there can be no

---

58. The story of Edward Wogan was given by Clarendon: see *The History of the Rebellion and Civil Wars in England,* ed. W. Dunn MacRay, 6 vols. (Oxford: Clarendon, 1888), 5:313–15.

secrets from duly constituted authority. The arguments on both sides rest; and the magistrate, with renewed civility, invites his prisoner to dinner, showing anew that they are really one. The prisoner refuses, this time, and withdraws "to a handsome bed room, where . . . he flung himself on the bed, and . . . sunk into a deep and heavy slumber" (31.155–61). Scott forgoes thoughts of the Inquisition this time and compares his hero's sleep to that of American Indians being tortured at the stake—but the entire examination has been as dreamlike in its way as the previous adventure with the blacksmith.

The second chapter in the sequence, "A Conference, and the Consequence," reveals why Scott has introduced Major Melville and Mr. Morton in tandem at the beginning of "An Examination." Here they are again in the new opening paragraph:

> Major Melville had detained Mr Morton during his examination of Waverley, both because he thought he might derive assistance from his practical good sense and approved loyalty, and also because it was agreeable to have a witness of unimpeachable candour and veracity to proceedings which touched the honour and safety of a young Englishman of high rank and family, and the expectant heir of a large fortune. Every step he knew would be rigorously canvassed, and it was his business to place the justice and integrity of his own conduct beyond the limits of question.

The explanation certainly speaks to the privileges of rank and fortune, while it admits that rank and fortune are also subject to law. But Scott has further use for Mr. Morton. As the chapter unfolds, Melville and Morton become paired as counsel in the case, one for prosecution and the other for defense.[59] Though neither of course is a lawyer, "both were men of ready and acute talent, and both were equally competent to combine various points of evidence, and to deduce from them the necessary conclusions." Their contrasting views of the case are due to "the wide difference of their habits and education" and "their respective deductions from admitted premises," which are explained in turn by the difference in backgrounds. "Major Melville had been versed in camps and cities . . . Mr Morton, on the contrary, had passed from the literary pursuits of a college . . . to the ease and simplicity of his present charge," his parish duties. The clergyman is in temperament a little like an older Waverley, perhaps, or the Author of Waverley himself.

59. The presence of the minister possibly recalls the presence of a parson at two of Jones's trials, though neither Thwackum (needless to say) nor the parson at Upton offers the hero any defense.

A love of letters, though kept in subordination to his clerical studies and duties, also distinguished the Pastor of Cairnvreckan, and had tinged his mind in earlier days with a slight feeling of romance, which no after incidents of real life had entirely dissipated. The early loss of an amiable young woman, whom he had married for love, and who was quickly followed to the grave by an only child, had also served, even after the lapse of many years, to soften and enhance a disposition naturally mild and contemplative.

The immediate recourse of the prosecutorial mind, "the severe disciplinarian, strict magistrate, the distrustful man of the world" who is Melville, is to narrate—to review the circumstantial evidence against Waverley as the coherent story of his guilt, up to that very day—and this he proceeds to do. " 'And, lastly,' continued Major Melville, warming in the details of his arguments, 'where do we find this second edition of Cavaliero Wogan? Why, truly, in the very track most proper for execution of his design, and pistolling the first of the king's subjects who ventures to question his intentions.' " For this summary, which occupies several pages, the major uses a present narrative tense, remaking the story for the reader as well as for his interlocutor in the novel. For the first time the reader can attend a narrative of Waverley's activities (or extended leave of absence) that is pointed to a specific conclusion. The magistrate as prosecutor makes a strong representation of the hero's guilt that ultimately contrasts with the novel's stance. Meanwhile Morton, for the defense, awaiting some more fortunate turn of events, announces his intention to confer with the prisoner (asleep for this night), "simply to make the experiment whether he may not be brought to communicate to me some circumstances which may hereafter be useful to alleviate, if not to exculpate, his conduct" (32.161–65).

Thus it falls to Mr. Morton, whose mind has been touched by literature and "a slight feeling of romance," to counsel Waverley in the third of the chapters on the arrest, entitled "A Confidant." And Morton, donning Scott's other hat as a member of the Faculty of Advocates in Edinburgh, really does approach his client as if he were attorney for the defense. "I do not intrude myself on your confidence, Mr Waverley, for the purpose of learning any circumstances, the knowledge of which can be prejudicial either to yourself or to others; but I own my earnest wish is, that you would intrust me with any particulars which could lead to your exculpation." Won over, Waverley confides in him, exclaiming, "I know, indeed, that I am innocent, but I hardly see how I can hope to prove myself so." He then tells his version of the story, omitting mention only of Flora and Rose. Morton, wearing the literary hat once more, cautions that certain motives—"the power of curiosity and the influence of romance as motives of youthful conduct"—are generally unknown to a person with the major's mind-set; and as in other construals of circumstantial evidence, the facts make sense only when attached to believable motives, which must be probed to the bottom. The pastor further prepares "a careful memorandum of the various particulars of Waverley's interview with Donald Bean, and the other circumstances which Waverley communicated" (33.167–68).

Thus Scott enlists a trio of characters—magistrate, prisoner, and confidant—to dramatize in as many chapters the turn from prosecutorial use of the evidence to its potential for defense. The hero never does come to trial, and *Waverley,* imitating *Tom Jones* and anticipating many more novels of the nineteenth century, mounts sufficient evidence in the end to exculpate him, just as Morton hopes. The hero's confidant persuades him to accept the magistrate's second invitation to dinner, and Waverley behaves at table "with ease, though he could not affect cordiality." Indeed, "Waverley, whose life was a dream, gave ready way to the predominating impulse, and became the most lively of the party." Joining in this polite society, he emphatically upholds his end "with ease and gaiety" (34.170). If he is now a prisoner of the law, the next day he is marched off as something like a prisoner of war, then recaptured by spies and skirmishers of the Jacobites. Soon he is caught up in more exotic circles, as the rebellion swirls past and Mac-Ivor introduces him to Charles Stuart in Edinburgh. "No master of cere-monies," avers the Chevalier, "is necessary to present a Waverley to a Stuart" (40.192). The hero gets his chance to struggle in arms against the establishment that has offered to try him for high treason, but he quickly shies away from rebellion and checks himself. At Prestonpans the death of Colonel Gardiner, his former commander, fills him with misgivings; his only role in the battle is to rescue another officer loyal to the government, Colonel Talbot. The latter, who is acquainted with Waverley's family, eventually helps smooth over the younger man's difficulties.

It should not surprise us that Scott thought of Fielding as "the first of British novelists," or that he preferred Fielding to Richardson on probabilistic grounds of "truth and human nature."[60] Along with such fantasies as striking up an acquaintance with the Chevalier, *Waverley* is

60. Scott, "Henry Fielding," 47, 52.

another carefully managed narrative analogous to a trial. With one hand, the novelist arranges the circumstances, sprinkled with a few falsehoods, so as to indict the hero; with the other hand, he constructs a defense from still more evidence. Ultimately the case hinges on intent, as it does in *Tom Jones,* and proof of intent awaits the summary of all the evidence rather than a confession. Scott does not pursue the analogy or reproduce the language of the law as incessantly as Fielding. He writes altogether less about what he is up to and what he expects of the reader, hence less about evidence as such. Criminal prosecution is less on his mind than on Fielding's. Still, it is hard to imagine him undertaking the Waverley Novels without the example of *Tom Jones* before him. Both writers regard themselves as realists, and their strong representations of Jones's and Waverley's innocence take roughly the same shape.

To appreciate the consequences Waverley's arrest has for literary history, however, it is important to try to grasp the differences in the two novels—differences inherent in the passage of sixty years. Jones and Waverley are by no means the exact contemporaries they are supposed to be. Notoriously, their manners differ, especially their manners in relation to women—though it was Thackeray, the Victorian disciple of Fielding, who complained of the greater constraints imposed on later heroes.[61] One possible way of generalizing about the differences in behavior is to point to the greater repression in nineteenth-century culture. Scott was highly aware of his own age's claim to new standards of decency, obedience to law, and truthfulness; his works were repeatedly praised, especially after his death in 1832, for the restraint they endorsed and their positive view of present times.[62] Yet repression is a concept too colored by later reflections—Nietzschean and Freudian reflections—on the progress of civilization, which was confidently extolled in Scott's time, following the defeat of the French Revolution and of Napoleon. The historical settlement that Waverley's own comfortable settling down suggests was taken for granted. The innocence of such a representative hero—representative of the gentlemen of England—requires a purely negative check, like the security checks still administered to officials of special trust in the West. The proof of Jones's innocence is quite different, since he is distinctly not a representative but an ideal hero—a good-natured man. Good nature, however defined,

61. Preface to *The History of Pendennis,* in *The Works of William Makepeace Thackeray,* 2:xlviii.
62. Welsh, *Hero of the Waverley Novels,* 18–29, 149–74, 199–207.

is a brand of innocence that tells against the local expectations.

Other differences that can be discerned between Jones and Waverley do have long-term significance for the backlash of repression, and these can best be glimpsed by narrowly comparing the outcomes of the heroes' trials. Whatever the reader feels about Fielding's pronouncements on his handling of the case or his didactic commitment to prudence in life, his management of the evidence results in something like carefree acquittal for Jones. Such an acquittal is possible partly because, as Ian Watt notes, Jones "is not in touch with his own past at all."[63] It is not so with Waverley, who retains something of his past about him. Waverley, as we have seen, endures his preliminary examination, is never formally tried, and is freed only in that his case is eventually dropped. For all Scott's reining in of behavior and more careful conveyancing of estates, his narrative somehow stops short of finding Waverley not guilty even as it stops short of finding him guilty. The hero is rewarded with marriage and property, and what is more, is rewarded by history. But he is not acquitted as Jones is acquitted. To understand this difference from *Tom Jones,* a number of factors have to be considered: *Waverley*'s subscription to a contractual theory of society, its modern construction of guilt, and its partial displacement of the hero's role. And these factors, implicit in the arrest of Waverley, are closely bound up with Scott's historicism: in the then-and-now of all historical writing, including historical novels, and in the graphic reminders of time and place in Scott's novels, right down to his repeated annotation of them; by what is *not* written about the intervening revolutions in America and in France—for as in the novels of Austen, a reaction to the French Revolution can only be inferred from the treatment of property and proprieties at home; and through a myth about the Glorious Revolution of 1688, which peaceable event supposedly put an end to violent revolution.

Peaceable agreement is more than a desideratum in the Waverley Novels, it is what history achieves; and this assumption holds whether Scott is writing of Henry Morton (in *Old Mortality*) on the eve of 1688, of Edward Waverley in the year 1745, or of Darsie Latimer and Alan Fairford (in *Redgauntlet*) about the year 1770. The heroes thrive under the auspices of an abstraction known as the social contract, and as modern heroes they pay a certain price for their freedom and security, in compliance with law and civil authority. "Every man," according to Blackstone, "when he enters into society, gives up a part of his natural

---

63. Watt, *Rise of the Novel*, 275–76.

liberty as the price of so valuable a purchase,"[64] and Scott's heroes are never behindhand in this respect. So Waverley steps forward with punctilio: "Duty, Major Melville, renders apologies superfluous." He has voluntarily decided to submit to examination before he is arrested; he subscribes to warrants drawn up "in full form," identifies with the law. "One of the first motives to civil society, and which becomes one of its fundamental rules," according to Burke, opposing the French Revolution, "is, *that no man should be a judge in his own cause.* By this each person has at once divested himself of the first fundamental right of uncovenanted man, that is, to judge for himself, and to assert his own cause."[65] When Scott situates his hero in history, he subscribes to this theory of a covenant or contract, the principal treatment of which in English goes back to Locke's Second Treatise on government, with its great pains to distinguish true political power from paternal power as exercised in the family. Fielding obviously respected the law and helped to enforce it too, but he was not really touched by contract theory, as nearly every thinker was by Scott's time. Fielding's notion of society was essentially paternalistic. There is no different or greater earthly authority in *Tom Jones* than Allworthy, fallible though he may be. The foundling hero, whose "history" is familial only, is loyal from filial sentiments; the plot restores his relation to Allworthy. His marriage to Sophia Western collapses her filial sentiments upon his own; in the end "the great Duty which she expresses and performs to her Father renders her almost equally dear to [Jones], with the Love which she bestows on himself" (18.13.981). And this pastoral denouement of patriarchy typifies Fielding's other novels as well.[66] In contrast, while far from disrespectful of fathers, Scott distinguishes even more sharply than Locke between political and filial loyalties. Waverley, though not an orphan, has closer ties to his uncle than to his father, but both are an embarrassment to him. The father's maladroit Hanoverian politics cause shame, and the uncle's Jacobitism proves dangerous to Waverley: a compromise and a way out are arranged for him only by Colonel Talbot,

---

64. William Blackstone, *Commentaries on the Laws of England,* vol. 1 (Oxford: Clarendon, 1765), 125.

65. Edmund Burke, *Reflections on the Revolution in France,* in *The Works and Correspondence of the Right Honourable Edmund Burke,* 8 vols. (London: Rivington, 1852), 4:199.

66. Cf. Malvin R. Zirker, *Fielding's Social Pamphlets: A Study of "An Enquiry into the Cause of the Late Increase of Robbers" and "A Proposal for Making an Effectual Provision for the Poor"* (Berkeley: University of California Press, 1966), 139–40. Dr. Harrison in *Amelia* and Parson Adams in *Joseph Andrews* provide a further dimension of Christian pastoralism, since both are portrayed as good fathers to their parishioners: see *Amelia,* 145 and Battestin's note.

who is personally indebted to the hero for saving his life. Taken together, the heroes of Scott, who are thoroughly conditioned to seek out in every crisis some duly constituted authority, are markedly independent of fathers. The text that best illustrates this straining for filial independence is *Redgauntlet,* but *Rob Roy* would do nearly as well.[67]

Waverley, whose examination occupies fewer pages than Jones's repeated trials, can never be wholly free because he is subject to a contract. Put simply, though one may outlive one's father, one cannot outlive the social contract: that is the distinction Locke was at pains to make. Waverley is far less subject to patriarchy than Jones, and for that reason is less easily acquitted of his escapades. He is also less subject to divine judgment, which in Fielding's writings is usually either visible or just over the horizon. Both Fielding and Scott composed secular narratives of life as a trial, but Scott's is the more secular of the two.[68] To a notable extent, the course of history in the Waverley Novels has subsumed the role of providence, and if Christianity has traditionally held out forgiveness for sins, modern historicism adapts this promise to a collective vision of the future. The promise, however, is inhumanly abstract; and again, the retreat from accessible authority, familial or divine, diminishes the felt possibility of acquittal for individuals. For Waverley there finally exist no authorities save those who, like Major Melville, he himself has theoretically placed in the judgment seat, and he must play his part as best he can. Having pretty well ceased to think of God, he has shouldered the burden of history and cannot turn back unless civilization itself were to turn back.[69] Hence it is that when Waverley

67. In *Redgauntlet* fathers very much stand for an outmoded and oppressive past. Alan Fairford's father, a lawyer in Edinburgh, dominates his son's life and career; Darsie Latimer's terrific uncle, Redgauntlet, kidnaps and threatens him before revealing their relationship. Latimer is the son, if he only knew it, of one whose skull is still perched above the walls of Carlisle, where it has been since Fergus Mac-Ivor's was set in the same place. "Its bleak and mouldered jaws command you to be a man," as his uncle tells him at last (378). These are only a few of the father figures in the novel, who go right back to the ancestral Alberick Redgauntlet, whose horse kicked the life out of the son opposing him. Cf. Gordon, *Under Which King?* 150–62.

68. This secularism was once registered more vividly than it is today. Notoriously, the Waverley Novels affected "the first unsettlement" of Mary Ann Evans's religion: see J. W. Cross, *George Eliot's Life as Related in Her Letters and Journals,* 3 vols. (New York: Merrill and Baker, n.d.), 1:369. But compare Northrop Frye, *The Secular Scripture: A Study of the Structure of Romance* (Cambridge: Harvard University Press, 1976), 5: "one of the roots from which these chapters grew was an abandoned essay on the Waverley novels of Scott."

69. Thus F. R. Hart, *Scott's Novels: The Plotting of Historic Survival* (Charlottesville: University Press of Virginia, 1966), charts something like a Christian existentialist viewpoint in Scott.

submits to examination, he both knows his innocence and feels guilty. There can be no personification of guilt and innocence as separate states of being, as in the prosecution's statement in *R v. Blandy* or Fielding's figure in *Amelia*. Waverley's posture, every bit as heroic as Jones's, permits the reader to perceive and share guilt as Jones's does not. This guilt can be thought of as the small print in the contract.

When Waverley submits to examination, he has and has not surrendered control, because the procedure is one he has agreed to in advance. So thoroughly has he identified with the powers of prosecution that he is perhaps ready to see himself as guilty without knowing it. So confidently has he already identified with society that he can afford to be guilty. And if there were no such ambiguity, what would be the point of checking his standing with some constituted authority? Mr. Morton's proposed defense extends to this possibility of diffuse motives. Morton, whose own mind was once "tinged" with romance, must caution the hero that the good but traditional magistrate, Melville, can probably distinguish only two kinds of motives, good and bad. By implication, there are many more diffuse and mixed motives than Melville knows of. (So the novel elsewhere speaks of tangled feelings and accommodates quite a few in its actions. "Love," for example, "with all its romantic train of hopes, fears, and wishes, was mingled with other feelings of a nature less easily defined" [27.133–34].) Waverley expressly brings no "conscious guilt" to his examination: when the charges are read, they catch him (and to some extent the reader) by surprise, and his "mind acquitted him of the crimes." But the same sentence in the narrative acknowledges that, inwardly and silently, "a hasty review of his own conduct" is taking place. Later, his plaintive outburst to Morton retells the same story: "I know, indeed, that I am innocent, but I hardly see how I can hope to prove myself so." A burden of proof has shifted to the hero along with the burden of history, and this burden will continue to be carried by heroes well into the nineteenth century and beyond. "We are all the victims of circumstances," the innocent Mr. Pickwick will protest, "and I am the greatest."[70]

Such potentially guilty innocence is not the issue with Fielding. Authority in *Tom Jones* is not contractual but traditional; its hero faces judges who are not even theoretically of his choosing and who perceive him as either innocent or guilty. Allworthy is such a traditional magistrate, of whom Major Melville is a truer contemporary than Waverley is of Jones. Allworthy may often forgive culprits, but not without first

---

70. Charles Dickens, *The Posthumous Papers of the Pickwick Club* (London: Oxford University Press, 1948), 245. See also Welsh, *Reflections on the Hero as Quixote*, 108–13.

being persuaded of their guilt. This is not to say that Fielding's psychology is less profound than Scott's; it is simply not depth psychology, not even inferentially. Though many criminal charges are leveled against Jones in the course of the novel, Fielding does not make the main fact in issue a criminal one; rather, the main issue is Jones's loyalty to Allworthy, his essentially filial love and gratitude. Yet even this love is measured the way intent is measured by a court of law: either he loved Allworthy or he did not.[71] Furthermore, when Jones's drunken rejoicing is mistaken for callousness and he is dismissed by Allworthy, he does not feel guilty the way Waverley and other moderns experience guilt—that is, prospectively. Rather, he blames himself after the fact for unthinking behavior and above all grieves—grieves for the breach with Allworthy that seems like death.

Fielding's novel is superficially more didactic than Scott's. One form the didacticism takes is the persistent moral satire of human types and behavior, and still another is the deliberate promotion of the concept of good nature, which derives from some of the most sophisticated moral philosophy of the time, from Hume and Adam Smith as well as from sermons and Shaftesbury.[72] Scott's achievement struck contemporaries as something quite different: he made the novel itself a respectable form, it was said, and his narratives could be perused for their own sake. The young Henry James explored this commonplace of literary history in a review of 1864. "With one or two exceptions," he disarmingly wrote, Scott was "the first English prose story-teller." In contrast, Richardson, Fielding, and "even" Smollett were didactic writers at heart. James spelled out the difference (which I have pinned to historicism and guilt) with reference to our very same two novels. The story of *Tom Jones* "is like a vast episode in a sermon preached by a grandly humorous divine; and however we may be entertained by the way, we must not forget that our ultimate duty is to be instructed." *Waverley,* on the other hand, "was the first novel which was self-for-

---

71. The language of Square's letter refers to Jones's most serious offense, his supposed rejoicing when Allworthy was near death, in criminal language: "As to the principal Fact, upon the Misrepresentation of which you discarded him, I solemnly assure you he is innocent" (*Tom Jones,* 18.4.927). Intention so narrowly defined is still difficult to prove, but it is clearly conscious intention that can be put to a common-law test.

72. With the concept of good nature, compare the idea of sympathy in Hume and Smith: David Hume, *A Treatise of Human Nature,* ed. L. A. Selby-Bigge (1888; rpt. Oxford: Clarendon, 1967), 316–89; and Adam Smith, *The Theory of Moral Sentiments,* selections in *British Moralists,* ed. Selby-Bigge, 2 vols. (1897; rpt. New York: Dover, 1965), 1:257–96. See also Bernard Harrison, *Henry Fielding's Tom Jones: The Novelist as Moral Philosopher* (London: Sussex University Press, 1975).

getful. It proposed simply to amuse the reader, as an old English ballad amused him. It undertook to prove nothing but facts. It was the novel irresponsible." James's lighthearted comparison was nothing short of brilliant—though he went on to acknowledge that Scott's success was owed to more than this "new style" or "method" of novel writing.[73] The rejection of overt didacticism became, in any case, a hallmark of nineteenth-century realism—one has only to think of James himself, or even of George Eliot, par excellence the Victorian realist.[74] But this rejection was possible precisely because didacticism had been absorbed into the culture and its fictions. The social contract, an all-absorbing myth, has swallowed up didacticism unnoticed. Individuals party to the contract, and novels party to the contract, have already succumbed to any essential teaching, since they have been written to the dictation of society. Only so could a novel undertake "to prove nothing but facts" and become, in this extraordinarily ambitious sense, "the novel irresponsible." James's words should thus be read very seriously. The novel after Scott still took the shape of a trial to prove the facts; since it also took for granted a social contract, it appeared "simply to amuse." The novel before Scott could only please *and* instruct (not unlike the prosecution's narrative in *R v. Blandy*). Yet James does not spell out the full implication of the story of nineteenth-century realism, for his novel irresponsible assumes an interminably responsible hero. Waverley believes that he is innocent but does not see "how I can hope to prove myself so"; the Jamesian chorus assures him merely that the novel will prove his innocence by proving nothing but facts. The same novel, or strong representation of innocence, may still not satisfy a hero's hope for clearing "myself." Psychological guilt is this loose end to the plot of realism.

History and the social contract, finally, induce a certain amount of displacement in the realistic novel. Impulse, waywardness, rebellion, even crime that is forbidden a hero or heroine may be projected onto

73. Henry James, *Literary Criticism: Essays on Literature, American Writers, English Writers,* ed. Leon Edel (New York: Library of America, 1984), 1200–1203. The review is of Nassau W. Senior, whose long essay on Scott first appeared in the *Quarterly Review* in 1821. See also James's perceptive remarks on "probable circumstances" in contemporary literature, in a review of Mary Elizabeth Braddon in 1865 (ibid., 742–43).

74. Like other realists, George Eliot believed that description was a sufficient lesson in moral truth. Thus, for example, she rejected Frederick Harrison's request that she write a novel inculcating Comtean positivism: see *The George Eliot Letters,* ed. Gordon S. Haight, 9 vols. (New Haven: Yale University Press, 1954–78), 4:284–89, 300–302. "I think aesthetic teaching to be the highest of all teaching because it deals with life in its highest complexity. But if it ceases to be purely aesthetic—if it lapses anywhere from the picture to the diagram—it becomes the most offensive of all teaching" (300).

another character, in some of realism's most ingenious moves to narrate irresponsibility within the fable of social responsibleness. All sorts of doubling of characters, needless to say, can occur in fiction, from the careful pairings of high comedy to the doppelgänger of romantic tales. Fielding introduces shining antitheses in his novel, the chief example being the contrast of Jones with Blifil.[75] But Blifil does not contain any motives secretly shared by Jones, and Jones acts out all of his feelings for himself. At the other extreme, a doppelgänger has only dreamlike being and little claim to any character independent of the protagonist's.[76] Since Scott, in his first novel, persistently compares his hero's adventures to a dream, it would not be strange to have doubling of that kind.[77] But much more prominent and typical of Scott's narrative is the deployment of Fergus Mac-Ivor, a character fully vested in the manners and motives of the times, whose attitudes Waverley might share were it not for the prior constraints of the contract. Since history denotes past action, this character may seem to have more historical presence than the hero, who is committed by the plot to society and the future. The very pastness of Mac-Ivor's role dictates its finitude and possibly tragic outcome.[78] Indeed, Tom Jones was a hero "born to be hanged," but no one is hanged after all in Fielding's comedy, and even Blifil, the hero's half-brother, is forgiven. "Born to be hanged" expresses character and fate as given, not as potential developments; the comparison of the brothers is therefore decisive, and dismissive of Blifil. In *Waverley,* Fergus Mac-Ivor *is* hanged and quartered by the end, for his part in the Stuart rebellion. Scott defuses the tension of the action with some quips from the dialect characters and justifies it with previous hints of Mac-Ivor's selfishness, but it is still told with a finality that, if not tragic, is drastic.[79] Precisely because Mac-Ivor dies to history, he can be said to die for—instead of—the hero.

The connection of the two characters is drawn much earlier, at the low point in the examination, when Waverley awakes "to a full con-

75. Cf. Andrew Wright, *Henry Fielding: Mask and Feast* (1965; rpt. Berkeley: University of California Press, 1966), 76–79.

76. Such figures appear not only in the tales of Hoffmann or Gogol, of course, but in major works of realism—Raffles in *Middlemarch,* Heep in *David Copperfield,* Rigaud in *Little Dorrit,* Orlick in *Great Expectations*—alongside countless examples of less eccentric displacement.

77. Cf. S. Stewart Gordon, "*Waverley* and the 'Unified Design,' " *ELH* 18 (1951): 116.

78. Welsh, *Hero of the Waverley Novels,* 58–70, 224–28; see also Robert Kiely, *The Romantic Novel in England* (Cambridge: Harvard University Press, 1972), 145, 151.

79. Cf. Bruce Beiderwell, "The Reasoning of those Times: Scott's *Waverley* and the Problem of Punishment," *Clio* 15 (1985): 15–30.

sciousness of the horrors of his situation" and before Morton offers his assistance. "How it might terminate he knew not," the hero reflects; but he fears either "military law, which . . . was not likely to be scrupulous in the choice of its victims, or the quality of the evidence," or the still more unfamiliar procedures of "a Scottish court of justice." Understandably, "a sentiment of bitterness rose in his mind against the government, which he considered as the cause of his embarrassment and peril," and he begins to wish that he had joined the Stuart cause. The rest is soliloquy, which concludes:

> Had I yielded to the first generous impulse of indignation, when I learned that my honour was practised upon, how different had been my present situation! I had then been free and in arms, fighting, like my forefathers, for love, for loyalty, and for fame. And now I am here, netted and in the toils, at the disposal of a suspicious, stern, and cold-hearted man, perhaps to be turned over to the solitude of a dungeon, or the infamy of a public execution. O Fergus! how true has your prophecy proved! and how speedy, how very speedy, has been its accomplishment!

It is, as I say, the low point, and Waverley is reproved by Scott in the next paragraph for "bestowing upon the reigning dynasty that blame which was due to chance, or, in part at least, to his own unreflecting conduct" (33.165–66). For anyone who has read to the end of the novel, the irony of the situation and reflection alike is striking. Fergus, not Edward, will endure the fate that the hero has envisioned for himself and tempted by his silence and despair. "Free and in arms, fighting, like my forefathers," the hero imagines he might break the social contract. For those archaic virtues—"for love, for loyalty, and for fame"— he would court the death his friend has courted. But the novel will not have it so: the arrest of Waverley leads inexorably to the execution of Mac-Ivor.

This degree of inward participation in another's fate accommodates a partial displacement of Waverley's own swiftly repressed rebellion. The displacement helps the hero to emerge from the examination of the novel as a whole with clean hands and a claim to future rewards, while it punishes wrong motives and antisocial actions more grimly than Fielding's comedy. Such a split, or a configuration of characters that invites this reading, is not present in *Tom Jones*.[80] It makes its

---

80. Cf. Alan Dugald McKillop, *The Early Masters of English Fiction* (Lawrence: University of Kansas Press, 1956), 128, on *Tom Jones*: "one of the conventions of comedy is that, unlike tragedy, it permits an escape from the past." Such is a generic account of Jones's acquittal—and forgiveness for Blifil, for that matter. But in *Waverley,* which is

appearance repeatedly, however, in nineteenth-century novels that depend on the management of circumstantial evidence. Most such novels take the same stance as Fielding's or Scott's: that is, up to a certain point or in certain episodes, the evidence supports any number of charges against the protagonist; then, in a complete view of the evidence, charges are dismissed. Because guilt cannot so easily be gotten rid of, novelists such as Dickens additionally work for the kind of displacement found in Scott. The evidence in *Bleak House* points to Lady Dedlock as the murderer of Tulkinghorn; when all the facts are known, she is exculpated. But not freely exculpated, as Tom Jones is, because she feels as much the murderer as if she had shot Tulkinghorn.[81] Her legal guilt is displaced entirely upon Hortense, the French maid, who has the happiness to pull the trigger. At still another remove, the most subtle guilt belongs to Esther Summerson. "If she ain't the t'other one, she ain't the forrenner," says Jo, the crossing sweeper. "Is there three of 'em, then?"[82] The masterpiece of such plotting is not an English novel at all but *The Brothers Karamazov,* in which Dostoevsky amasses every conceivable kind of evidence against Dmitri Karamazov, from his motive and threats to his presence at the scene of the crime and his behavior afterward, but does not allow Karamazov to commit the murder after all, though he insists upon his guilt and punishment for the same. Still another scenario is worked through for Ivan Karamazov, while of course the actual killer is their half-brother Smerdyakov. Are there three of them, then?

Thus a historicizing of the trials of Tom Jones results in psychological guilt and displacement, and management of evidence more and more curiously directed. Note how the social contract, as opposed to sources of authority in traditional society, provides an assumption of guilt as pervasive as the doctrine of original sin, without the notion of inheritance. One can never fully propitiate the demands of an undying contract. The assumption of guilt presses upon the logic of inference as it does in a criminal trial, and it can be no accident that so many memorable—as well as forgotten—novels of the later nineteenth century

---

part comedy, the past cannot be escaped entirely. This historicity is accommodated by a double fable with, in effect, two heroes.

81. "Her enemy he was, and she has often, often, often, wished him dead. . . . The horror that is upon her, is unutterable. If she really were the murderess, it could hardly be, for the moment, more intense": *Bleak House,* ed. George Ford and Sylvère Monod (New York: Norton, 1977), 666. Dickens devotes several paragraphs to delineating the feelings of Lady Dedlock in this conditional state, *as if* she were the murderer.

82. Ibid., 383.

have sensational detective or blackmail plots.[83] In this development of realism, a scrap of evidence or the slightest omission often unravels the whole truth, as it does in so many psychoanalytic investigations, only because of the assumption of guilt behind the management of the narrative. The assumption lies in the culture and, philosophically speaking, in the social contract. After the arrest of Waverley it became commonplace in the novel.

Consider once more the prosecution's case in *R v. Blandy*. The prosecution made out that the arsenic used to kill Francis Blandy was supplied by the prisoner's boyfriend along with the gift of Scottish pebbles. Was the powder merely for cleaning the pebbles? Serjeant Hayward called attention to what Blandy and her friend had *not* said. "From time to time mention is made of the pebbles; but not a syllable about the powder."[84] Why would suspected poisoners mention one and not the other? Under suspicion their silence — "not a syllable about the powder" — becomes evidence of their intention, just as Burke contends that "silence where he was called to speak" is evidence of Hastings's state of mind, or the silences of Blifil in *Tom Jones* ultimately tell against him. Inferences of this narrow kind depend on first constructing a suppositious or partial story of guilt and then indirectly affirming it by the actor's evasions. The access to the person's mind depends wholly on circumstantial evidence; the significance of a single fact or omission, at least until the whole story is known, depends on an assumption of guilt. The latter assumption, as well as the evidentiary point, was historically generalized for modern times through the social commitment dramatized in *Waverley*. The modern hero's purpose to submit to examination before he is arrested reflects his innocence *and* prospective guilt, since he must not be his own judge. He expects that silence will be used against him, and so he generally talks. These are conditions preparing a way for psychoanalysis[85] and, more obviously, other novels.

"Someone must have traduced Joseph K., for without having done

83. See Alexander Welsh, *George Eliot and Blackmail* (Cambridge: Harvard University Press, 1985), and for the differences between blackmail and detective plots, 8–10.

84. The Trial of Mary Blandy, *State Trials*, 18:1132.

85. Freud would not have insistently deployed the evidence of small omissions or constantly invoked the resistance to analysis were it not for the nineteenth-century conjunction of contract theory with the popular notion of pursuing criminals by means of circumstantial evidence. The implicit theory and detective practices were made widely familiar through novels. Cf. "Psycho-Analysis and the Establishment of the Facts in Legal Proceeding" (1906), in *The Standard Edition of the Complete Psychological Works of Sigmund Freud*, ed. and trans. James Strachey et al., 24 vols. (London: Hogarth, 1953–74), 9:103–14; and Welsh, *George Eliot and Blackmail*, 337–77.

anything wrong he was arrested one fine morning."[86] If Edward W.'s adventures are dreamlike, Joseph K.'s are such that dream and reality are indistinguishable. Kafka's formula for postrealistic narrative fully expresses the hero's bewildered eagerness to appear before the court, where his very conscious and unconscious thoughts will be sorted out for him. And still the novelist is conducting a defense, however futile, against the indictment he has also arranged.

86. Franz Kafka, *The Trial,* trans. Willa and Edwin Muir (1937; rpt. New York: Modern Library, 1956), 3.

3

The Evidence of Two Shakespearean Lives

Having once acquir'd this notion of causation from the memory, we can extend the same chain of causes, and consequently the identity of our persons beyond our memory, and can comprehend times, and circumstances, and actions, which we have entirely forgot, but suppose in general to have existed.

—David Hume, 1739

If circumstances leade me, I will finde
Where truth is hid, though it were hid indeede
Within the Center.

—A Councillor of State, 1604

V ERBAL REPRESENTATIONS ARE LIMITED neither to narrative nor to writing. Of the several models of strong representation I have been invoking, the outstanding one of the modern criminal trial is itself the product of an oral tradition. We may pore over the record of *R v. Blandy* or of *R v. Donellan*—as Burke did, in the second instance—in order to grasp the relation of circumstantial evidence to narrative and conviction, but the words on the page were originally spoken aloud and listened to by a jury. To be sure, witnesses, prosecutors, and judges generally have to limit themselves to telling and arguing about the facts rather than attempting to reenact them before the jury, whereas in other, equally venerable institutions such as the theater, representation can be both verbal *and* visual—not nearly so dependent on the use of words as a trial, but enhanced by acting and different conventions for reflecting time. Both kinds of representations—or productions, if you will—succeed in making present the absent, sometimes fictitious, events in question. Trials, however, whenever there are no eyewitnesses, readily invite strong representations of events, whereas theater need not expressly develop any evidence of things not seen.

Such basic differences between narrative and drama, while necessary to keep in mind, should not exclude drama from consideration here, if only because of the importance of Shakespeare's plays in English. For one thing, though a play is not itself a strong representation, it may contain within it narratives with that tendency as well as characters strenuously and conclusively arguing from indirect evidence. Iago fakes enough circumstantial evidence to persuade Othello of the guilt of Desdemona and Cassio; Leontes perceives enough evidence of infidelity to convince himself of a similar story without the intervention of an Iago, and this in opposition to the testimony of everyone in his court. From these two examples, we may surmise that Shakespeare opposed convictions about things unseen that are only inferred from circumstances, and that surmise merely tends to confirm my historical argu-

102

ment: Shakespeare indeed lived and wrote for the stage before the heyday of circumstantial evidence. But second, no account of modern representation—in history or psychology, let alone poetry, plays, or novels—can very well ignore the construction of character. Novels, of course, are famous for the representation of characters, some of whom we are persuaded we know better than the people next door or even our own families. But in English literature, since the eighteenth century Shakespeare's plays have been no less known for their characters, and a commitment to character is a much disputed ground of Shakespeare criticism. Character, it could be said, did not mean the same thing after the reception of Lockean and Humean notions of the self as an accumulation of sensations over time—a sort of narrative construct of individual being. And that brings us to a third observation—that methods of interpreting Shakespeare changed at roughly the same time as the realistic novel and the modern criminal trial evolved, when natural religion achieved its intellectual supremacy and not only psychology but geology and biology came to be based on developmental ideas. Accordingly, nineteenth-century Shakespeare criticism has sometimes been seen as a departure from the study of dramatic art into the study of narrative, and written narrative at that, more appropriate to the study than the stage.

In a book devoted not to Shakespeare but to nineteenth- and twentieth-century poetry, Robert Langbaum reviews the ways characters can seem to exceed the bounds of dramatic action, and specifically the history of "the isolation of character from plot" in certain Shakespeare criticism. "Are the characters agents of the plot with only as much consciousness as the plot requires; or have they a residue of intelligence and will beyond what the plot requires and not accounted for by it, so that they stand somehow above the plot, conscious of themselves inside it? The latter view assumes that we can apprehend more about the characters than the plot tells us, assumes our sympathetic apprehension of them." Langbaum deliberately recalls the development of the second view, from the later eighteenth century to the early twentieth, in order to establish a parallel or precedent for the representation of character in the dramatic monologue, with its simultaneous appeals to the sympathy of readers and to their moral verdict. In the dramatic monologue, especially, it seems that the supposed events, or occasion of the poem, are "merely an episode in the character's career, an episode whose beginning and end shades off into the rest of his biography."[1] He ap-

1. Robert Langbaum, *The Poetry of Experience: The Dramatic Monologue in Modern Literary Tradition* (1957; rpt. New York: Norton, 1963), 177, 170, 180.

propriately singles out Maurice Morgann's work of 1777, *An Essay on the Dramatic Character of Sir John Falstaff,* as a harbinger of this view of character, though the eighteenth-century writer was necessarily constrained by the conceptions of argument and evidence of his time.

Undoubtedly Maurice Morgann's effort has to be seen today as advanced in some respects and antiquated in others. But if one considers the rhetorical design of his *Essay,* its place in the history of strong representations becomes suddenly very clear. Morgann, after straining to place Falstaff on trial, appoints himself the task of defending the character—on the basis of *all* the evidence, he insists. With the ingeniousness of a novelist and with language as blatantly forensic as Fielding's, he charges Falstaff with cowardice and then proceeds to acquit him of the charge: he conducts another popular defense, like that in *Tom Jones* or *Waverley* but in a different mode of discourse, based on circumstantial evidence. Morgann will accept the testimony of other characters in the play when it supports his case, but he is more prone to examine the absence of testimony, some silence or omission that seems to tell on behalf of his client. Indirection strongly appeals to him, and he praises Shakespeare's indirection. His is a genuinely complicated piece of criticism—a bit perverse, one may think—and when the going gets tough Morgann sometimes takes refuge from his readers by calling it sport. Nevertheless, far from being constrained by preromantic psychology, the forensic impetus of the *Essay* should set one thinking about the contribution circumstantial evidence made to the writing and reading of dramatic monologues themselves.

Morgann's *Essay* created some stir at the time and then was largely forgotten. Like other early forays of Shakespeare criticism on diverse fronts, it did not hold out long against the comprehensive contributions of eighteenth-century editors or the incipient character criticism of Hazlitt and Coleridge. But partly the fault was Falstaff's: a great clown may unsettle our very perceptions of ourselves, but for that reason he is not likely to be a focus of steady and wholehearted identification. Langbaum is rather generous, in fact, to claim that "the Falstaff question has only been less important than the Hamlet question in establishing the psychological interpretation of Shakespeare."[2] In the course of the nineteenth century, interest in Hamlet far and away predominated over interest in any other character, even though there were certain underground connections between Falstaff and Hamlet, a few of which I shall try to dig out. It is no more possible to trace character criticism purely

2. Ibid., 171.

in evidentiary terms than it is to explain in these terms Scott's important alteration of Fielding's novel. A certain thematic difference over time has to be understood before one can judge that "Hamlet is his own Falstaff."[3] But A. C. Bradley, whose *Shakespearean Tragedy* of 1904 I shall treat as an epitome of character criticism, understood well enough this modern link between Hamlet and Falstaff. Bradley also appreciated Morgann, regretted that the *Essay* was not better known, and accepted some of its arguments rather unguardedly.[4]

At about the time Scott was arranging for the arrest of Waverley and, worse, releasing him on his own recognizance, Shakespearean critics arrested Hamlet in a slightly different sense. From the romantic period on, the question became why Hamlet had arrested himself. Why did he delay? No magistrate or voluntary defender had anything to do with this question, which became mainly psychological. As with Waverley, the initial constraint on the character seemed to originate with himself, but the romantic Hamlet had no modern political standing comparable to that of Scott's hero: the social setting for Hamlet had been arranged by Shakespeare well before the age of contract and of romantic criticism. In *Waverley,* a forensic model for testing the hero's guilt or innocence was presented as a part of the action, whereas in *Hamlet,* composed two hundred years earlier for the stage, such a model had to be inferred if it existed at all — unless Shakespeare playfully predicted the course of strong representations still to come in the thinking of Polonius. Out of the anachronism of romantic criticism, in short, emerged a new story of Hamlet, which *was* a story and invited a deeper consideration of motive on the strength of circumstantial evidence. For Bradley, Hamlet had thus been arrested and examined for a hundred years or more, and the need for a defense of Hamlet, on the same grounds of circumstantial evidence, could be taken for granted. Bradley succeeded admirably — pulled off that defense, as we might say — but only, in one of *his* critics' words, by "forcing a nineteenth-century legalistic interpretation upon sixteenth-century material."[5]

A little triangulation with the dramatic and narrative representations of Falstaff or Hamlet can be instructive, therefore, about the history of

3. Harold C. Goddard, *The Meaning of Shakespeare,* 2 vols. (1951; rpt. Chicago: University of Chicago Press, 1967), 1:341.
4. A. C. Bradley, "The Rejection of Falstaff," *Oxford Lectures on Poetry* (London: Macmillan, 1909), 266–67.
5. Lily B. Campbell, "Bradley Revisited: Forty Years After," *Studies in Philology* 44 (1947), reprinted as appendix A of *Shakespeare's Tragic Heroes: Slaves of Passion* (New York: Barnes and Noble, 1968), 251.

circumstantial evidence itself. Bradley, of course, was a contemporary of Freud, and their respective analyses of Hamlet's delay were worked out within a few years of each other. That Freud was a maker of strong representations, a master storyteller of things not seen, an ingenious miner of evidence hidden not only from sight but from consciousness, who could deny? But though his affinities for English culture were marked, Freud was not an English writer like the others studied here, and his daring management of evidence in psychoanalysis has far too intricate a history to trace easily. Very conveniently, it was Ernest Jones who, writing in English for an American journal in 1910, first elaborated the explanation of Hamlet's delay offered in a mere footnote (later a paragraph) in Freud's *Interpretation of Dreams*. His version of a Hamlet both arrested and psychoanalyzed certainly counts as a strong representation and, because of its redoubtable forensic rhetoric, can be compared to Morgann's eighteenth-century efforts on Falstaff's behalf. In fact, Jones's analysis of Hamlet is so curiously and relentlessly prosecutorial that it is reminiscent of still earlier claims for circumstantial evidence than Morgann's. It is as if the psychoanalysis of Hamlet, assuming a general guilt, was able to deploy prosecutorial and defensive modes of representation in tandem.

Morgann's Defense of Falstaff

The public career of Maurice Morgann (ca. 1725–1802) followed the wake of the earl of Shelburne, whom he served as a secretary concerned mainly with American affairs in the late eighteenth century. Though he had no training as a lawyer, he studied Canadian judicature at first hand preparatory to the Quebec Act of 1774, and he seems to have had a penchant for drafting strong representations. While Shelburne was out of office, Morgann wrote not only his amateur defense of Falstaff but a precocious attack on the slave trade, his *Plan for the Abolition of Slavery in the West Indies* (1772).[6] In the preface to *An Essay on the Dramatic Character of Sir John Falstaff*, he cheerfully accepts "rather the character and tone of an Advocate than of an Inquirer." As the preface also allows, the *Essay* is an "Exercise" and an "Experiment"; but the author consistently presents himself throughout as Falstaff's "Voluntary defender." His concessions as to his client's moral failing and lying, for example,

6. For biographical details see Maurice Morgann, *Shakespearean Criticism*, ed. Daniel A. Fineman (Oxford: Clarendon, 1972), 3–11. This edition provides not only a comprehensive introduction to the *Essay* but revisions of the same that have survived in manuscript.

are for the purpose of damage control: lying may have "precluded *Falstaff* from all rational defence of his own person; —but it has not precluded me, who am not the advocate of his *lyes* but of his *Courage.*"[7]

Morgann's decisive move was to try Falstaff on a charge as narrow as that of a criminal indictment, then to defend him on grounds of circumstantial evidence that he could arrange in his own fashion. He was neither the first student of Shakespeare to warm to Falstaff nor the first to protest against the rejection scene at the end of *2 Henry IV.* Nicholas Rowe had driven a small wedge between the character and the play in 1709; and in 1744 Corbyn Morris had used the example of Falstaff in an important essay on humor, which already covered many of the grounds for finding the character likeable despite his faults.[8] In the same spirit Morgann rises to the defense, first conceiving of an opposing opinion that serves as the indictment of Falstaff—"the character so generally given him of an absolute Coward" (2). This charge he then narrows still further to the question whether Falstaff was "a *Constitutional Coward*" (15), so that no single incident or expression of cowardice can weigh of itself in a verdict against his client. No one, perhaps, has ever accused a character of anything quite so technical as constitutional cowardice, but this model of accusation and defense permits Morgann to work up the circumstantial evidence and to trace the "*mental Impressions*" that, in his Humean psychology,[9] differ from our "*Understanding*" of Shakespeare's play (4–6).

At a number of moments Morgann takes refuge behind the position that his defense of Falstaff is only a sport, and he compares the entertainment to that of a novel. He even pleads, on this comparison, a certain license in argument, or freedom from "the strict severity of logical investigation," though he would hope that the entertainment is of a sort "more rational than the History of Miss *Betsy,* eked out with the Story of Miss *Lucy,* and the Tale of Mr. *Twankum*" (47, 113). Such pleas and concessions, spoken near the commencement of a long dominant and still significant strain of Shakespeare criticism, raise the question whether second-order analysis of character, no matter how serious or probing, does not become speculatively more free, more licensed to

7. [Maurice Morgann], *An Essay on the Dramatic Character of Sir John Falstaff* (London: Davies, 1777), 112, 141. Subsequent page references are given in parentheses.

8. For Corbyn Morris and Morgann, see especially Stuart M. Tave, *The Amiable Humorist: A Study of the Comic Theory and Criticism of the Eighteenth and Early Nineteenth Centuries* (Chicago: University of Chicago Press, 1960), 118–34.

9. Fineman, in his notes for Morgann's *Shakespearean Criticism,* 362–63, makes the comparison with Hume.

narrate, than the original fiction. When Shakespeare puts a make-believe character like Falstaff on the stage (or when Fielding and Scott describe characters in novels), he proposes, however extravagantly, to represent life; but when the character critic comes along, he proposes, however respectfully, to represent a fiction. Falstaff, to be sure, is first of all Shakespeare's character, and Morgann frequently sees his responsibility—still within a forensic model—to establish Shakespeare's intention as well as the character's. But the critic has his own relation to an audience to think about as well, his pride in his own ingenuity. Thus Morgann chooses to represent a notorious client against an almost sure verdict: Falstaff, he argues, is not a coward. The constraints of a difficult brief provide a still greater challenge, for the evidence "lies so dispersed, is so latent, and so purposely obscured, that the reader must have some patience whilst I collect it into one body, and make it the object of a steady and regular contemplation" (4).

Maurice Morgann, amateur critic and attorney, promises to master the evidence even while imputing conspiracy and concealment to the other side—not merely those who suppose Falstaff a coward but the artist Shakespeare. For though he argues as Shakespeare's advocate as well as Falstaff's in the *Essay,* the evidence has been "dispersed" and "purposely obscured" by the dramatist to produce his special effect, a kind of pleasure of drawing inferences that can be enjoyed by the audience or reader. Morgann, who is one of the early idolators of Shakespeare, patterns his mastery of circumstantial evidence on the dramatist's mastery of the same, much as a natural theologian works out all the inferences planted in the universe by Creation.[10] He is a far more modest critic than the ones Fielding addresses in *Tom Jones* and more modest than Fielding, too, since he attributes to Shakespeare all the ingenuity demanded of the defense. In a long footnote to the *Essay*—"something which may be thought too heavy for the *text,*" as he modestly states— Morgann spells out the aesthetic premise of his criticism:

> A felt propriety and truth from causes unseen, I take to be the highest point of Poetic composition. If the characters of *Shakespeare* are thus *whole,* and as it were original, while those of almost all other writers are mere imitation, it may be fit to consider them rather as Historic than Dramatic beings; and, when occasion requires, to account for their con-

---

10. "All the incidents, all the parts, look like chance, whilst we feel and are sensible that the whole is design" (67). In some places Morgann capitalizes personal pronouns referring to Shakespeare, and one could almost annotate this text's seeming theological ambitions as Martin Battestin has been able to annotate Fielding's novels.

duct from the *whole* of character, from general principles, from latent motives, and from policies not avowed. (58, 62)

In other words, Shakespeare's is the art of inference, of unseen causes, and his critic has therefore to get up the evidence of things not seen. From a brief dialogue on stage, especially as studied in the book of the play, a character with a history can be inferred. In this footnote, Morgann's speculative elevation of "Dramatic" to "Historic" being is a compliment that rankles with many students of Shakespeare, who believe that characters in a play should not be confused with real people. Yet the primary contrast here is between dramatic and narrative being — a character about which a story might be told, a history lifted from the "latent" evidence in the play and not from life. We have heard before the call to await the full story in a trial based upon circumstantial evidence: now Morgann calls for a determination of the *"whole"* character — character, as his analysis of Falstaff shows, existing over time. Langbaum is correct to single out from this viewpoint "the isolation of character from plot," if plot is thought of in an Aristotelian sense. But Morgann, after all, is invoking a different plot — the plot of remotely relevant facts, the roundabout and expansive plot of circumstantial evidence.

Rhetorically, the model of a fair trial serves Morgann as the model of science serves Freud, as an inspiration not to be stalled by opposition — a way to examine all the relevant evidence and to pursue the facts wherever they lead. No sooner has he defined his terms and explained why he will not follow the order of events presented in *Henry IV* than he runs enthusiastically ahead to Falstaff's "strategem" of playing dead at the battle of Shrewsbury. But then he checks himself, disarmingly, with the following earnest deliberation:

> But I am too much in advance, and must retreat for more advantage. I should not forget how much opinion is against me, and that I am to make my way by the mere force and weight of evidence; without which I must not hope to possess myself of the reader: No address, no insinuation will avail. To this evidence, then, I now resort. The Courage of *Falstaff* is my Theme: And no passage will I spare from which any thing can be inferred as relative to this point. It would be as vain as injudicious to attempt concealment: How could I escape detection? The Play is in every one's memory, and a single passage remembered in detection would tell, in the mind of the partial observer, for fifty times its real weight. Indeed this argument would be void of all excuse if it declined any difficulty; if it did not challenge opposition. (26–27)

How could he escape detection? In thus inviting us to observe closely his advocacy, Morgann lets on that strong representations create their own trial. His little colloquy, obviously, does not concede any argument to anyone but, on the contrary, fancies an opposition when none is actually present. The bold adversary manner, absent the other side, merely lulls the reader into accepting what he has to offer. Morgann's submission to the text ("the Play is in every one's memory") is similarly rhetorical: the text is whatever he can persuade his reader to believe.

In the two-part play that concludes with Falstaff's arrest, Shakespeare cannot be said to have placed his character's courage on trial. Falstaff's courage is not a fact in issue, so to speak, except in the joke played by the Prince and Poins at the beginning of Part 1—the robbing of the robbers at Gad's Hill—and even there the expectation that Falstaff will run away, as he does, is incidental to the purpose of hearing the extravagant lies he will tell afterward in excuse. Yet the dramatic importance of the joke—and practical jokes often make their particular demonstration—might be guessed from Morgann's determination to avoid it. He all but reproves Shakespeare for beginning the play with an experiment so prejudicial to the character now on trial, and in his *Essay* he deliberately postpones consideration of Gad's Hill to the end:

> The scene of the robbery, and the disgraces attending it, which stand first in the Play, and introduce us to the knowledge of *Falstaff*, I shall beg leave (as I think this scene to have been the source of much unreasonable prejudice) to *reserve* till we are more fully acquainted with the whole character of *Falstaff*; and I shall therefore hope that the reader will not for a time advert to it, or to the jests of the *Prince* or of *Poins* in consequence of that unlucky adventure. (17)

When Falstaff's advocate, having rearranged the action of the play, eventually has to cope with the "unlucky" incident, he does so by further isolating it. He examines the circumstances as they would appear to Falstaff at the time, divorced from the "braggadocioes *after the fact*" (134). He thus disrupts the aspect of proof built into the joke by Poins and the prince and, in this instance, refuses to complete the temporal sequencing customary for circumstantial evidence. "We have now gone through this transaction considered simply on its own circumstances," he writes, "and without reference to any future boast or imputation. It is upon these circumstances the case must be tried" (notice how fixed by now is the notion that the character is on trial). Regardless of the defendant's subsequent behavior (compare Burke's "every circum-

110

stance, precedent, concomitant and subsequent"), he asks that the case be considered "as it stands hitherto, with reference only to its own preceding and concomitant circumstances" (125). To give Morgann credit, he works over the Gad's Hill episode from every possible angle that does not entail his client's cowardice, distracts the jury by taking a few pokes at Poins's character, and prefaces this final performance with one more hint that, given what we now know about Falstaff, the whole matter is "unessential" and, besides, can be thought of as a "weak moment" such as other heroes occasionally experience (113–14).

Morgann's decision to give Falstaff a fair trial nevertheless makes its contribution to criticism. The task he sets himself, after all, is to explain the doubleness, the contradiction of liking and severity, in our response to the character. He wants to explain rationally the unstable impressions the play produces on its audience or readers. To do this, he reduces the issue to "a question of fact" (12), such as might be adjudicated before a jury or debated among students in a classroom. His choosing to defend Falstaff against the general opinion, as he conceives it, ensures a vigorous adversary stance that will call for a thorough examination of the evidence. At times he pretends that he is not serious, or is only playing devil's advocate, but each backing away then becomes an excuse for filling in more evidence, and more and more of the play comes in for close study. Morgann's attention, like Fielding's in *Tom Jones,* is fixed on evidence. If he seems less scrupulous than Fielding, that may be a measure of the man but appears more, I have suggested, the result of a certain license in second-order analyses of fictional characters invented by others. "We will examine, in course," he writes, "such evidence, either of *persons* or *facts,* as are relative to the matter" (16). Although he does not attack testimony with Fielding's persistence, he knows well how to counter testimony by discrediting witnesses—most notably Poins and Shallow in their respective parts of *Henry IV* and Falstaff's royal enemy, Prince John of Lancaster. Chiefly he transforms the absence of direct testimony on the point at issue, Falstaff's constitutional cowardice, into more circumstantial evidence in his favor: "though this silence," he boldly states, "be a negative proof only, it cannot, in my opinion, under the circumstances of the case, and whilst uncontradicted by facts, be too much relied on" (77). He understands the requirement that such evidence be complete and descend to the smallest matters: "if *Shakespeare* meant sometimes rather to *impress* than explain, no circumstances calculated to this end, either directly or by association, are too minute for notice" (47). He champions Shakespeare's reliance on in-

111

ference and believes that his characters cannot fully be comprehended without a study of inferences. In the footnote "too heavy" for his text (and reaching beyond the trial of Falstaff), he writes:

> The reader will not now be surprised if I affirm that those characters in *Shakespeare,* which are seen only in part, are yet capable of being unfolded and understood in the whole; every part being in fact relative, and inferring all the rest. It is true that the point of action or sentiment, which we are most concerned in, is always held out for our special notice. But who does not perceive that there is a peculiarity about it, which conveys a relish of the whole? And very frequently, when no particular point presses, he boldly makes a character act and speak from those parts of the composition, which are *inferred* only, and not distinctly shewn. (61–62)

Such is Morgann's theory of Shakespearean representations, and to apply it one must pay the closest attention to small points lest an inference be lost. "*Shakespeare* deserves to be considered in detail," he declares—and cannot help boasting, "a task hitherto unattempted" (16).

In keeping with this sense of his own originality, Morgann anticipated the objection that he was writing about something foreign to dramatic art. No sooner has he announced that the evidence he counts on is dispersed in the text, latent and obscured, than he imagines the other side protesting, "But what have we to do . . . with principles *so latent, so obscured?* In Dramatic composition the *Impression* is the *Fact*" (4). Yet persons in a theater as well as readers are capable of arguing about a play and its characters, and there is no way of confining their argument strictly to the performance or the text. They may simply express pleasure or displeasure with the play, but if they hope to persuade others to share a particular response, they usually propose to attach this to the facts invented by the play. Differences about the *Henry IV* plays and the need to debate differences are uppermost in Morgann's mind throughout the *Essay:* so much is implicit in his adversary approach. He does not actually confuse Falstaff or other characters with historical persons, except in praise of Shakespeare's mimetic powers or for convenience in writing about the characters.[11]

> With a stage character, in the article of exhibition, we have nothing more to do; for in fact what is it but an Impression; an appearance, which we are to consider as a reality; and which we may venture to applaud or condemn as such, without further inquiry or investigation? But if we

---

11. Cf. Alfred Harbage, *As They Liked It: An Essay on Shakespeare and Morality* (New York: Macmillan, 1947), 77.

would account for our Impressions, or for certain sentiments or actions in a character, not derived from its apparent principles, yet appearing, we know not why, natural, we are then compelled to look farther, and examine if there be not something more in the character than is *shewn*; something inferred, which is not brought under our special notice: In short, we must look to the art of the writer, and to the principles of human nature, to discover the hidden causes of such effects. (152–53)

In the case of Falstaff, even a single reader or member of the audience is likely to experience mixed feelings—or, as Morgann generally believes, a mixture of affection and moral disapproval. The incongruity of the character stirs debate within the individual perceiver too. Thus a rational account of a single individual's response to Falstaff entails a review of the circumstantial evidence and cannot avoid inference. Such inferences are in every sense authorized by Shakespeare, in Morgann's view, though his theory scarcely guarantees that the critic can always penetrate to the author's intention. One of the obstacles to agreeing with Morgann *as* a critic is his persistent disregard for some evidence.[12] But as A. D. Nuttall, a recent defender of Shakespearean representations against various formalist positions, has noted, it is possible to accept Morgann's principle of attending to inferences without always concurring with his reading of the plays.[13]

For better or worse, Morgann's practice exchanges drama for narrative, a move that makes it easier to impute cause and effect. After a few preliminaries and almost without warning—except that circumstantial evidence warrants it—Morgann produces a number of conjectures about his client's past. Falstaff's "leading quality" is his wit, and this quality "led him probably very early into life, and made him highly

12. It is fair enough to blame actors, as Morgann does a couple of times, for perpetuating some unbecoming antic of Falstaff's (25, 127), but surely not to deny, for example, that Falstaff *roared* at Gad's Hill in the face of undisputed testimony from Poins and the prince, at separate times in the play, merely because the text includes no stage direction to the effect that he roared (124–25). More often, Morgann simply blinds himself to any circumstances from which Falstaff's cowardice *can* be inferred, such as why it would ever have occurred to Poins to play this particular joke on such a person or how he could accurately foretell its success.

13. A. D. Nuttall, *A New Mimesis: Shakespeare and the Representation of Reality* (London: Methuen, 1983), 174. Probably the best-known rejoinder to character criticism is L. C. Knights's lecture of 1933, "How Many Children Had Lady Macbeth?" in *Explorations* (1947; rpt. New York: New York University Press, 1964), 15–54. In "The Argument about Shakespeare's Characters," *Critical Quarterly* 7 (1965): 107, Nuttall suggests that "Knights' real objection is to the practice of drawing inferences from the seen to the unseen with respect to persons of the play." Nuttall, incidentally, also draws a connection between Morgann and Freud, of whom he is more critical (*New Mimesis*, 177).

acceptable to society; so acceptable, as to make it seem unnecessary for him to acquire any other virtue. Hence, perhaps, his continued debaucheries and dissipations of every kind." This beginning over again with the character's youth decidedly shifts the grounds for moral judgment to the past. One might think that Falstaff would fare better being charged with a single offense rather than having his whole career thus exposed to view, but of course the jury is being asked to consider what habitual behavior must be like, with its myriad impersonal causes as well as personal failures. "By degrees" Falstaff "acquires bad habits, becomes a humourist, grows enormously corpulent, and falls into the infirmities of age," Morgann draws to a close this first excursion into the character's past. At what point can Falstaff be especially blamed, in such a long drawn-out story? At what point can he be said to have intended to become what he is? The inferences about his past life, however strained, alter the focus of criminal intention, for while it might be easy to prove highway robbery on the evidence of *Henry IV*, it would still be awkward to try to prove the defendant's intent to acquire bad habits or his desire to grow old. A few conclusions as to intent Morgann drops into his narrative a priori: "a mind free of malice or any evil principle"; "innocence as to purpose, and wickedness as to practice" (17–20). Other proofs depend on the assumption that wellborn and well-to-do characters are likely to be innocent. Because "the ideas of Courage and *birth* were strongly associated in the days of *Shakespeare*," Falstaff's social class is warranty of his courage (46). Though Morgann duly historicizes this argument, it reflects more nearly the eighteenth-century assumptions of his own class. He even wastes more pages vainly trying to prove that his client's means are greater than his empty pockets lead one to believe. Be that as it may, both the past and present conditions of Falstaff's life must be taken into account—"the circumstances and conditions of his whole life and character, which yet deserve our very particular attention"—and such a narrative construction is distinctly analytic, since it is invented not for the sake of its own interest but to establish the cause of those "particular transactions" that are offensive. It cannot be called *psycho*analytic, because Morgann does not attribute unconscious motives to Falstaff or to Shakespeare; yet the narrative of the character's early experience and the quest for indirect evidence—"something more in the character than is *shewn*; something inferred, which is not brought under our special notice"—may be thought of as potentially psychoanalytic.

To appreciate Morgann's activity on behalf of Falstaff and understand his recourse to narrative, one finally has to adopt his own methods, and possibly some hints from Freud—the Freud of *Civilization and Its Discontents*. As Harold Bloom has claimed, "One can read Freud on our discomfort in culture backward, and get somewhere close to Falstaff,"[14] and midway back there one comes upon Falstaff's defender. What latent or dispersed evidence can one find in *An Essay on the Dramatic Character of Sir John Falstaff* that will explain why its author should appoint himself the character's "Voluntary defender"? Can he merely be enjoying the stretch of his reasoning powers and asking to entertain us, as he sometimes suggests? But why defend the witty Falstaff by maintaining his courage instead of trying to justify the wit? Morgann defends Falstaff, I suggest, because the character appeals to him from out of the play, not by what he is but by what he says. In the rapid series of scenes of the battle of Shrewsbury, in *1 Henry IV,* Falstaff stands over the body of Sir Walter Blunt and says, "Give me life, which if I can save, so: if not, honour comes unlooked for, and there's an end."[15] Or after he has pretended to be dead in order to escape being killed by Douglas, he exclaims, "Counterfeit? I lie, I am no counterfeit: to die is to be a counterfeit, for he is but the counterfeit of a man who hath not the life of a man" (5.4.113–16). Falstaff frankly does appear to act the coward in these battle scenes, Morgann to the contrary notwithstanding; but Falstaff's position is very much pro life. A principle of honor argues that a man who is shamelessly afraid deserves to die; and Christian belief allows death to be in God's hands. "Why, thou owest God a death," the prince has told him before the battle (5.1.126). But Falstaff wants to live: give me life; I am no counterfeit. Morgann has heard this appeal and takes up Falstaff's cause.

The critic first represents the character against the charge of cowardice—a lost cause but a strong representation. He then extends the case, pursuing Falstaff's very appeal for life, to a narrative of the whole life and character. One can understand these moves generically, as akin to Fielding's downplaying comedy in favor of true representation in a novel. Morgann (I infer) does not wish to dispose of Falstaff as a figure of comedy, exorcised in the rejection scene at the end of *2 Henry IV,* and his alternative is to represent him as a real person. And one can also understand the moves thematically, as a defense of what Falstaff stands for in the play. Morgann (I infer) does not quite realize how far

---

14. Harold Bloom, *Ruin the Sacred Truths: Poetry and Belief from the Bible to the Present* (Cambridge: Harvard University Press, 1989), 85.

15. Shakespeare, *1 Henry IV,* 5.3.58–61. Quotations from *Henry IV* are from the new Arden edition of both parts by A. R. Humphreys (London: Methuen, 1960 and 1966). References are to act, scene, and lines.

he has altered the fact in issue by insisting on so-called constitutional cowardice. By more and more narrowly arguing that Falstaff possesses merely "natural" courage, he seems only to be saying that Shakespeare conceived of the character as a real person.[16] If natural "Courage and Ability are first principles of Character, and not to be destroyed whilst the united frame of body and mind continues whole and unimpaired" (165), then every voluntary defender's client who remains in one piece and does not get off by pleading insanity must be acquitted.

For all his admiration of Falstaff's wit, Morgann much diminishes the comedy of the two plays. He does not examine very far why the wit appeals to him, for he is busy standing up to those characters in *Henry IV* who would make a fool of Falstaff. Subsequent literary historians have shown, to the contrary, that Falstaff has many analogues in comic literature, a goodly number of which are at once witty and the butts of wit,[17] and latterly a critic like C. L. Barber has accounted still better for the conventions of Shakespearean comedy by associating them with folk ritual. Thus Barber showed how Falstaff, as a carnival king of misrule, might so impressively occupy a history play and yet be the same Falstaff as in *The Merry Wives of Windsor* (where almost any critic who bestows life upon the character is embarrassed to find him a different person). Oldcastle or Falstaff—the comic knight by any name—seems to have made it easy for Shakespeare to accommodate the legend of Prince Hal's wild youth within his own naturalizing history, the royal succession portrayed familiarly as the succession of son to father. The figure of misrule can be exorcised for the harmony of parenting and of history alike, as for the entertainment of the bourgeoisie in the village of Windsor.[18] Morgann would find himself at a loss before this now popular interpretation of the plays, however, because he could not very well defend misrule in a court of law; and even if he were knowledgeable of the carnivalesque, it would make little sport to defend Falstaff as a scofflaw. Morgann is not quite successful in defending him, on the evidence of facts and persons, against a charge of cowardice, though by making a strong representation to this effect he moves in his own fashion from comedy to history and addresses the role of inference in the writing and reading of character.

16. Langbaum, *Poetry of Experience,* 173, suggests that the issue for Morgann "would seem to be whether Falstaff is to exist at all."

17. For example, Elmer Edgar Stoll, "Falstaff," *Modern Philology* 12 (1914): 197–240. Stoll appointed himself the chief adversary of Morgann in the first half of the twentieth century.

18. C. L. Barber, *Shakespeare's Festive Comedy: A Study of Dramatic Form in Its Relation to Social Custom* (1959; rpt. New York: Meridian, 1967), 67–73, 192–221.

This much Morgann might have achieved by defending any Shake-spearean character against some such reasonable charge as cowardice. But he chose to appoint himself the voluntary defender of Falstaff, a world historical Shakespearean character. To understand thematically what he is up to—and has "purposely obscured," to use his own ex-pression—one has to ask why he chose the very character who is not only the great carnival figure of comedy or the character "whole and unimpaired" whose history can be inferred and told in a book, but the infamous propagandist against the code of honor, and most pertinently that code's repudiation of cowardice. Morgann takes almost no notice of what Falstaff says about honor, a subject upon which so much of the admired wit is concentrated. Falstaff's catechism of honor on the occasion of the battle of Shrewsbury, for example, he never refers to. There Falstaff recognizes honor as the personal motive to battle and an invitation to casualties. "But can honour set to a leg?" he queries. "No. Or an arm? No. Or take away the grief of a wound? No. Honour hath no skill in surgery then? No. What is honour? A word. What is in that word honour? What is that honour? Air" (5.1.131–35). The jest turns on the truth that honor *is* a word of commitment, as in the expression "one's word of honor" or a solemn oath.[19] Honor is not equivalent to a demonstration of courage but is rather a commitment of an exact kind, a commitment for which the pledge or surety given is one's life (or sometimes a collective life, like that of a gang or an army). The word of honor prescribes courage because it always pledges that one shall do or die, or at the very least suffer a loss that is partial death—an arm or a leg certainly, but also, for austere refinements of the code, say one's income or general reputation. Falstaff keeps nagging away at the nature of the pledge, the potential cost to the body of every such commitment. His world historical infamy, which follows from this opposition, thrives on the private acknowledgment of the cost, the potential depletion of the body in every such commitment to civilized behavior.

Morgann, as I say, tends to be silent about his client's formidable contribution to the debate on honor as such, but he does not overlook Falstaff's formidable body, that great counterweight to every vow and

19. Though Verdi at the end of his lifetime set to music *The Merry Wives of Windsor,* he and his librettist Boito included this speech from *1 Henry IV* in the first scene of the great operatic *Falstaff.* When their version of the catechism arrives at a *word,* the orchestra stops completely and Falstaff's "una parolle" solemnly fills the theater, a cappella. This precise reply, in the Renaissance play or the nineteenth-century opera, is no mere chance witticism in the matter of honor.

shade of opinion in the plays. What Morgann celebrates as natural courage, in fact, often reduces to the character's determination to preserve his body in one piece. And to be sure, while the principal male characters in *Henry IV*—with fateful exceptions like Northumberland— put their lives on the line, Falstaff regularly remarks the weight of his body and his margin of safety: "I am as hot as molten lead, and as heavy too: God keep lead out of me, I need no more weight than mine own bowels" (Part 1, 5.3.33–35). He just as persistently calls attention to his weight problem when a highwayman as when called to war, and in the tavern scenes as well, Falstaff's eating, drinking, and sleeping—to say nothing of the constant stream of verbal abuse that he endures on the same score—all call attention to his bulk. That body attracts a certain fascinated friendship even as it signals an antisocial absence of commitment: "there's no room for faith, truth, nor honesty in this bosom of thine," as Hal at once protests and admires; "it is all filled up with guts and midriff" (3.3.152–53). Morgann confronts this aspect of the play fairly and is a little carried away himself. As we have seen, his argument sometimes seems to be that one cannot dismiss Falstaff without ignoring that body, or the character's whole life fleshed out with circumstances.

By modeling his argument on a trial at law and carefully managing the evidence, Morgann can pressure the reader to agree in a finding of fact: it is as if failure of courage were a capital offense, since one cannot hold body and mind together without it, and by getting Falstaff off that charge Morgann can give him life. Yet he does not openly acknowledge the temptation that underlies Falstaff's great infamy; he does not openly support the subversion of honor or commitment. He substitutes for the dramatic exposure of the code of honor in *Henry IV* his own trial of Falstaff, which then becomes increasingly quaint as it turns more and more on the question whether a person can survive without courage. Here is one of the places in the *Essay* where Morgann comes closest to revealing the other issue, the one that has always made it possible to think about Falstaff as well as laugh at him and the one that, I believe, actually attracts the critic to the case:

> *Constitutional Courage* extends to a man's whole life, makes a part of his nature, and is not to be taken up or deserted like a mere Moral quality. It is true, there is a Courage founded upon *principle,* or rather a principle independent of Courage, which will sometimes operate in spite of nature; a principle, which prefers death to shame, but which always refers itself, in conformity to its own nature, to the prevailing modes of honour, and

the fashions of the age. —But Natural courage is another thing: It is independent of opinion; It adapts itself to occasions, preserves itself under every shape, and can avail itself of flight as well as of action. (23)

Thus nature and Falstaff are the same. Only the second sentence touches any commitment that would subordinate the body, and it is a very slippery sentence, posing as a concession but ending as dismissal. Morgann's attitude here is as Falstaffian as can be, though his terms of argument are much more up-to-date. What is honor? A prevailing mode, he replies; a fashion of the age; a mere moral quality. Morgann's is an Enlightenment version of Falstaff's more churchly catechism, and the critic gives away his inner conviction here: he has been seduced by Falstaff's arguments after all. But one can only infer this interest from a few such glimpses and from the absence of any other motive for defending Falstaff on his terms. For if the point is to advocate natural courage, why choose Falstaff of all the characters in these plays? And if the point is that no one can be without natural courage, how will that presupposition serve Morgann's client?

It seems odd that, since Shakespeare's Falstaff was apparently an immediate popular success, he should have to wait nearly two hundred years before Morgann could provide him with a fair trial and sketch his whole life and character. One explanation for this anachronism is that somehow theatrical conventions of the earlier time were forgotten, or that Morgann simply did not know much about theater or comedy in his own time. And I have argued that a new set of conventions positively inspired this eighteenth-century critic: the jury trial, a model for narrative then popular and frequently in print, without which it would be hard to explain Morgann's enthusiasm for circumstantial evidence. But there is also the possibility that, long after he first set foot on stage, Falstaff is now to be cheered on because his subversion of honor as commitment has a fresh contemporary appeal. The somewhat misnamed *Essay on the Dramatic Character of Sir John Falstaff* more than defends Sir John's courage and elucidates Shakespeare's skill in planting evidence. It comes to defend everyone's "natural" courage to be oneself against a general feeling of social expectation or reproval; and like the novels *Tom Jones* and *Waverley,* it turns the management of circumstantial evidence against the prosecution of its main character. This prosecution Morgann as surely invents as if he were writing a novel, but not without some feeling that there might be prosecution of sorts in the air. In his preface, after all, he admits right away that he has taken a stand "contrary to the general Opinion."

Consider one other point in the *Essay* where Morgann's private attraction to Falstaffian principles shows through the case for constitutional courage: "And is it the duty then, *think we still,* of true Courage, to meet, without benefit to society, *certain death?* Or is it only the phantasy of honour?" (101). The implication, for once, is that there is such a motive as honor, apart from natural courage, and the defense of Falstaff is merely that the motive does not apply to his situation (no benefit to society in this instance). It is the utilitarian "benefit to society" that no speaker in *Henry IV,* with whatever view of honor, could utter. On Shakespeare's stage there were depicted warring factions, dynastic and family crises, fighting and thieving, but no benefit to society as a measure of commitment. While excusing Falstaff on any terms, Morgann thinks of society here as a man of the Enlightenment. As in Renaissance conceptions of honor, a potential loss or sacrifice, even certain death, must be contemplated; but in these more modern times that ideal has been homogenized, distributed among the members of society as a condition of membership. As an excuse for Falstaff the argument is rather specious, since Falstaff (or for that matter Hal or Hotspur) was not likely to encounter any opportunity to sacrifice himself to "society." On the other hand, the specific anachronism still attacks commitment, in these particular circumstances, as a "phantasy." The potential cost of commitment to the body, which Falstaff refuses in the play, is still operative in the modern sense of "duty," though it is diffused, present all of the time to all but criminals (now redefined as nonmembers of society) who have refused to agree to it.[20] Hence Morgann, whose initial reasons for putting Falstaff on trial and getting him off again were perhaps sportive, is also protesting a little at the idea of anyone's being forced to choose between sacrifice for the benefit of society and accepting criminal status; and hence other modern readers of *Henry IV* may identify with this storied Falstaff against a diffuse and continuous expectation of unheroic sacrifice or may hope as Morgann does to exonerate the character from imagined criminal charges.

By enclosing the dramatic character of Falstaff in narrative—or providing the foreground of the play with background, as he might put it—Morgann has also intervened in the levels of style in *Henry IV* and come up with a representation of reality much different from Shakespeare's. In the language of Northrop Frye's historical criticism,[21] he

20. The most explicit equation of criminality with violation of the contract and exclusion from society is Rousseau's, in *The Social Contract,* bk. 2, chap. 5.

21. Northrop Frye, *Anatomy of Criticism: Four Essays* (Princeton: Princeton University Press, 1951), 33–67.

has flattened out the mixture of prose and blank verse of Shakespeare's high mimetic mode and produced a low mimetic or novelistic Falstaff; or alternatively, if he takes a Shakespearean clown and makes a hero of him, as his critics often protest, he produces a distinctly modern essay in Frye's ironic mode. He brings an efficient modern solution to the inherent strain of Shakespeare's contrast of styles as memorably described from the very same plays by Erich Auerbach.[22] In brief, Falstaff emerges as a modern hero because Morgann conceives of him as almost exclusively the victim of circumstances. "If we will but examine a little into the nature of those circumstances which have accidentally involved him," the *Essay* proposes early on, a quite different man may be glimpsed, "a character of much Natural courage and resolution" (15). Of course this notion of the man as victim of circumstances is meant to palliate his sins, or perhaps to convince us that he has not sinned at all and has merely been "involved in circumstances productive of imputation" of wickedness, as his advocate suggests a few pages later (20). But if one can argue so for Falstaff, then possibly any character can be thought of as a victim of circumstances "which have accidentally involved him," a thought that is endemic to the very procedure of narrating a "whole life and character." Morgann's *Essay* registers a slippage in the hold of Providence over lives and welcomes a new role for accident. In that respect the author may be closer to Sterne than to Fielding, among novelists.[23] Yet if so, he has been infected more by the sentimental moralism of Sterne than by the laughter. For all his praise of Falstaff's wit and his promise to provide more entertainment, Morgann takes care not to laugh before the jury has come in with a verdict.

Bradley's Character of Hamlet

The youngest son of a twice-married clergyman, A. C. Bradley (1851–1935) grew up in a large Victorian family. An older brother was F. H. Bradley the philosopher, and both were Oxford men. Andrew Cecil, also trained in philosophy, became a fellow of Balliol College in 1874 when Benjamin Jowett was master, but he left Oxford in 1882 for modern literature chairs at Liverpool and Glasgow; Francis Herbert stayed on at Merton College for life. Until he was fifty, Bradley pub-

---

22. Erich Auerbach, *Mimesis: The Representation of Reality in Western Literature,* trans. Willard R. Trask (Princeton: Princeton University Press, 1953), 312–33.

23. Morgann is certainly acquainted with Sterne's *Tristram Shandy* (1760–67), because he mentions it at one point in his *Essay* (164).

lished virtually nothing, though on two occasions he edited volumes by the idealist T. H. Greene. In 1901 his *Commentary on Tennyson's "In Memoriam"* appeared, and he was elected poetry professor at Oxford for the usual five-year term. To the opening years of the twentieth century, then, belong the works for which Bradley is chiefly remembered: the lectures entitled *Shakespearean Tragedy* (1904) and two subsequent volumes of essays and lectures. In 1907 he turned down the Edward VII chair at Cambridge, and he was not active after the First World War.[24] About 120 years separate his writings on Shakespeare from Morgann's, and Bradley was far more knowledgeable, thoughtful, and consistent than his jaunty forebear. Yet he too was a gentlemanly bachelor and an amateur of sorts, another close critic of select plays rather than a literary historian. In the introduction to *Shakespearean Tragedy*, he fairly stated that the dramatist's "life and character, the development of his genius and art, the genuineness, sources, texts, interrelations of his various works"—the standard fare of Shakespeare scholarship, in short—would not be discussed.[25] That book is often said to epitomize the kind of criticism that Morgann's *Essay* on a single character began; and if the earlier critic had largely been forgotten in the nineteenth century, Bradley warmly welcomed him home in his own lecture on Falstaff.[26] Here I wish only to show that Bradley's treatment of Hamlet is another defense of a fictional character on the ground of circumstantial evidence.

Bradley never scraps with an imagined prosecution as Morgann does, arguing over the evidence with those who—he would have us believe—would condemn his client to ignominy or to death. Bradley does not think of himself as an advocate, voluntary or otherwise, in an adversary role. If anything, his forensic role resembles that of the examining magistrate of Continental practice, whose duty it is to uncover the facts and weigh the possible explanations of those facts: this may be another respect in which he is un-English, as critics sometimes complain of his Hegelian idea of tragedy. Patently he is concerned with evidence and with proof in his examination of Hamlet's character, in the play by

24. For these and other details of the life, see Katharine Cooke, *A. C. Bradley and His Influence in Twentieth-Century Shakespeare Criticism* (Oxford: Clarendon, 1972), 13–46.

25. A. C. Bradley, *Shakespearean Tragedy*, 2d ed. (London: Macmillan, 1905), 1. Subsequent page references are given in parentheses.

26. "That Falstaff sometimes behaves in what we call a cowardly way is certain; but that does not show that he was a coward." Bradley then summarizes some of Morgann's evidence and asks, "What do these facts mean? Does Shakespeare put them in with no purpose at all, or in defiance of his own intentions? It is incredible" (*Oxford Lectures on Poetry*, 266–67).

Shakespeare that best suits his approach. The analysis of Hamlet spans two of the lectures that constitute *Shakespearean Tragedy,* and midway Bradley disclaims any conclusive proof, for "to attempt such a demonstration here would obviously be impossible." Quite simply, "the only way, if there is any way, in which a conception of Hamlet's character could be proved true, would be to show that it, and it alone, explains all the relevant facts presented by the text of the drama." Thus he seems to shy away from any strong representation. Yet Bradley expresses his reservations neither as a rule of inference nor as a matter of policy, so much as a practical constraint upon him in the present lecture. What is impossible "here" hints at a wealth of possibilities greater than two lectures can command, or a virtually endless array of facts and inferences from the facts potentially available to analysis, for which he must at present substitute a narrative of "the course of the action [in *Hamlet*] in so far as it specially illustrates the character" (129). Thus qualified the argument begins to seem familiar, and the procedure reminiscent of the summary of the evidence in a trial. Though Bradley is no one character's advocate, the character Hamlet has been accused of inaction; the critic's task is to review the facts and come up with a convincing explanation, which serves at least as a partial defense. With the reader's sympathy for Hamlet already taken for granted, the fact in issue is silently shifted to the cause of inaction (compare Morgann's shift to a proof of constitutional courage), which can be settled in the light of circumstantial evidence. Indeed, Bradley's general assessment of tragedy invites this intensely circumstantial account of the case. All behavior ought to be seen in relation to the whole character, which can be construed only from a narrative. As Harold Jenkins, a recent editor of the play, remarks of Bradley, "no-one can excel him in the careful summing up of evidence which bears on both character and story."[27]

Bradley did not have to invent a trial for Hamlet as Morgann did for Falstaff. Hamlet had long been charged with inaction—though not, to be sure, "until late in the eighteenth century," when critics began to interest themselves in the character as such. Bradley's exposition of the matter reveals how taken for granted the process of indictment and defense of Hamlet had become. After pronouncing that "the whole story turns upon the peculiar character of the hero" as a proposition no longer disputed, he passes directly to "the central question of Hamlet's

---

27. Harold Jenkins, "*Hamlet* Then till Now," *Shakespeare Survey* 18 (1965): 40. Note that when Bradley feels himself called upon to defend Shakespeare the writer from charges of "inconsistencies, obscurities, or passages of bombast," he has recourse to narrating the conditions under which Shakespeare presumably wrote (68–70).

character" and the many "insufficient or mistaken" theories that bear upon it, without even pausing to state what the question is. Obviously he cannot begin to sort and expound these theories—divided among external causes, internal causes, sentimental Hamlets and reflective Hamlets—without soon indicating that all are theories of "Hamlet's delay" (89–94). Yet not until Bradley is well launched upon his own explanation does he refer to delay as the fact in issue—"the main fact, Hamlet's inaction" (122). The inadvertences here merely show the complaisance with which Shakespeare's play has become, for criticism, Hamlet's trial. One may ask, Why not charge the real criminals, Claudius and Laertes? To protest so, however, would be as vain as to ask Scott's novel to feature the arrest of Fergus Mac-Ivor and Donald Bean Lean instead of the arrest of Waverley. In other words, some guilt or complicity of the hero inheres in the modern view of the play, and one immediate result is that Bradley treats Claudius almost too kindly and regards the second poisoner, Laertes, as a model son and avenger.

The hero's delay is still the fact in issue for most twentieth-century criticism of *Hamlet*. Jenkins, for example, after a very Bradley-like examination of Hamlet's self-accusations and his repetition of the word "dull," firmly concludes that the play is "about a man with a deed to do who for most of the time conspicuously fails to do it."[28] Yet any criticism that thoughtfully returns to the fact of delay, instead of plunging directly into the causes, soon recalls how narrowly the question depends on the hero's own testimony. The charge of inaction originates largely from Hamlet's self-blame in act 2, scene 2 and act 4, scene 4, in the soliloquies cited by Jenkins and many others. The character critic typically takes up this charge and proceeds to show, with the help of circumstantial evidence, that Hamlet's testimony is still inadequate to the case. A study of the whole character will show that the accused was in some sense not to blame, because character develops over time and for purposes of analysis can be separated from action.

Bradley for his part is at great pains to examine the circumstances of Hamlet's delay. Of the various theories before him, he favors those that attribute delay to internal causes or character, and most especially "the Schlegel-Coleridge theory" of an excessively reflective Hamlet. He is sharply critical of that theory, however, insofar as it would predict the character's behavior "at *any* time and in *any* circumstances." The Schlegel-Coleridge theory, though finely descriptive of irresolution, by

28. Harold Jenkins, Introduction to the new Arden edition of *Hamlet* (London: Methuen, 1982), 136–40. My quotations from *Hamlet* are from this edition. References are to act, scene, and lines.

itself "degrades Hamlet and travesties the play. For Hamlet, according to all the indications in the text, was . . . a man who at any *other* time and in any *other* circumstances than those presented would have been perfectly equal to his task." With this objection stated, he has reached the moment for revealing his own theory of the delay: "the direct cause was a state of mind quite abnormal and induced by special circumstances, —a state of profound melancholy." Then to confirm this amendment of Schlegel-Coleridge (and to exemplify splendidly the use of circumstantial evidence) he next turns to a brief narrative of "what we can gather from the play, immediately or by inference, concerning Hamlet as he was just before his father's death" (107–8). In the remaining pages of this first of the two *Hamlet* lectures, Bradley persuasively argues that the hero's unusual state of mind was caused not by "his father's death" nor by "the loss of the crown," but by "the sudden ghastly disclosure of his mother's true nature" (117–18). The thrust of this psychological explanation is insistently circumstantial; the character's disposition is important, but the circumstances are even more so. Bradley still probes the character for "seeds of danger," "any special danger," or what "might prove dangerous to him" (109, 115, 116). The danger envisioned, of course, is the failure to act: the locution implies both that Hamlet was still free to act and that not to act was morally wrong. Thus Bradley supposes that circumstances are not strictly decisive, while his belief that "the psychological point of view is not equivalent to the tragic" (127) allows that the catastrophe of *Hamlet* need not follow from any character's action or inaction.[29]

The theory, in short, constantly seeks to adjust individual responsibility to circumstances. In the opening lecture of *Shakespearean Tragedy,* Bradley also insists on a degree of human agency: "the calamities of tragedy do not simply happen, nor are they sent; they proceed mainly from actions, and those the actions of men." The point is seconded, however, by a paragraph that begins: "We see a number of human beings placed in certain circumstances; and we see, arising from the co-operation of their characters in these circumstances, certain actions. These actions beget others, and these others beget others again, until this series of inter-connected deeds leads by an apparently inevitable sequence to a catastrophe." These sentences insist on circumstances, as

---

29. Horatio's summary of the action of *Hamlet* is a useful corrective to any interpretation exclusively concerned with the hero's motives: "So shall you hear / Of carnal, bloody, and unnatural acts, / Of accidental judgments, casual slaughters, / Of deaths put on by cunning and forc'd cause, / And, in this upshot, purposes mistook / Fall'n on th' inventors' heads" (5.2.385–90).

even "inter-connected deeds" surround and constrain subsequent deeds, though the paragraph as a whole argues that the tragic hero is a doer, and Bradley is approaching a well-known aphorism about deeds and doers: "the centre of the tragedy, therefore, may be said with equal truth to lie in action issuing from character, or in character issuing in action" (11–12). Something similar happens when he seeks to define the "one-sidedness," "predisposition," or "tragic trait" of Shakespearean heroes: the trait operates only "in certain circumstances"; or "in the circumstances where we see the hero placed, his tragic trait, which is also his greatness, is fatal to him" (20–21). Again we can glimpse the retreat of plot in the Aristotelian tradition before the wider plot of circumstantial evidence. Mere action issuing from character or character issuing in action (the character in either case coming first), though frequently cited as Bradley's theory, would violate his own injunction against Schlegel-Coleridge on *Hamlet*: unless the special circumstances are taken into account, the principle must degrade the character and travesty the play.

Typically Bradley has been accused, not of travestying plays, but of mistaking them for nineteenth-century novels.[30] Of course the complaint arises from his interest in character over time and his willingness to extend inferences in the form of narrative, though it might also seem a compliment to the novel's mastery of circumstantial evidence. About thirty years ago, for example, John Bayley suggested that "there is a sense in which the highest compliment we can pay to Shakespeare is to discuss his great plays as if they were also great novels."[31] Bradley himself did not make the connection between his enterprise and novel criticism. Precisely while claiming that Shakespeare's interest lay "in action issuing from character, or in character issuing in action," he rejects any interest in "mere 'plot' " and instances Wilkie Collins's *The Woman in White* as the kind of thing for which Shakespeare "cared even less" (12–13). Like Morgann, he is rather disdainful of some novels, perhaps because they are mere make-believe as contrasted with his own much more careful analyses of an earlier writer's fictitious characters. His two lectures on *Hamlet* employ inference and narrative such as many

30. The suggestion that Bradley treats plays as novels has been made—to give just a sampling culled from the pages of Katharine Cooke—by T. J. B. Spencer, Clifford Leech, Helen Gardner, George Watson, and F. R. Leavis (Cooke, *A. C. Bradley,* 10, 119, 119n, 121, 218–19).

31. John Bayley, *The Characters of Love* (London: Constable, 1960), 41. The argument could be developed historically if we had some better current understanding of Shakespeare's true impact on the English novel.

novels themselves provide, and thus the comparison should be with novels rather than novel criticism. Bradley's procedure has much in common with Freudian analysis, which also weaves inferences into narrative, stresses character alteration rather than action, and adduces special circumstances from minute evidence.

Bradley and Freud were as far as I know unacquainted with one another's writings, but I am hardly alone in noting the partial resemblance.[32] One thing they have in common is a readiness to trace unusual symptoms to traumatic experiences. According to Bradley, the circumstances that distinguish Hamlet's experience were traumatic:

> Suppose that violent shock to his moral being of which I spoke; and suppose that under this shock, any possible action being denied to him, he began to sink into melancholy; then, no doubt, his imaginative and generalising habit of mind might extend the effects of this shock through his whole being and mental world. . . . Thus the speculative habit would be *one* indirect cause of the morbid state which hindered action; and it would also reappear in a degenerate form as one of the *symptoms* of this morbid state.

Here the language could easily be mistaken for a translation of Freud. To enhance the scientific aspect of his explanation, Bradley first presents it as a hypothesis and then displays the evidence to confirm it: "now this is what actually happens in the play" (116–17). As he expounds the evidence, he arrives swiftly at the point of thematic resemblance to Freud's analysis of Hamlet. Leaning heavily on the first soliloquy but bolstering it with narrative, he dismisses "mere grief" for the father's death or loss of the crown and settles for the sudden violation of Hamlet's love for his mother.

> It was the moral shock of the sudden ghastly disclosure of his mother's true nature, falling on him when his heart was aching with love, and his body doubtless was weakened by sorrow. And it is essential, however disagreeable, to realize the nature of this shock. It matters little here whether Hamlet's age was twenty or thirty: in either case his mother was a matron of mature years. . . . He can do nothing. He must lock in his heart, not any suspicion of his uncle that moves obscurely there, but that

32. Jenkins, "*Hamlet* Then till Now," 40, might once again represent Shakespeareans. Ernest Jones, in *Hamlet and Oedipus* (1949; rpt. New York: Norton, 1967), makes no particular comparison of Bradley with Freud, but notably when he discusses Hamlet's relation to his mother, he approvingly writes, "As Bradley well says" and "as Bradley well remarks" (82, 84).

horror and loathing; and if this heart ever found relief, it was when those feelings, mingled with the love that never died out in him, poured themselves forth in a flood as he stood in his mother's chamber beside his father's marriage-bed. (117–19)

Though Bradley makes explicit—"however disagreeable"—the sexual content of this shock to Hamlet's sensibility, he remains leaps and bounds behind Freud's imputation of Hamlet's desire, Hamlet's ambition, and Hamlet's murderous impulse. According to him, the hero's very goodness has been shocked, and he imports no notion of infantile sexuality.[33] Bradley, where Hamlet is concerned, has no theory of the unconscious except as entailed by his ordinary nineteenth-century idea of character, with its "inward struggle." To be sure, he is interested in Hamlet's trauma as a wounding by knowledge rather than passion, and this was Freud's angle of inquiry also. The assumption of psychological conflict *is* basic to Bradley's reading of Shakespeare: "the concentration of interest, in the greater plays, on the inward struggle emphasises the fact that this action is essentially the expression of character" (18–19).

So Bradley does not suppose that he is analyzing a novel, though he is engaged in an activity somewhat analogous to writing one. He employs narrative and deflects attention from the staged dramatic action of *Hamlet* to a psychological reading of the main character. A little like Freud, he seeks an explanation of the action in the case history, and this procedure results in a double narrative like that of nineteenth-century detective novels: a narrative of what must have already happened, designed to explain what is happening in the present time of action. Also as in Freudian analysis, the crucial happening of the past begins to loom more noticeably than the manifest present. The sheer evidentiary task of recovering the former results in a narrative that, for the sake of argument or in the course of analysis, first dominates and then substitutes for the latter. The interest in the cause even distracts from the effect that was the occasion of this interest, and such distraction would no doubt be healthful as well as pleasurable if the character were an actual person. A full substitution of past for present action takes place in Bradley's first lecture on *Hamlet,* though the trauma he defines is still recent. "That violent shock" to Hamlet is nothing other than his

33. Bradley's analysis is closer to the liberal Freudian reading by Theodore Lidz, *Hamlet's Enemy: Myth and Madness in "Hamlet"* (New York: Basic, 1975), than to Freud. On the other hand, his directing attention to sexuality "however disagreeable" shows his contemporaneity with Freud in another way: Freud never lets his readers forget that his investigations are disagreeable, and this badgering necessarily relies on those readers' avoidance of sexual matters.

realization of his mother's "astounding shallowness of feeling" for his father and her "coarse sensuality . . . speeding post-haste to its horrible delight" (118). This mental event, which is conscious on Hamlet's part and the key to Bradley's analysis, has occurred before the action represented on stage.[34] The critic's chosen trauma thus substitutes for the unmistakably traumatic moment in the play: the ghost's charge that he was murdered by his brother and his call for revenge, which leaves the hero, brave as he is, hysterical. That dramatic moment also has its story, its sorrowful personal account of circumstances from which the lives of several characters might be inferred, but Bradley does hardly anything with it. As he fills in the evidence in support of an antecedent mental shock to Hamlet, this visible shock and along with it Hamlet's father tend to be forgotten. This is a little curious, because the analysis that was undertaken to explain Hamlet's delay has the effect of reproducing his forgetfulness in the reader and referring everything uncomfortable in the relationship with his father to his mother.

As in trying to fathom Morgann's extensions of circumstantial evidence, we ought to ask why Bradley chose this particular Shakespearean play (along with three other tragedies), or why indeed the nineteenth century chose *Hamlet* for him.[35] Here it may be sufficient to take note of a certain convergence of the fate of Hamlet with that of Falstaff where Bradley is concerned. Two years before the publication of *Shakespearean Tragedy* he delivered and published his lecture "The Rejection of Falstaff,"[36] and in it he very readily associated the two characters. To see how this comparison could be offered, one has to look first at what Bradley has to say of Falstaff, which is far shrewder than the bit he takes over explicitly from Morgann. He gives a fine short explanation of Falstaff's appeal, by summarizing what the character stands for (or more especially against) in the play: "His humour is not directed only or chiefly against obvious absurdities; he is the enemy of everything that would interfere with his ease, and therefore of anything serious, and especially of everything respectable and moral. For these things" —

34. Though Bradley may seem to conflate two revelations, that of Hamlet's mother's behavior and that of the ghost, the long paragraph beginning "Now this is what actually happens in the play" and detailing "the moral shock of the sudden ghastly disclosure of his mother's true nature" has exclusively to do with the first: it concludes with the reference to "any suspicion of his uncle that moves obscurely" in Hamlet's heart (quoted in my text), which situates this trauma distinctly prior to the ghost's revelation (117–19).

35. Bradley himself is fully aware that *Hamlet*'s ascendancy can be associated with "the great ideal movement which began towards the close of the eighteenth century" (127).

36. "The Rejection of Falstaff" was delivered as a lecture 5 March 1902 and first published in the *Fortnightly Review* 71 (1902): 849–66. See Cooke, *A. C. Bradley,* 240.

and this once the increasing historical appeal of Falstaff's ease becomes clear—"impose limits and obligations, and make us the subjects of old father antic the law, and the categorical imperative, and our station and its duties, and conscience, and reputation, and other people's opinions, and all sorts of nuisances." There follows a long and eloquent paragraph, easily ridiculed if taken to mean that the clown actually triumphs over these concerns,[37] in which Bradley enumerates the causes that Falstaff "by his words, sometimes by his actions too," takes on: truth, honor, law, patriotism, duty, courage, war, religion, and—a Morgann touch, this—the fear of death. Most remarkably, and in the spirit of the wit he is expounding, he characterizes these sweeping and ubiquitous commitments as nightmares. Falstaff, he says, "delivers us from the oppression of such nightmares." Then comes the astonishing comparison, in the best and worst tradition of sentimental criticism: "No one in the play understands Falstaff fully, any more than Hamlet was understood by the persons round him. They are both men of genius."[38]

Since Bradley drops the comparison as soon as it is made—dismisses it, in effect, with the epithet "genius"—it scarcely seems worth pausing over. Yet he quite means it, as the range of the subject matter he attaches to Falstaff's wit and his readiness to characterize these human commitments as nightmares attest.[39] Falstaff's attack on commitments is founded on ease and the welfare of his body. His protest—"give me life"—issues in clowning and droll wit that elicit laughter: laughter that we cede to him, Bradley intimates, because the opposing demands upon us are both a nuisance and a nightmare. Hamlet's voice is a parallel one, though it is founded in depression and despair. Commitments come to him *as* a nightmare in the visitation of his father's ghost; death makes its crude demand upon him. His protest issues in plotting, in more grief and meditation, in antic disposition and his own jesting, of such brilliance that few can resist identifying with him. Bradley's response to both characters is significantly but not unwarrantedly anachronistic. If Falstaff puts him in mind of "the categorical imperative" (compare Morgann's "benefit to society"), he obviously does not respond to Falstaff as Shakespeare's original audience did. Nor can he hear Hamlet's voice as that audience heard it: Hamlet was born a prince, and princes at one time were born to rule; but in modern times a Hamlet complaining

37. Cf. Stoll, "Falstaff" (note 17 above), 228.
38. Bradley, *Oxford Lectures on Poetry,* 262–63.
39. Bradley would later make a more specific comparison of Falstaff to Shakespeare's Cleopatra: see "Shakespeare's *Antony and Cleopatra*" (1906), in *Oxford Lectures on Poetry,* 299–301.

that the time is out of joint speaks more widely of shared responsibilities of governance—hence of what Bradley, in writing about Falstaff, calls "all sorts of nuisances" and "the oppression of such nightmares." To a modern contractual society, the easeful genius of Falstaff and the wretched genius of Hamlet can and do speak similar messages.

Whatever one thinks of Bradley's linking of the two characters, the plays from which the characters have stepped constitute an exceptional pair. *Henry IV* and *Hamlet* are Shakespeare's most concerted studies of the relation of fathers and sons, and each in its own way is an honor play. *Henry IV*, a two-part comedy and history, concludes with a reconciliation of father and son that is, in the tradition of new comedy, compatible with the triumph of the younger generation. Famously, Shakespeare naturalizes and brings home the dynastic drama by playing out the familiar paternal and filial experiences. Bradley no doubt sees Falstaff's role as transcending either royal part, but Falstaff—one of whose best jokes is his supposed youth—is the abettor of Prince Hal's wildness; Bradley is wrong to say that no one in the play fully understands Falstaff, because Hal pretty well does (he is Falstaff's royal audience). *Hamlet*, so naturalized as to be partly a domestic tragedy, concentrates even more closely on fathers and sons and concludes, as tragedies often do, with the destruction of both generations. Whatever action was presented in the so-called *Ur-Hamlet*, we can judge from Shakespeare's handling of his sources for other plays, most notably *King Lear* but also *Henry IV*, that the wholesale development of the Polonius-Laertes relationship was his own emphasis. The sheer number of lines given to Hamlet and his soliloquies results in a play with a dominant point of view, the hero's, and as if this were not enough, the representatives of the older generation are cast in such dubious light that the audience cannot help but side with the young, as in a comedy. *Hamlet* and *Henry IV* are, then, the two great "Oedipal" plays in the Shakespeare canon. They are also honor plays: one focusing on the commitment of lives in battle that sometimes alters history; the other, on revenge that sometimes feels like justice. Because Shakespeare is also an unmatched dramatist of ideas, the motive of honor is challenged and partially subverted in both plays. Falstaff is the principal agent of subversion in *Henry IV*; Hamlet, in *Hamlet*. The very soliloquies in which Hamlet blames himself for delay, contrasting his inaction with playacting in one and with vain military action in the other, make a mock of honor.[40]

40. Not only do the occasions of these two soliloquies subvert the lessons Hamlet tries to draw from them, but his own words mock the very comparisons he is engaged in. From the first, for example: "Am I a coward? / Who calls me villain, breaks my pate

For the aristocratic code of Shakespeare's time, precisely because honor was understood as a means of self-government, it was a principle of government as well; yet even so, from Shakespeare's intensely dramatic presentation, honor can repeatedly seem a nuisance and a nightmare.

Possibly *Hamlet* achieved its nineteenth-century status as Shakespeare's most profound play because it could be reconstrued as a story of things not seen but inferred from circumstances. The ghost himself, after all, was a poor witness to crime, for unless he had kept one eye open while he slept in the orchard, he would not have seen who poured poison in his ears—he apparently knows these things only as ghosts know them. His son, not satisfied with this singular testimony or with his own premonitions of his uncle's guilt, arranged one circumstantial proof that a secret murder had occurred and that Claudius was aware of it. Yet for all that, the script written by Shakespeare is far from being a detective story.[41] *Hamlet* affords no receipts for poisons purchased or recollections of shadowy figures leaving the orchard, no searching after bottles or footprints; from the conventional ordering of evidence that has come into being before, during, and after the crime, the hero avails himself only of the last—with the result that the focus of the play within the play is on Claudius's guilty afterthoughts. To enable the audience to watch the king even more closely than Hamlet or Horatio can, Shakespeare also breaks the suspense before the trap is sprung ("O heavy burden!" the king has already exclaimed at the beginning of act 3). There is no other investigation of the murder but this, and *Hamlet*'s mystery is not the mystery of what happened in that orchard. On the contrary, the pertinence of *Hamlet* to the history of circumstantial evidence rests on the instructive differences between the play and the narrative substituted for it by Bradley and other interpreters.

The play scene enacting Hamlet's indirect proof of Claudius's guilt illustrates these differences very well, as modern readers inadvertently reveal when they complain of the redundancy of the dumb show or

---

across, / Plucks off my beard and blows it in my face, / Tweaks me by the nose, gives me the lie i' th' throat / As deep as to the lungs—who does me this?" (2.2.566–70). Hamlet is pretending he is on stage, and possibly a puppet stage at that. He has admired the first player's acting, but here he is mock acting. Or in the later soliloquy, he chooses to chide himself by comparison to "twenty thousand men / That, for a fantasy and trick of fame, / Go to their graves like beds, fight for a plot / Whereon the numbers cannot try the cause, / Which is not tomb enough and continent / To hide the slain" (4.4.60–65). There is perhaps no way to drown out the Falstaffian notes of these two soliloquies.

41. Peter Alexander, *Hamlet, Father and Son* (Oxford: Clarendon, 1955), may have been the first to compare the play outright to a detective story, but of course the notion of the mystery of Hamlet's own motive carries back to romantic criticism.

the laboriousness of Lucianus's show-and-tell.[42] The redundancy and laboriousness reflect the small faith in circumstantial evidence in Shakespeare's time. In act 1 the ghost of Hamlet's father testifies that he was secretly poisoned, and in act 3 the touring players act out such a poisoning. They proceed to make their crime seen, and the reaction of Claudius to their performance is scarcely more notable than the process of making seen that reflects a certain helplessness when it comes to the validity of indirect proofs. Lucianus's highly explicit language, as he "pours the poison in his ears" (the Folio's stage direction for the play within the play), is a reminder that even if there were twenty eyewitnesses in an orchard, all they would have seen is someone pouring and not poisoning as such. The script therefore has Lucianus supply the circumstantial, psychological, pharmaceutical, and magical evidence in words, which also testify directly to malice aforethought:

> Thoughts black, hands apt, drugs fit, and time agreeing,
> Confederate season, else no creature seeing,
> Thou mixture rank, of midnight weeds collected,
> With Hecate's ban thrice blasted, thrice infected,
> Thy natural magic and dire property
> On wholesome life usurps immediately.
>
> (3.2.249–54)

Lucianus thus shows *and* tells it all. While in this dramatic production the court and theater audience become eyewitnesses to crime, Hamlet's experiment with indirect evidence is also being wound back into the direct discourse that was thought necessary to establish guilt. *That* sets Claudius going, perhaps, but for good measure Hamlet, the presumed author of these lines and this poisoning, still names the crime and its motive: "A poisons him i' th' garden for his estate." One can appreciate Shakespeare's dramatic purposes in this ritual reenactment of Hamlet's father's murder and still read in the lines an old-fashioned idea of proof that lacks nothing of conviction, since the criminal confesses his wickedness outright.

The dramas of Shakespeare obviously assumed a quite different stance toward circumstantial evidence from that which prevailed in the eighteenth and nineteenth centuries. For Shakespeare, reliance on such ev-

---

42. J. Dover Wilson, *What Happens in "Hamlet,"* 3d ed. (1951; rpt. Cambridge, England: Cambridge University Press, 1961), 138–97, notoriously revised the play scene to meet with modern sensibilities; Lucianus's six lines are usually omitted from productions of *Hamlet,* presumably from a sense of embarrassment at their obviousness, though these are lines supposedly composed for the players by Hamlet himself.

idence for conviction seems to have been either a poor joke or a vicious game: Polonius, not Hamlet, was his master detective and maker of representations; and his evil genius of circumstances was Iago. Between Shakespeare's subsequent tragedy about indirect proof and trust, love and a handkerchief, and William Paley's reproof to juries about rejecting "such proof, from an insinuation of uncertainty . . . and a general dread lest the charge of innocent blood should lie at their doors," for example, the ways of reaching a conviction with which an English population could be comfortable would seem to have changed a good deal.[43] *Hamlet* and *Othello* were Shakespeare's own dramatic revisions of stories of things not seen, perhaps, but only in an age that encouraged strong representations could the hero of the first play and the villain of the second be associated as Shakespearean lives that share the same depths. Before writing *Shakespearean Tragedy,* as we have seen, Bradley drew a fine thematic line from Falstaff to Hamlet, but within the lectures on tragedy, and specifically in the second lecture on *Othello,* he far more deliberately compared the character of Iago to that of Hamlet, precisely along the axis of hidden motives: "This question Why? is *the* question about Iago, just as the question Why did Hamlet delay? is *the* question about Hamlet. Iago refused to answer it; but I will venture to say that he *could* not have answered it, any more than Hamlet could tell why he delayed" (222). But circumstances can be thought to explain Hamlet's *in*action, of course, without accumulating in something strictly like an unconscious motive, whereas Iago's actions call out for a motive, conscious or otherwise.

Bradley promoted Falstaff, Hamlet, Iago, and Cleopatra[44] as the four "most wonderful" characters of Shakespeare, and of these, in order of their creation, the middle two "are perhaps the most subtle." He also ventures that "if Iago had been a person as attractive as Hamlet," as much would be written about Iago as is written by critics about Hamlet (208). But a "warning" is to be introduced at this point, a warning that silently confesses to a difference and at the same time reveals how insistently an interpreter ought to dismiss testimony in favor of indirect evidence: "one must constantly remember," Bradley writes, "not to believe a syllable that Iago utters on any subject, including himself, until one has tested his statement by comparing it with known facts

43. See chapter 1, note 24, above.
44. Bloom, *Ruin the Sacred Truths,* 54, lists Falstaff, Hamlet, Iago, and Edmund as Shakespeare's "free artists of themselves," but surely Edmund does not quite rank with the others or with Bradley's fourth choice, Cleopatra.

and with other statements of his own or of other people, and by considering whether he had in the particular circumstances any reason for telling a lie or for telling the truth" (211). This time, nevertheless, Bradley's management of the evidence and construction of a narrative in this lecture result in the full imputation of unconscious motive—though it is a little unclear, when he is done, why the pleasures of power, excitement, and artistry that he adduces for Iago should remain unconscious when the criminal designs of the character are generally outspoken. Iago can only be explained

> as a man setting out on a project which strongly attracts his desire, but at the same time conscious of a resistance to the desire, and unconsciously trying to argue the resistance away by assigning reasons for the project. He is the counterpart of Hamlet, who tries to find reasons for his delay in pursuing a design which excites his aversion. And most of Iago's reasons for action are no more real ones than Hamlet's reasons for delay were the real ones. Each is moved by forces which he does not understand; and it is probably no accident that these two studies of states psychologically so similar were produced at about the same period. (226)

From this determined comparison of the two characters, I would single out Bradley's own emphasis on hidden motives. At this level of analysis it makes little difference that Iago is a criminal and Hamlet a victim, yet the model for both investigations of character seems to be modern criminal prosecution, or closely related uses of circumstantial evidence, for which motives are regularly and with good reason supposed to be hidden. In his pursuit of the "secret springs" of a plot (222), Bradley treads a path remarkably close to Freud's at the time.[45] To be sure, he does not intend to trump Shakespeare's achievement by arguing that the playwright's motives are hidden from himself, though he writes of the subtle Iago—what everyone takes for granted about Hamlet—that as artist "at any rate Shakespeare put a good deal of himself into Iago" (231).

Bradley's book is about four plays—*Hamlet, Othello, Lear,* and *Macbeth*—regarded as the epitome of Shakespeare's achievement. Why trag-

---

45. For example, Freud formally argues that all dreams represent the fulfillment of a wish; but *The Interpretation of Dreams,* published four years before *Shakespearean Tragedy,* shows the writer exclusively concerned with dreams as they betray "hidden wishes." It is not only the unconscious or the censorship that is at stake in this account of dreams, but the evidentiary problem, the solution of which would be obviated if dreams represented wishes or their fulfillments directly.

edy and these four plays in particular should be regarded as the highest form of art is a complicated question for literary history, and a question inextricable from the assumptions about character that Bradley exploits. But one thing about this consensus should not go unremarked: if the subplot of *Lear* is taken into account, all four tragedies feature *secret crimes of great heinousness*—a kind of action not common to all Shakespearean tragedy by any means. Thus the four tragedies consorted well with the Victorian persuasion that evil is generally suppressed and not seen, though revealed indirectly by circumstances—as we shall see, the association of circumstantial evidence with poisoning, in particular, was continuous from the eighteenth century to the nineteenth. *Hamlet, Othello, Lear,* and *Macbeth* also consorted well with Bradley's theory of tragedy, which pits evil dialectically against an "ultimate power" for good. Bradley placed as much faith in history, after all, as in circumstances: evil in this theory is not relentless, but the advancing repression of evil is.

> These defects or imperfections are certainly, in the wide sense of the word, evil, and they contribute decisively to the conflict and catastrophe. And the inference is again obvious. The ultimate power which shows itself disturbed by this evil and reacts against it, must have a nature alien to it. Indeed its reaction is so vehement and "relentless" that it would seem to be bent on nothing short of good in perfection, and to be ruthless in its demand for it. (35)

This dialectical idea of progress instills repression more obviously than a social contract does, perhaps, since wickedness is bound to seek concealment from forces so incessantly good.

Hamlet Arrested and Psychoanalyzed

The classic psychoanalytic study of Hamlet in English is that by Ernest Jones (1879–1958), Freud's early disciple and eventual biographer. Though his *Hamlet and Oedipus* was published as a book in 1949, its argument was first set forth in an article of 1910, and—in order to respect the rough time frame of the present study—that is the version referred to here.[46] Steeped in nineteenth-century Shakespeare criticism, German as well as English, the diagnosis of Hamlet's difficulty (the delay again) is based directly on Freud's idea, first printed as a footnote

46. Ernest Jones, "The Oedipus-Complex as an Explanation of Hamlet's Mystery: A Study in Motive," *American Journal of Psychology* 21 (1910): 72–113. Page references to this publication are cited in parentheses.

to *The Interpretation of Dreams* in 1900.[47] At the end of a decade that saw the publication of Freud's decisive books, Jones writes as a convinced acolyte; his article, besides pursuing character criticism to new depths, illustrates the special import of circumstantial evidence for psychoanalysis.

Though Jones cites numerous books and articles on *Hamlet,* he does not betray any historical perspective such as led Bradley to realize that Hamlet's problem was not reckoned with before the late eighteenth century. Rather, in "The Oedipus-Complex as an Explanation of Hamlet's Mystery," he takes a progressive scientific stance toward the subject and remarks "the inadequacy of all the solutions of the problem that have up to the present been offered" (73–74): thus he indicates at the start that he believes a breakthrough has occurred. His ambition to confirm Freud's thesis of the Oedipus complex and to provide an unassailable psychological account of Hamlet's delay is accompanied by an aggressive, no-nonsense attitude toward the character himself. Hamlet, charged with inaction, is implicitly on trial in virtually all the secondary literature invoked, but Jones evidently writes for the prosecution once more and blames the character not only for evading action but for evading the truth about himself. By analogy to psychoanalytic practice, the ultimate purpose here ought to be to help the character, but curiously the procedure is to attack Hamlet rather sharply, to attain a conviction against him by proving a motive ("A Study in Motive" is the subtitle of the article) that he cannot worm his way out of because it alone makes sense of his story. Prospectively, no doubt, one can imagine the character helped by self-knowledge, but for now he is helped only by the improved understanding of Jones's readers. The implied defense of Hamlet is finally the universality of the Oedipus complex: Hamlet did not act because he was inhibited by that complex. Bradley, by way of contrast, does not impute psychological guilt to the hero, and his implied defense rests on almost the opposite principle—extenuating circumstances.

47. Freud raised this footnote to the text of *The Interpretation of Dreams* in 1914. The key sentences are these: "Hamlet is able to do anything—except take vengeance on the man who did away with his father and took that father's place with his mother, the man who shows him the repressed wishes of his own childhood realized. Thus the loathing which should drive him on to revenge is replaced in him by self-reproaches, by scruples of conscience, which remind him that he himself is literally no better than the sinner whom he is to punish. Here I have translated into conscious terms what was bound to remain unconscious in Hamlet's mind." See *The Standard Edition of the Complete Psychological Works of Sigmund Freud,* ed. and trans. James Strachey et al., 24 vols. (London: Hogarth Press and Institute of Psycho-Analysis, 1953–74), 4:265.

Jones does not stop to ask whether every play illustrates the Oedipus complex. The beauty of *Hamlet* for his purposes is that the hero does not act, and therefore the play is bound to represent an action that is psychological. The high valuation ceded to the play by all is now co-opted by psychoanalysis. *Hamlet* is the summa of "Shakespeare's philosophy and outlook on life" as well as of "the deeper working of Shakespeare's mind," and it "so far excels all his other writings that many competent critics would place it on an entirely separate level from them" (74); at the same time (with help from Freud) Jones has seen through *Hamlet*, by seeing through the character Hamlet, to the unseen fictional character. Weirdly like Morgann on Falstaff, he tries Hamlet for cowardice, acquits him on two counts, and convicts him on a third—the count that makes the character human:

> Action is paralyzed at its very inception, and there is thus produced the picture of causeless inhibition which is so inexplicable both to Hamlet and to readers of the play. This paralysis arises, however, not from physical or moral cowardice, but from that intellectual cowardice, that reluctance to dare the exploration of his inner mind, which Hamlet shares with the rest of the human race. (102)

Resistance! defense! as Freud was already exclaiming of those who would not be analyzed or who balked in the course of analysis: those very expressions argue that psychoanalysis had to become prosecutorial in order to name the guilt it would exorcise. For Jones, neither Hamlet nor *Hamlet* can be innocent.[48]

In outline, Jones's argument is similar to Bradley's. He takes for granted that the critic's job is to solve "the central mystery," which he specifies variously as Hamlet's "hesitancy," "inhibition," or "difficulty in the performance of the task"; and he divides the available hypotheses into three groups, as they attribute the difficulty to "temperament," "the nature of the task," or "some special feature in the nature of the task which renders it peculiarly difficult or repugnant to Hamlet" (74–75). The task, of course, is revenge, and like most critics of delay, Jones does not think of revenge as analyzable at all. With Bradley, he quickly rules out grief as a convincing explanation of "general aboulia" (77), and alas for Bradley, he rules out the sudden revelation of Hamlet's mother's sexuality as well; for "in real life speedy second marriages occur commonly enough without leading to any such result as is here

48. It gives one pause to realize how commonly the charge of cowardice *is* bruited by psychoanalysis. Patients are thus exhorted to recover thoughts they have repressed and readers dared to face the truths of the theory in general.

depicted" (92). On such matters Jones takes a tone much like Gertrude's in the play. After disposing of the traditional hypotheses, he carefully presents the psychoanalytic explanation as a refinement of the third type, names it the Oedipus complex, and once more credits Freud. Only then—and here very much like Bradley again—does he arrange the facts in narrative form: "The story thus interpreted would run somewhat as follows: As a child Hamlet had experienced the warmest affection for his mother, and this, as is always the case, had contained elements of a more or less dimly defined erotic quality . . ." (98–102).

Until Jones commences this narrative, his delivery of any evidence is rather thin. He may criticize Goethe, for example, for failing to consider "the whole picture" (78)—and we recognize this as the ordinary stance of an argument from circumstantial evidence—yet he himself tends to wrap the picture in a number of generalities, whether scientific, such as "psycho-pathology has clearly demonstrated" (77), or semantic, such as "simple revenge in the ordinary sense of the word" (79), or observational, such as the subject not behaving "as a man confronted with a straight-forward task" (81). Some details the critic is merely holding in reserve for a convincing narrative once the psychoanalytic explanation is on the table. As he prepares to set forth that explanation (or Freud's hypothesis), it becomes clear that he expects to organize the circumstantial evidence around the subject's motive. Once the motive is stated, as in a criminal investigation, the facts will no longer be so mysterious:

> In short, the whole picture presented by Hamlet, his deep depression,
> the hopeless note in his attitude towards the world and towards the value
> of life, his dread of death, his repeated reference to bad dreams, his self-
> accusations, his desperate efforts to get away from the thoughts of his
> duty, and his vain attempts to find an excuse for his recalcitrancy; all this
> unequivocally points to a tortured conscience, to some hidden ground
> for shirking his task, a ground which he dare not or cannot avow to
> himself. We have, therefore, again to take up the argument at this point,
> and seek for some evidence that may serve to bring to the light of day
> the hidden motive. (89)

To narrow the question down to a hidden motive, moreover, is already to infer a source of shame or guilt. For psychoanalysis it is sure to be guilt.[49]

---

49. I have tried to sketch some of these differences between shame and guilt in *George Eliot and Blackmail* (Cambridge: Harvard University Press, 1985), 153–56.

The search for a motive for Hamlet's *in*action shows the extraordinary powers that Jones claims for circumstantial evidence, which can be reduced to these three propositions: testimony is further stripped of its pretensions to represent the facts; nontestimony, or silence itself, is often the best possible evidence of guilt; and at the same time, concealments that take place below the level of consciousness can be brought to light, precisely by the subordination of direct to indirect evidence in the construction of a narrative. Only the third of these propositions necessarily assumes a depth psychology, and all three presuppose the expert management of evidence—the professional claim already familiar to us in forensic, novelistic, and literary-critical arenas. But familiarity should not dull our sense of the extremes to which the claims for circumstantial evidence are pressed in Jones's interpretation of *Hamlet,* and each is worth pausing over.

Hamlet speaks more lines than any other character in Shakespeare, and a critic who can dispose of all that testimony is in good shape to press for a determination of the case on circumstantial grounds. Jones argues that Hamlet says too much, and most particularly expresses too many reasons for delay. To such a witness, Jones can give a criminal prosecutor's reply: "when a man gives at different times a different reason for his conduct it is safe to infer that, whether purposely or not, he is concealing the true reason." By formalizing the character's musings and chidings of himself as "alleged motives," he none too subtly ascribes to him deception of the prosecution and most definitely "self-deception." By averring that "the more specious the explanation Hamlet puts forth the more easily does it satisfy him," he stretches the evidence merely to scold; and by adding "[the more specious the explanation] the more readily the reader will accept it as the real motive," he seems to suggest—if not that Hamlet himself has written the play to fool someone—that readers are as easy to fool as a jury. Moreover, though Hamlet famously addresses a great many subjects, most of his talk can be reduced to cover-up, for as Jones complains on the same page, "he eagerly seizes every excuse for occupying himself with any question rather than the performance of his duty" (87). Such an onslaught upon testimony makes earlier asseverations of the superiority of circumstantial evidence seem primitive, and here the attack is centered on the testimony of the patient-defendant himself rather than that of hostile witnesses. A long forensic tradition assumes that some witnesses lie and others get the facts wrong; furthermore, circumstantial evidence could show how falsehoods helped to betray the true story. Even so psychoanalysis might turn dream distortions, parapraxes, and resistances to account, while further suggesting that well-meaning witnesses do not know when they are lying, or that testimony is not of much interest *unless* the facts are got wrong, and thus expose some unexpected motive.

With the hero's testimony disposed of, his silences tell for more. "Why did Hamlet in his monologues give us no indication of the nature of the conflict in his mind?" (83). This insinuation is also prosecutorial: the rhetorical question has to be uttered very knowingly, because logically it goes nowhere without a previous imputation of guilt. Silence cannot betray unless (*a*) there is something to uncover and (*b*) there is a cover-up. Given both conditions, silence becomes presumptive though scarcely specific evidence of guilt: it becomes specific only as an isolated response to some specific question. Of course criminal prosecution—with varying degrees of specificity—supplies such conditions, since the accused has been formally charged and can be presumed to cover up in order to escape punishment. "Between delinquency on the one hand, and silence under inquiry on the other, there is a manifest connexion," in Bentham's words—"a connexion too natural not to be constant and inseparable."[50] Just so Jones, in drawing inferences from Hamlet's silence, or what he does not say, must already be convinced that the character is concealing something. He already suspects Hamlet of (*a*) harboring incestuous, murderous thoughts (because Freud has both specifically fingered Hamlet and claimed these thoughts are universal) and believes Hamlet has (*b*) repressed these very same thoughts (because Freudian analysis "has amply demonstrated that certain kinds of mental processes shew a greater tendency to be 'repressed' (*verdrängt*) than others"—89). Not only is the prosecutorial tone Jones adopts consistent with these premonitions of guilt and preconceptions of concealment, it distantly echoes the prosecutorial uses that gave circumstantial evidence a powerful impetus in the eighteenth century. Absent the same tone and presumptions, Hamlet's silence evidences nothing whatever.

50. Jeremy Bentham, *Rationale of Judicial Evidence,* 5 vols. (London: Hunt and Clarke, 1827), 5:209. For Bentham's arguments against the exclusion of "self-disserving" evidence in common law, see 192–299; also 3:131–48. In the eighteenth and nineteenth centuries, just when the virtues of circumstantial evidence were most celebrated, defendants in English criminal trials were not permitted to testify; the present practice of allowing them to take the stand but subjecting them to cross-examination was instigated by the Criminal Evidence Act of 1898, as the era of strong representations—in the view of the present book—drew to a close. For a concise history of the rights of an accused person not to be questioned, see Glanville Williams, *The Proof of Guilt: A Study of the English Criminal Trial,* 3d ed. (1963; rpt. London: Stevens, 1979), 37–72.

From the way Jones presents the second condition, the matter of concealment, it is hard to say whether the existence of the unconscious explains Hamlet's silence or Hamlet's silence proves there is such a thing as the unconscious. As in much of the literature of psychoanalysis, the case study is neither quite the application of a theory nor its proof, but a little of both. To prove "Hamlet's non-consciousness of the cause of the repugnance to his task," Jones appeals (for once) to the intelligence of the chief actor: if the causes of delay were available to consciousness, this argument goes, then such "a keen and introspective thinker, as Hamlet was, would infallibly have recognised them, and would have openly debated them instead of deceiving himself with a number of false pretexts" (84). Thus the silence *and* the false testimony go to argue that it is possible not to know one's own motives for not doing something. But this inference of the existence of unconscious motives is obviously too weak (though it again suggests that *Hamlet* is a very special play, because Hamlet is so exceptional a nonwitness of such motives). Jones does not acknowledge that the argument is weak, but he has not finished yet. He turns about and comes at the existence of the unconscious from the other direction, from the cumulative proofs of psychoanalysis.[51]

> Now instances of such specific aboulias in real life invariably prove, when analyzed, to be due to an unconscious repulsion against the act that cannot be performed. In other words, whenever a person cannot bring himself to do something that every conscious consideration tells him he should do, it is always because for some reason he doesn't want to do it; this reason he will not own to himself and is only dimly if at all aware of. That is exactly the case with Hamlet. (86)

This argument regards the existence of the unconscious as proved repeatedly ("invariably" may be an exaggeration) by the science that has demonstrated its effects. But notice how the second sentence, though pitched at universality, summarizes the case at hand as Jones sees it and thereby suggests that *Hamlet* shows what always happens, while the reference this time to a specific aboulia begins the narrowing of the argument from silence necessary to an indirect proof. This specific aboulia will soon be narrowed further to the question of confronting

---

51. Jones documents earlier Shakespeare criticism much more strictly than he does the psychoanalytic literature on his subject. The former, of course, is more easily identified, as writing about a play called *Hamlet*. Of the latter, Jones already writes as an insider who exempts the practice of psychoanalysis from documentation.

someone who has murdered one's father and slept with one's mother, as *Hamlet* still more remarkably shows the universality of the unconscious at work in the Oedipus complex. Shakespeare's play has become a sort of bootstrap by which Jones is lifting psychoanalysis.

Bootstrap arguments are not necessarily a bad thing and are common in science, when hunches have to be played out and what is thought invariably to happen can be grasped only by a few instances. (They tend to be frowned upon, to be sure, by a careful judiciary when reviewing a criminal conviction.) From an evidentiary point of view, what is especially weak in Jones's two-directional argument, from Hamlet's evasions to the theory of the unconscious and from the theory to Hamlet's evasions, is the supposed ground for the theory: the rather condescending generalizations about what always proves to be the case "when analyzed." Such generalizations appear to protect the actual evidence for the theory from scrutiny, and certainly more indexing of sources for the generalizations would be reassuring. Approaching this depth psychology from the perspective of forensic models, I am also tempted by an argument that is merely a hunch: namely, that the same prosecutorial attitude that inspires Jones's analysis of Hamlet's "specific aboulia" has helped produce the theory on which it partly depends. Because psychoanalysis always portrays the unconscious as a condition of concealment, it is possible that the science has silently internalized the forensic scene: guilty thoughts are concealed from consciousness just as a person's conscious guilt is concealed from prosecution; and murderous and incestuous thoughts are concealed above all, since murder and incest are crimes certain to be punished if detected. In the process of briefly explaining repression, Jones draws such a parallel himself, at least with respect to its sexual component, when he writes: "as the herd unquestionably selects from the 'natural' instincts the sexual ones on which to lay its heaviest ban, so it is the various psycho-sexual trends that most often are 'repressed' by the individual" (90). And his "so it is" expresses a relation stronger than mere analogy, for the analogy to social life tells one what to look for below the level of consciousness and names what one will find there: that is, a ban on sexual thoughts. Similarly, I am suggesting, the conditions of guilt and concealment have worked their way from a forensic model of the argument from silence into the psychoanalytic model of the mind. From such a construction emerges, as one of its end results, the extraordinary compliment that Shakespeare's greatest play is *Hamlet,* because no one can directly comprehend it; or what Jones calls "the apparent paradox"—but apparent only—"that the hero, the poet, and the audience are all profoundly moved by feelings due to a conflict the source of which they are unaware" (85).[52]

To say as much is to pay an even greater compliment to Freud and psychoanalysis, since Hamlet's mystery has now been subjected to a fresh investigation, using indirect evidence, and thereby solved. Not the least claim made for circumstantial evidence since the eighteenth century has been reserved for its expert management, and that remains true for Jones's article as well. This claim was always partly based on the need for an external means of representing someone else's thoughts, most particularly someone's intent to commit a crime. In Bentham's words, once again, "unless stated by the individual himself in whose mind the fact is considered as having place, the existence of any such psychological fact can only be a matter of inference."[53] But in psychoanalytic belief, no individual ever states or knows completely the facts present in his or her mind; indirect evidence is all the more requisite for an account of motives; and the need for expert management of that evidence and shaping into narrative is paramount. "Fortunately for our investigation," as Jones puts it, "psycho-analytic study has proved beyond doubt that mental trends hidden from the subject himself may come to external expression in a way that reveals their nature to a trained observer," and there exist "special objective methods of penetrating into obscure mental processes." This is a boost for psychoanalysis, of course, and Jones follows Freud in deferring credit from himself personally to the achievements of the school. At the same time, the good news conveyed here has an almost religious appeal, especially in combination with Freudianism's customary deflation of human pretensions. That powerful combination (call it religious or rhetorical) is certainly present here, as Jones contrasts this expert view of the evidence with old subjective notions of motive. "Man's belief that he is a self-conscious animal, alive to the desires that impel or inhibit his actions, and aware of all of the springs of his conduct," he writes in these same paragraphs, "is the last stronghold of that anthropomorphic outlook on life which so long has dominated his philosophy, his theology and, above all, his psychology" (84–86). Deflation of the subjective narrative and inflation of the objective method of getting at the subject have been implicit in

52. Dan Jacobson, "Hamlet's Other Selves," *International Review of Psycho-Analysis* 16 (1989): 265–72, takes issue with Jones on the matter of the artist's unconsciousness. Jacobson also challenges the idea that Hamlet is unconscious of his feelings where his mother is concerned.

53. Bentham, *Rationale of Judicial Evidence,* 3:6.

the claims for circumstantial evidence all along. Here this claim has been topped with news of see-what-we-can-do that Jones fully expects to have its own appeal, the appeal *of* a large evidentiary claim by itself. If the "anthropomorphic" view is to be abandoned, what would seem to be left is a certain religiosity, the appeal of which is precisely its story of things not seen.

The importation of unconscious motives and special methods for fathoming them are extensions of circumstantial evidence not exploited by Morgann or Bradley (though the former, as we saw, laid some claim to show how Shakespeare's audience might be moved unconsciously). To the substantive interpretation of Hamlet's character, Jones also brings some new features—the projection of the hero's desires upon his enemy Claudius, the tracing of his history back to childhood, and the significance of the father in the story (not touched upon very seriously by Bradley). All these features have an interest for psychoanalysis, and that of projection belongs with its recognized transformations, which serve the theory almost like presumptions of law. Thus, in the narrative by which Jones tests the hypothesis that revenge has been stymied by an Oedipus complex, he argues that Claudius has come to stand, in Hamlet's unconscious, for Hamlet himself. Very early on the hero has wished to replace his father in two different senses; now someone, Claudius, has murdered the hero's father and married his mother. "More, this someone was a member of the same family, so that the actual usurpation further resembled the imaginary one in being incestuous," and thus both of Hamlet's guilty wishes are "realised by his uncle" (99). By the rule of projection, such resemblance can constitute a powerful identification between nephew and uncle, which becomes in Jones's analysis the proximate cause of delay: "the call of duty to slay his uncle cannot be obeyed because it links itself with the call of his nature to slay his mother's husband, whether this is the first or the second; the latter is strongly 'repressed,' and therefore necessarily the former also" (101). Yet is "links itself" a causal relation? Remember the difficulties experienced over two centuries with "chains" of circumstance. The argument surely makes its own dramatic revelation, rivaling that of the play, for Jones has substituted for the secret crime of Claudius an earlier and still more secret crime, or thought, of which Hamlet is unconscious.[54] The analysis differs from Bradley's in respect to the substitution and the

54. The Freudian hypothesis is not needed to see a resemblance between Hamlet and Claudius. See especially the reading of the play by Francis Fergusson, *The Idea of a Theater* (1949; rpt. New York: Anchor Books, n.d.), 109–54.

assessment of the main character. Bradley requires no projection, because he substitutes for the shock to Hamlet in the dramatic action an earlier mental shock, also to Hamlet. His Hamlet suffers from melancholy and the revelation of his mother's sexuality, not from his own guilt. But Jones also could well have argued, in Bradley fashion, that Hamlet was too overwhelmed with guilt to act. The additional idea of projection appears to get him his proximate cause.[55]

Bradley was not concerned to trace his character of Hamlet back to childhood. The temporal range of Bradley's narrative is better typified by those appended notes that have so irritated his critics, such as "Note B: Where Was Hamlet at the Time of His Father's Death?"[56] Even Jones feels no need to mention childhood until he is well launched upon his Freudian hypothesis, for which "infantile jealousies" are pro forma. By contending that Hamlet's current suffering is "an obscure aftermath of his childhood's conflict," however, he provides a certain defense for the hero; and this argument, while not as affecting as Bradley's study of Hamlet's melancholy, is at least sympathetic, because he goes out of his way to explain that a child may demand a parent's undivided attention, or even wish a parent dead, without understanding the direness of the thought (93–97). Jones does not quite suggest that relegating conflict to early childhood provides an excuse or alibi for Hamlet-like depression and self-blame.[57] Nor does he speculate on the evidentiary implications of this customary direction of psychoanalytic investigations, their insistent leap backward in time to an era of each individual's past that has virtually been forgotten and for which the evidence is mostly irrecoverable. Again, successful inquiries into what happened in infancy have their own appeal, as feats of narrative not easily undertaken; and the sheer recovery of some memory of that time can seem remarkable. The intermittent record of this — comparatively speaking — ancient past requires skill and imagination to piece together. In this use

55. Projection is unexamined by Jones, who says nothing of what force it takes to "link" the idea of oneself with that of another person or of what forces result from the linking. One can accept both projection and repression (as I certainly do) without seeing why Hamlet's repression of his own secret desires "necessarily" entails the repression of his animosity to Claudius. Projection could just as easily cause him to take out his self-hatred against his uncle or cause him to take out hatred of the uncle against himself, by suicide. But Hamlet delays, and therefore projection has produced his delay and not revenge or suicide — or so Jones's argument goes.

56. Bradley, *Shakespearean Tragedy*, 321–24.

57. By ascribing sexual jealousy to children "below the age of puberty" (94), Jones expressly counters the American psychologist Stanley Hall, the editor of the journal in which he is publishing. It was Hall who invited Freud to lecture at Clark University in 1909.

of circumstantial evidence, the models for psychoanalysis were the stunning achievements of archaeology and paleontology in the nineteenth century, and particularly the biological discovery that ontogeny recapitulates phylogeny.[58]

Though Bradley has not much to say about Hamlet's father, Jones allows him at least that role acceded by the Oedipus complex. Like Bradley, he makes primary Hamlet's relation to Gertrude: "whereas the murder of his father evokes in him indignation, and a plain recognition of his obvious *duty* to avenge it, his mother's guilty conduct awakes in him the intensest horror" (91). And even after expounding the Freudian thesis, he perceives Hamlet as one "in whom 'repressed' love for the mother is even more powerful than 'repressed' hostility towards the father" (110). (The idea of repression, which Jones always hedges with quotation marks in his article, allows the said hostility to contradict the first assertion and all naive interpretations of *Hamlet*, with its hero's expressed awe, if not love, for his father and marked hostility to his mother; still, the statements are consistent in stressing some relationship with his mother.) Hamlet's father is dead: we hear testimony of what he was like as a person, and his ghost even appears on stage, but not surprisingly a production or a reading of the play deposits more clues about Hamlet's mother, who has not died. The grim realization of Hamlet's father's death as a poisoning initiates the dramatic action of *Hamlet*, an action that happens to and around Hamlet and not the deceased father. Dramatically the hero's feelings about his mother are amply warranted by his discovery that his father was murdered, which knowledge occupies nearly the entire play. Hamlet never actually avenges his father's death unless one counts his actions after he too has been poisoned at the end.

Hamlet and the Oedipus complex have in common this readiness to see the death of fathers as murder, with the aftermath falling short of "simple revenge" (79) after all. Everyone's father dies; if the Oedipus complex is universal, every child therefore feels guilty. Hamlet's father dies, was murdered; and luckily for Hamlet, someone else did it. This brief sampling of character studies cannot possibly compass the history of *Hamlet* criticism or of the Oedipus complex; yet one cannot fail to note the coincidence of these close investigations of humanity and of Hamlet at the end of the nineteenth century. They are investigations with marked and similar points of view: a view by sons of their fathers,

---

58. See Frank J. Sulloway, *Freud, Biologist of the Mind: Beyond the Psychoanalytic Legend* (New York: Basic, 1979), 199–204, 259–64.

or to some extent by children of parents, but not the other way around. Neither the Hamlet story nor the Oedipus complex summarizes the father's point of view; rather, they suggest the younger generation's experience of the death of fathers and the transformation of this death to murder. It is the two generations that are crucial to the construction of guilt in each case, not the incidental scandal that sexual feelings have been aroused (feelings that are not always troubled because they are not always possessive, and if possessive not always so for the parent of the same sex). But every human child takes a long time before growing as tall as a parent, a time during which the parent's potential for punishing the child is real, whether exercised or not. Narrative time, or personal history, is crucial, for while the parent has stopped growing, the child catches up. Thereafter, as far as physical might is concerned, conflict could be resolved either way, but open conflict with the parent, especially the privileged father, is unthinkable. It is unthinkable from habit, by the custom of family life, and now in the refinement of nineteenth-century middle-class life.

If there is a historical reason for the twin discoveries of Hamlet analysis and psychoanalysis, therefore, it almost certainly resides in adult feelings about fathers. One has to assume that children have always grown up in families, but they traditionally stayed with their families or nearby. The nineteenth-century industrial, commercial, financial, and professional economies demanded not only much greater social mobility but also the maximizing of every individual's efforts, whether mean or prestigious. Though women were not expected to be other than drudges at the lower end of the social scale and refined housewives at the upper end, men were regularly expected to do better than their fathers, especially in the newly created professional classes. Fathers went on dying but also lived longer, while sons were positively counted on to outstrip them early. But they were not humanly authorized by anyone to do so; it was what the system demanded and permitted.[59] It is common today, especially because of the concentration of so much feminist criticism on the period, to regard the nineteenth century as the age of patriarchy. The age certainly paid much respect to fathers; but not as much respect as fathers paid to themselves, or even as much as Freud

59. At the very end of his life Freud expressed a rivalry with his father not derived solely from infancy but springing from their diverging careers: "it seems as though the essence of success was to have got further than one's father, and as though to excel one's father was still something forbidden." See "A Disturbance of Memory on the Acropolis" (1936), *Standard Edition*, 22:246–48.

paid to fathers. The truth of the matter is that patriarchy as such was finished: children naturally still experienced the fear of fathers as they grew up, and fathers may even have become reactionary—more patri-archal—in the knowledge that they were finished; but what Freud and others began to describe was the experience of a male-dominated family once the practical and theoretical grounds for it had been withdrawn.[60]

As I suggested earlier with regard to the novel after Scott, part of the price of civilization was a sense of never surrendering oneself fully enough to society, when the only basis of that society is surrender of self. The living of a social contract, after all, is very much what Freud meant by repression, and repression is the work not of fathers but of civilization.[61] Freud is essentially another contract theorist in most of what he assumes, and notably fails to argue, about repression. The contract, obviously, did not do away with fathers; but it may possibly have bequeathed an Oedipus complex to Freud and all those who adopt the view of the younger generation. One has only to think of the principal document of contract theory in English, Locke's Second Trea-tise on government, to see how unalterably opposed the theory is to patriarchy as such. Locke was at great pains to distinguish true political power from paternal power as it is exercised in the family—or from what he liked to call parental power, not out of eagerness to include mothers but to embarrass his opponents, whose arguments could *not* logically exclude mothers, as he pointed out. In his First Treatise he attached Robert Filmer's *Patriarcha,* and now he set out to define true political power, in which obedience to law made fathers and sons equals over time. As Locke wrote in his chapter on paternal power, if respect for law "*made* the Father *free,* it shall make the Son free too."[62] By and large, the prescription for political power that gradually came to be accepted in western Europe and most of the colonial world put fathers out of the picture. But Freud directed his gaze on the family, and he could scarcely leave fathers out of that. Freud wrote about living with the contract, as the nineteenth-century novelists had done before him.

60. Of course *male* dominance did not end with the power of fathers: see Carole Pateman, *The Sexual Contract* (Oxford: Polity, 1988).

61. I am thinking primarily here of the Freud of *Civilization and Its Discontents* (1930), but even as Freud initially thought of *Hamlet* in connection with Sophocles' *Oedipus Rex,* he remarked "the changed treatment of the same material . . . the secular advance of repression in the emotional life of mankind." See *Interpretation of Dreams, Standard Edition,* 4:264.

62. John Locke, *Two Treatises on Government,* ed. Peter Laslett (Cambridge: Cambridge University Press, 1960), 325.

He thus wrote of the experience of guilt in surpassing fathers. Without that experience, obviously, there would be no Oedipus complex and no fresh construction of the mystery of Hamlet.[63]

Without fathers there could be no Hamlet or Oedipus. These same fathers, however, were already emasculated by modern times and modern political theory: hence Freud's fearlessness, perhaps, and Jones's too, while their own knowingness often seems at odds with modernism in the arts and their claims for circumstantial evidence are possibly exaggerated. About forty years ago the resemblance of Shakespearean character criticism to criminal investigation was summarized by E. E. Stoll with a kind of growl: "criticism is but open-minded comprehension," Stoll insisted, "not dubiety and detection."[64] That protest may remind us that a hermeneutics of suspicion is older than Freud or Marx; it coincides with the era of circumstantial evidence, with the distrust of testimony inherent in strong representations. Psychoanalysis partakes in that move, and Freud himself did not fail to recognize a connection between his discoveries and legal proceedings.[65] Psychoanalysis distrusts testimony: it hearkens to dialogue, but only for the dialogue's indirect revelation of what cannot attain to consciousness, let alone to speech. It privileges dreams, parapraxes, or hapless evasions precisely because those verbal expressions are not intended. Thus it seeks, with the early proponents of circumstantial proof, evidence that has not been subject to deliberation: the unconscious cannot lie. Psychoanalysis also hearkens to silence, as the most ordinary form taken by resistance. But silence is not suspicious in itself unless there is a presumption of guilt, so that analysis has possibly a greater affinity for prosecution than for neutral investigation of the facts. Just as surely as literary narratives from Scott to Kafka, psychoanalysis depends on some general and historical discovery of guilt since the Enlightenment. This guilt seems to be a marked nineteenth-century phenomenon, whether one derives it from contract theory, a dialectic of good and evil, or the primal murder of a father.

---

63. In *Totem and Taboo* (1912–13), Freud essentially worked up a primitive anthropology that would explain the origin of the Oedipus complex. The overthrowing of the primal father is another deliberately constructed myth, a Freudian alternative to the social contract. Repression is a condition accounted for by both of these philosophical—as opposed to folkloric—myths.

64. Elmer Edgar Stoll, "A Falstaff for the 'Bright,' " *Modern Philology* 51 (1954): 158.

65. Freud, "Psycho-Analysis and the Establishment of the Facts in Legal Proceeding" (1906), *Standard Edition,* 9:103–14.

4

The Evidence of a Great Many Deaths

And the inference is obvious. If it is chiefly evil that violently disturbs the order of the world, this order cannot be friendly to evil or indifferent between evil and good, any more than a body which is convulsed by poison is friendly to it or indifferent to the distinction between poison and food.

—A. C. Bradley, 1904

Proof of a life to come must be given. In fire and in blood, if needful, must that proof be written. In fire and in blood do we trace the record throughout nature. In fire and in blood does it cross our own experience. Sufferer, faint not through terror of this burning evidence.

—Lucy Snowe, 1853

A SUSPICION OF MURDER HANGS about many of the most enterprising uses of circumstantial evidence, especially the imaginary uses. *Hamlet,* to a modern audience, seems a well-worn murder mystery, and the very phrase "circumstantial evidence" is widely known because of its celebration in detective novels and films. Murderous impulses are assumed to inhabit the unconscious commonly enough to make psychoanalysis worthwhile, and at least since Hobbes, the mere existence of a civil state has seemed to call for inferences about a prior state of violence. Yet we all of us mostly consult evidence and draw inferences without respect to crimes of violence. So is there any sense to this special fondness for evidence of murder?

That such a fondness exists is clear: one has only to think of the little pamphlet on the detection of murder that Fielding compiled after he had written four novels, two of them classics in the language.[1] But it is better to avoid another literary authority if possible and to consider a text from the maturity of the law of evidence and even skepticism about the virtues of circumstantial evidence. A beautiful example comes to hand from the writings of James Fitzjames Stephen, whose authority in English criminal law is as great as Fielding's in the novel and who quite disliked detective novels—to say nothing of his particular dislike of Dickens.[2] Stephen was the author of the first comprehensive and critical history of the criminal law and half a dozen other books, and he happened to draft the Indian Evidence Act of 1872. In the same year he published, in 130 pages prefatory to a copy of the act, a lucid *Introduction* to the subject of evidence. The Indian Evidence Act, which is still the law in the Republic of India today, governed both civil and criminal practice. Stephen himself declared to the Legislative Council of India in 1872, and repeated in the preface to this publication, that

1. See above, chapter 2, note 1.
2. See [James Fitzjames Stephen], "Detectives in Fiction and in Real Life," *Saturday Review* 17 (1864): 712–13; and for the best known of his attacks on Dickens, his review of *Little Dorrit* in the *Edinburgh Review* 106 (1857): 924–36.

"the subject is one which reaches far beyond the law," and that "the law of evidence is nothing unless it is founded upon a rational conception of the manner in which truth as to all matters of fact whatever ought to be investigated."[3] Yet when he employs sixty-five of his pages to present five cases—four English and one Scottish—as illustrating the relevancy of evidence, two things immediately stand out. In the first place, these so-called abstracts of the evidence in five trials are already shaped as narratives, not in the form in which the evidence had been presented in court or in which analogous evidence would in future be presented in Indian courts. And second, though the act and Stephen's discussion of it apply over the full spectrum of litigation—and by extension, in the author's words, to "all matters of fact whatever"—the five cases selected for the reader's instruction and better understanding are criminal cases, and all five are cases of murder.

The reduction of trial evidence to narrative cannot surprise us. Evidence of every kind seems to call for strengthening as a continuous narrative—even as Shakespeare's plays are altered to narrative in the process of examining their evidence of character. As we have seen, the full transcripts of criminal trials provided narratives made out by the prosecution at the opening of the trial and by the bench in the summary of evidence at the close. These models were quickly supplemented by pamphleteering in sensational cases, or soberly condensed by barristers to orient the readers of their law reports and treatises. In four of the five trials Stephen presents, this ordinary reworking into narrative was already accomplished for him by his source: he simply cross-references the resulting short stories, by means of footnotes, to the appropriate sections of his Indian Evidence Act. It is the second point, his partiality for murder—virtually an insistence on murder cases to illustrate the use of evidence—that concerns me now. "Even a dog," Oliver Wendell Holmes wrote in 1881, "distinguishes between being stumbled over and being kicked";[4] and Stephen could certainly distinguish, in the same era, other liabilities than the criminal. But despite his knowledge of the common law and despite the wider purposes of the act and his *Introduction,* a certain gut instinct led him to choose five murder cases to

3. James Fitzjames Stephen, *The Indian Evidence Act (I. of 1872), with an Introduction on the Principles of Judicial Evidence* (Calcutta and London: Macmillan, 1872). The essay is hereafter referred to as the *Introduction,* with page references given in parentheses.

4. Oliver Wendell Holmes, *The Common Law,* ed. Mark de Wolfe Howe (1963; rpt. Boston: Little, Brown, n.d.), 7. In this work of 1881, Holmes uses Stephen respectfully enough; a few years later, he calls him "rather a model of a fine old 18th century controversialist than a philosopher" and "an adult male animal": see *Holmes-Pollock Letters,* ed. Mark de Wolfe Howe, 2d ed. (Cambridge: Harvard University Press, 1961), 21.

illustrate in detail what he calls the relevancy of evidence. And his selection of cases is still more special than murder: because he was mainly writing about circumstantial evidence—notwithstanding his objections to the phrase—no fewer than three of the five trials are for poisoning.

Since Stephen was not the only writer on evidence to give disproportionate space to murder, the matter is worth pursuing. The identification of murder with circumstantial evidence, I believe, stems partly from the valuation of the evidence of things not seen that was shared by law and natural religion since the seventeenth century in England, and especially from the emphasis on the future life of individuals that was exemplified by Bishop Butler, whose writings remained so attractive to Victorians—even to nonbelievers among them. In this chapter I shall explicate Stephen's comparatively little known *Introduction* to the Indian Evidence Act and suggest some reasons why murder might serve as *the* object of strong representations for others besides detective novelists. Then, with the help of Butler's well-known *Analogy of Religion,* I shall argue that the development of natural religion may account for the special devotion of circumstantial evidence to murder, whether in the popular imagination or in the minds of sophisticated professionals. And third, I shall review briefly how still another discipline closely allied with natural religion—the new science of geology—made death such a remarkable fact in issue for the nineteenth century: no widespread fear of violence, certainly, but insistent ordinary death compels attention to the evidence for murder.

The Victorians' most celebrated literary rendering of death is *In Memoriam,* which, unlike the fiction of Hamlet and his father, offers itself as a poem about an actual death—that of Tennyson's friend Arthur Hallam, age twenty-two, in 1833. This loss was surely uncommon,[5] yet much as an unnatural murder teaches Hamlet to endure death in the play, a new outrage that was ostensibly natural—the extinction of whole species—seems to have made Hallam's death easier to accept than it might otherwise have been. The paradox results, in both cases, from the psychological chance that outrages may finally be easier to take personally than respected inevitabilities, such as ordinary death, that are every bit as cruel. In this same poem, Tennyson took some satisfaction in contemplating the representation of death and extinction that

5. "Thou know'st 'tis common," Hamlet's mother chides (*Hamlet,* 1.2.72); and the nineteenth-century poet seems to reply, "That loss is common would not make / My own less bitter, rather more" (*In Memoriam,* 6.5–6). See *The Poems of Tennyson,* ed. Christopher Ricks, 2d ed., 3 vols. (Berkeley: University of California Press, 1987), 2:323 and n.

he found in Charles Lyell's classic *Principles of Geology,* published from 1830 to 1833. The poet, though drawn to such arguments and generally amenable to Lyell's uniformitarianism,[6] refused the consolations of natural religion just because they imposed arguments from circumstantial evidence and did not address what he felt. So closely were natural religion and the new science of geology intertwined that even writers who were not actually trying to prove creation from the evidence of rock formations were at least careful to show that evidence consistent with a divine plan. But Lyell, indeed, was a barrister as well as the most successful theorist of geology for a century: as Stephen Jay Gould has at once good-humoredly and bitterly complained, Lyell came up with "the most brilliant brief ever written by a scientist . . . a passionate brief for a single, well-formed argument, hammered home relentlessly."[7] Such a strong representation of geological facts bears looking into along with Tennyson's response, and that response is not altogether unrelated to the way one might feel about murder.

Stephen's Introduction to Evidence

James Fitzjames Stephen was the older of two surviving sons of a worthy Clapham Sect family. His brother was Leslie Stephen, biographer and intellectual historian, and the main source of our knowledge of Fitzjames as a person.[8] Their father, James, another extraordinarily energetic man, at once more and less worldly than his sons, held appointments in the Colonial Office for over thirty years, served as its undersecretary from 1836 until his retirement in 1847, and wrote for the *Edinburgh Review.* Fitzjames, like Leslie after him, attended Eton and Cambridge, where he was more prominent as a member of the Apostles than as a student. He was called to the bar in 1854 and for the next fifteen years pursued a divided career as a moderately successful barrister on the circuit and as a prolific journalist.[9] In the tradition of Bentham, and by tempera-

6. William Whewell coined the term "uniformitarianism" in his review of Lyell's *Principles of Geology,* vol. 2: "these two opinions will probably for some time divide the geological world into two sects, which may perhaps be designated as the *Uniformitarians* and the *Catastrophists.*" See *Quarterly Review* 47 (1832): 126.

7. Stephen Jay Gould, *Time's Arrow, Time's Cycle: Myth and Metaphor in the Discovery of Geological Time* (Cambridge: Harvard University Press, 1987), 104–5.

8. Leslie Stephen, *The Life of Sir James Fitzjames Stephen* (London: Smith, Elder, 1895). This *Life* has now been seconded by a thoroughgoing intellectual biography, K. J. M. Smith's *James Fitzjames Stephen: Portrait of a Victorian Rationalist* (Cambridge: Cambridge University Press, 1988).

9. An extensive bibliography is available in Leon Radzinowicz, *Sir James Fitzjames*

ment, Stephen could never adapt to the profession of law as an insider, convinced though he might be that there was no system superior to the English. He characteristically pursued an independent line of thought, and his *General View of the Criminal Law of England* (1863) anticipated the logic and critical perspective of his three-volume *History of the Criminal Law of England* (1883). In the last weeks of 1869 he succeeded Henry Sumner Maine as legal member of the Governor General's Council in India, where in less than two and a half years he authored a good deal of legislation besides the Evidence Act.[10] On the return voyage he worked on his most memorable book outside the law, *Liberty, Equality, Fraternity* (1873), a trenchant and still valuable response to Mill's *On Liberty*.

As with other Victorians, an exalted position in the administration of the empire confirmed Stephen's conservatism and his essentially Hobbesian view of human society. A more immediate effect, however, was to intensify his Benthamite enthusiasm for codification.[11] Upon his return to England, he was involved in two strenuous and frustrated efforts at codification at home: a code of evidence in 1872 and a homicide law amendment bill the following year. In order not to waste the energy devoted to these bills, which failed partly because of changes of government but equally because of the law's resistance to codification, Stephen diverted it into the writing of two successful digests. He brought out *A Digest of the Law of Evidence* in 1876 and, since a principal criticism of the homicide bill had been that a single portion of the criminal law should not be codified by itself, he enlarged his work on the latter to write *A Digest of the Criminal Law,* long in print after 1877. The Indian experience had stiffened his reforming zeal, and in a foray of Liberal campaigning during the same years he compared codification in the law to Bradshaw's *Railway Guide*: according to Stephen's brother, he argued that Bradshaw "is puzzling enough as it is; but what would be our state if we had to discover our route by examining and comparing all the orders given by the directors of railways from their origin, and

---

Stephen, 1829–1894, and His Contribution to the Development of Criminal Law (London: Quaritch, 1957), 49–66.

10. For Maine's assessment of the conditions inherited by Stephen in India, see his speech "Evidence" (1868), in M. E. Grant Duff, *Sir Henry Maine: A Brief Memoir of His Life* (New York: Holt, 1892), 294–300.

11. See Stephen's address to the Social Science Association, 11 November 1872, "Codification in India and England," *Fortnightly Review* 18 (1872): 644–72. "To compare the Indian Penal Code with English criminal law is like comparing cosmos with chaos" (654). Thomas Babington Macaulay, the first legal member of the council, was the author of the penal code.

interpreting them in accordance with a set of unwritten customs, putting special meanings on the various terms employed?"[12] It is hard to imagine Fitzjames Stephen offering any such comparison lightheartedly, witty as it may be. He did not have Bentham's penchant for satire, and he scorned lightheartedness in such matters. But it ought to be stressed how refreshingly and substantially modern were his typical contributions: for example, his reduction of the ancient concept of "malice aforethought" in defining murder to a particular state of knowledge.[13] Whether because of his intellectual or his political contributions, Stephen was appointed a judge of the Queen's Bench Division in 1879. In truth, he appears to have served in that capacity rather indifferently.[14] He could exercise his independence more freely in writing, and it was as a kind of outsider that he most successfully championed the common law.

Many of Stephen's best traits are demonstrated by his *Introduction* to the Indian Evidence Act, an essay primarily for students and almost entirely free of the usual citations of case law in such works. The argument is congruent with common-law practice but untrammeled by much regard for history: the author wants to present a method for the true representation of facts as a perfectly reasonable business. He begins by implying, if not quite stating outright, that making sense of the evidence is more important than memorizing technicalities of the law, and one feels he is talking to himself as much as to students. He cannot refrain from criticizing the usual rules of evidence even as he summarizes them. For example, the rule against hearsay, to which a dozen or so exceptions were admitted by the nineteenth century, would be better construed as exclusion of irrelevant evidence—"but the English law contains nothing which approaches to a definition of relevancy." That, to Stephen, is the most staring fault. Directly he advocates a single distinction between "facts in issue," from which some right or liability depends in substantive law, and "relevant facts," which "may affect the probability of the existence of facts in issue." "All the facts with which it can in any event be necessary for courts of justice to concern themselves, are included in these two classes" (5–10). With this dichotomy in hand, in true Benthamite style, he can begin to provide the guide to relevancy that English law lacks. It is, of course, the Indian context of

12. Leslie Stephen, *Life of Sir James Fitzjames Stephen,* 347.

13. The argument was set forth in Stephen's *Digest of the Criminal Law* (London: Macmillan, 1877), 354–66. See also his *A History of the Criminal Law of England,* 3 vols. (1883; rpt. New York: Franklin, 1964), 3:50–87.

14. Cf. Leslie Stephen, *Life of Sir James Fitzjames Stephen,* 437–50; and Radzinowicz, *Sir James Fitzjames Stephen,* 37–43.

his effort that amplifies Stephen's ambition to supply this lack. Though his tone is not condescending, the occasion for writing is inevitably so, and the imperial task makes for stunning simplification.

Accordingly, the second chapter of the *Introduction* broadly identifies reasoning from evidence in a court of law with reasoning from evidence in science. Stephen begins with perception as the test of fact and with propositions as the means of conveying facts through words. Then he expands a little on the nature of induction, with principal reference to Mill's *System of Logic* (1843), and still more widely on the differences between scientific and judicial inquiries. In this entire chapter he makes but two references to actual cases, though a number of paradigmatic cases illustrate forms of inductive reasoning. The aim of the discussion is still preparatory to the third chapter, "The Theory of Relevancy, with Illustrations," where the argument is deferred to the five narrated murder trials. These are not case law either, in the accepted sense. Stephen's illustrations come from the sort of materials that were collected in successive editions of the *State Trials*.[15] His purpose is not to cite precedents for the rules of evidence but to show what sort of representations of fact are relevant. The unusual thing about the Evidence Act was the inclusion, in sections 6 to 11, of an attempt to define relevant facts. "These sections," according to their author, "are by far the most important, as they are the most original part of the Evidence Act, as they affirm positively what facts may be proved, whereas the English law assumes this to be known, and merely declares negatively that certain facts shall not be proved" (55). The entire *Introduction* reflects this emphasis. In the remainder of this chapter, after sixty-five pages of the illustrations, Stephen allows only seven pages to "Irrelevant Facts," or the ordinary exclusions of the common law that are recited in the remaining sections of the act itself. The fourth and last chapter of the *Introduction* consists of a few pages on presumptions and general matters.

How then are relevant facts defined? Admittedly, sections 6 to 11 of the act are "worded very widely, and in such a way as to overlap each other." They are each very briefly stated, and for our purposes an even briefer paraphrase can suffice. Relevant facts are (in the order enacted into law) facts that are part of the same transaction as the fact in issue; facts that are the occasion, cause, or effect of the fact in issue; motives or preparations and previous or subsequent conduct of the doer of a

15. In "The State Trials," *Cornhill Magazine* 6 (1862): 351–63, Stephen writes of their value as recreational reading when he was studying law.

fact in issue; facts necessary to explain or introduce relevant facts; things said or done by conspirators in reference to a common design; and facts not otherwise relevant that become relevant either because they are inconsistent with a fact in issue (thus tending to disprove it) or because they make a fact in issue or relevant fact highly probable or improbable (tending to prove or disprove it). It will be seen that the act's definitions of relevancy cut such a wide swath that they are likely to defeat one of Stephen's implied purposes, which is to eliminate unnecessary testimony or wayward narrative in court. Moreover, he does not defend but illustrates the definitions, by means of the five criminal trials. Four of these trials are so boiled down in his source that he is able, by means of footnotes, to attach nearly every sentence in their narratives to one or another of sections 6 to 11 of the act. Rather defensively, he declares that these trials were "the most intricate that I could discover" (55–56), though many civil trials would run to greater intricacy. None of the narrative versions of the trials is so intricate that he points to any *ir*relevant evidence that was introduced.

The five "remarkable trials" need not be summarized in any detail, since they can readily be named and typed. That Stephen employs the word *remarkable* pretty well announces that they are of the general type to be found in the *State Trials* and originally published in something close to a stenographic record. The first four are reproduced verbatim from the brief versions given in the third edition of William Wills, *An Essay on the Principles of Circumstantial Evidence,*[16] followed without any break or typographical indication by a paragraph or so of commentary by Stephen. *R v. Donellan,* tried at the Warwick Assizes in 1781, as described earlier, was well known in the literature of circumstantial evidence because it had been cited by Burke in the impeachment of Warren Hastings.[17] *R v. Belaney,* the next case, was tried at the Central Criminal Court in 1844. Belaney, a surgeon, was acquitted of poisoning his pregnant wife on a visit to London. This is the only acquittal that Stephen introduces among the five narratives illustrating relevancy. He does not suggest that any of the evidence presented was irrelevant; his concluding comment barely hints that if it were up to him Belaney

---

16. William Wills, *An Essay on the Principles of Circumstantial Evidence,* 3d ed. (London: Butterworth, 1850), 192–96, 175–78, 225–29, and 230–34. The first edition of this work (1838) bore the title *Rationale* instead of *Principles.*

17. Stephen had included *Donellan* among the cases appended to *A General View of the Criminal Law of England* (London: Macmillan, 1863) and would give another version of it in *History of the Criminal Law,* 3:371–88. In both works it is immediately followed by *R v. Palmer.*

might have hanged. He had offered no separate comment on *Donellan,* but he now comments that the two cases together demonstrate "the amount of uncertainty which constitutes what can be called reasonable doubt" and "the all-important principle that every case is independent of every other, and that no decision upon facts forms a precedent for any other decision."[18] *R v. Richardson* was a Scottish case of 1786. Richardson was convicted of slashing the throat of a young woman who was pregnant, presumably by him. He was identified by matching shoes of men attending the funeral with footprints at the scene of the murder, and both Wills and Stephen (citing Wills) record that Walter Scott borrowed this bit of detection for use in *Guy Mannering.*[19] In his comment this time, Stephen applies Mill's "method of agreement" in analyzing the narrative, enumerating ten correspondences between known facts about the murderer and known facts about Richardson. In *R v. Patch,* a case tried at the Surrey Assizes in 1803, the accused was convicted of shooting his business partner to gain the latter's property and to conceal his own fraudulent dealings with him. *Patch* is mainly interesting for the murderer's elaborate preparations, which included first shooting at his victim in rehearsal, as if to set up the inference that the man had some other enemy in the vicinity. And finally, in *R v. Palmer,* tried at the Old Bailey in 1856, a medical practitioner and betting man from Staffordshire was convicted of poisoning his friend, another betting man, to cover up for fraud and theft. This trial lasted a highly unusual twelve days, and it was of course too recent for Wills to have discussed. Stephen uses the version of it given in his *General View,* where he cites as his authority the contemporary shorthand report.[20] Presumably this narrative summary was Stephen's own work. He devotes more space to *Palmer* than to the other four cases combined and

18. Stephen, *Introduction,* 66–67. But see his remarks in *History of the Criminal Law,* 3:388, where he suggests that both men were guilty and that the evidence against Belaney is "rather stronger" than that against Donellan.

19. In Walter Scott's *Guy Mannering* (1815), however, the culprit and his exposure (chap. 56) differ markedly from the original. See also Scott's letter to John B. S. Morritt, 12 January 1813, in *The Letters of Sir Walter Scott,* ed. H. J. C. Grierson, 12 vols. (London: Constable, 1932–37), 3:225–26.

20. *A Verbatim Report of the Trial of William Palmer . . . Transcribed from the Short-hand Notes of W. Angelo Bennett* (London: Allen, 1856). Stephen gave another version of *Palmer* in the appendix to *History of the Criminal Law,* 3:389–425, where he reveals that he "was present throughout the greater part of this celebrated trial" and instances Palmer as a type deserving capital punishment (422–25). Robert Graves, ostensibly irritated by the version of this trial in the Notable English Trials series (1912), wrote a fictionalized account and asserted his own opinion of Palmer's innocence: see *They Hanged My Saintly Billy: The Life and Death of Dr. William Palmer* (New York: Doubleday, 1957).

in the process details some of the evidence as it was presented in the trial. At least a dozen pages concern the expert medical testimony on both sides. Were the symptoms of the deceased to be associated with tetanus or with strychnine? Stephen for once hints that some of the evidence might have been irrelevant, for Dr. McDonald of Garnkirk, near Glasgow, "assigned the most extraordinary reasons for supposing that it was a case of . . . epilepsy. He said that the fit might have been caused by sexual excitement, though the man was ill at Rugeley for nearly a week before his death; and that it was within the range of possibility that sexual intercourse might produce a convulsion fit after an interval of a fortnight" (116–17).

This, then, is the core of Stephen's introduction to the subject of relevant facts: five British murder cases from the previous one hundred years—three poisonings, one throat cutting, and one shooting—all presented in narrative form with only one focusing much attention on evidence as it was presented in court. The Indian Evidence Act of 1872, with its unusual attempt to give positive instruction in relevancy, is still the law. In India today the whole of Stephen's *Introduction*—with minor changes in wording to eliminate his use of the first person—and the five murder cases as he presented them are enshrined within nearly four thousand closely packed pages of commentary that have grown up around the act.[21] As might be expected, the very notion of defining relevancy drew criticism, and some of this criticism has also been preserved by the commentary.[22] From the point of view of a general history of representation since the Enlightenment, the ambition of Stephen's design has a very direct and disarming appeal. Yet its exposition is unbelievably special. As the same exhaustive commentary on the act makes clear at a glance, the consideration of evidence reaches to every form of litigation, yet Stephen's exposition of relevancy begins and ends with murder. And to this limitation none of his commentators seems to object.

Stephen was at least aware of the special nature of his illustrations, for the five cases in the *Introduction* are preceded by this paragraph of explanation:

21. *Woodroffe and Ameer Ali's Law of Evidence in India,* ed. E. S. Subrahmanyan, 13th ed., 4 vols. (Allahabad: Law Book, 1973–75), 1:22–108. The first edition, which I have not seen, was published in 1898. According to the preface to the ninth edition (1930, p. vii this edition), "We have acquired the copyright of the Introduction to the Evidence Act of the late Sir James Fitzjames Stephen and have incorporated it in our own."

22. Ibid., 1:109–40. See also James Bradley Thayer, *A Preliminary Treatise on Evidence at the Common Law* (1898; rpt. New York: Kelley, 1969), 266–70n. Thayer characterizes Stephen's effort as that of one who attempted "to take the kingdom of heaven by force."

I may observe upon these cases that the general principles of evidence are, perhaps, more clearly displayed in trials for murder, than in any others. Murders are usually concealed with as much care as possible; and, on the other hand, they must, from the nature of the case, leave traces behind them which render it possible to apply the argument from effects to causes with greater force in these than in most other cases. Moreover, as they involve capital punishment and excite peculiar attention, the evidence is generally investigated with special care. There are accordingly few cases which show so distinctly the sort of connection between fact and fact, which makes the existence of one fact a good ground for inferring the existence of another. (56)

The explanation stops short of saying what needs to be explained, since it does not directly say that the trials all *are* for murder: the paragraph would equally well serve to introduce trials of which some were for murder and some not. Only if the notoriety of Donellan, Belaney (acquitted), Richardson, Patch, and Palmer—whose trials Stephen has so far merely listed in a column—is such that the reader knows them for murderers is the exclusive nature of the club clear. If their notoriety is indeed such, then the trials were obviously selected on some different or additional ground than their evidentiary interest.

If one seeks to unpack the explanation, the immediate result is frustrating. Stephen's argument comes in two halves, separated by "moreover." The first half is a mysterious statement about concealment and "traces" of murder that supposedly attract inductive reasoning of some "force." This statement at least obliquely suggests why three of the five cases should be poisonings, notoriously a secret crime affecting parts of the body not seen. Beyond that, the argument seems to aim at the "greater force" of circumstantial evidence in prosecuting murder as compared with other litigation, but it makes no sense of this claim. The assertion that murders "must, from the nature of the case, leave traces behind" may hint at some providential design in nature, but if so this claim too is unsupported. "Traces" very likely refers to the bodies of those murdered, among other things, but their bearing on the special force of induction must be taken for granted. As for the second half of the explanation, the admission that evidence in capital cases is customarily examined with "special care" seems to give the wrong signal to prospective students of the *Introduction* and litigants under the act, whose everyday concerns will seldom be with murder. The source of the "peculiar attention" attracted by murder is undoubtedly strong community feeling, but this connection too is left open. "Accordingly," the nearly inadvertent paragraph of explanation hints rather than explains anything. Absent "accordingly," Stephen's last sentence would articulate precisely the question to be asked: why *murder* cases "show so distinctly the sort of connection between fact and fact, which makes the existence of one fact a good ground for inferring the existence of another."

We can begin to see that mystery lingers in the five trials that Stephen chooses to illustrate the workings of his enlightened Evidence Act, as well as mystification in the paragraph of explanation that good sense suddenly obliges him to provide.[23] He could not choose three trials for poisoning, out of all the possible trials, civil and criminal, that he might present, without distilling in his argument some vapors of death unseen—some sniffing at bottles, some autopsies, and some sense of desecration that persists into modern times. Yet by 1872, when he offered these illustrations, the crime of murder had been importantly demystified, in part by Stephen himself.[24] Perhaps murder will never be assimilated to the idea of mere harm to another, and probably this is a good thing, but before the nineteenth century it bore much heavier associations with desecration and pollution than it does today.[25] In general, the common law has called for a higher degree of probability—"beyond reasonable doubt," as the saying goes—in criminal as distinct from civil cases, which are to be decided according to a "preponderance" or balance of probabilities.[26] Trials for homicide, in particular, engage a wider community interest than other trials, and this difference can be explained quite apart from the marked sense of violation of human life. The truth of the matter is that the principal complainant to homicide is dead, and so is the principal witness in most cases. The prosecution for homicide has to be carried on by kith and kin or by the state, and

23. Cf. Stephen, "The Sacredness of Human Life," *Saturday Review* 17 (1864): 776: "there is a mystery about human life which we do not thoroughly understand, and . . . the existence of this mystery to some extent ties our hands in dealing with it."

24. See note 13 above.

25. The curious institutions of deodands and forfeiture register the sense of violation that murder aroused. Deodands required that the instrument of death be sacrificed: hence old indictments for murder had to specify the value of the weapon employed. Forfeiture meant that the state inherited the property of a convicted murderer. These customs were abolished, however, by legislation of 1846 and 1870, respectively (9 & 10 Vict. c. 62 and 33 & 34 Vict. c. 23). For an account of the same, drawn up for another purpose, see Jacob J. Finkelstein, "The Goring Ox: Some Historical Perspectives on Deodands, Forfeitures, Wrongful Death, and the Western Notion of Sovereignty," *Temple Law Quarterly* 46 (1973): 169–212.

26. A good account of the anomalies of applying these elusive standards of proof is L. Jonathan Cohen, *The Probable and the Provable* (Oxford: Clarendon, 1977), 49–120.

hence in any period requires a greater measure of community support than the prosecution of other wrongs. Before the end of the eighteenth century nearly all prosecution for crime in England was managed by private means.[27] The increasing practical involvement of the state and the establishment of a police force in the nineteenth century undoubtedly heightened, if not the abhorrence of unnatural death, at least the scope of public responsibility for its prevention and prosecution.[28]

The criminal law had long singled out the need to establish the intent of the doer of a fact in issue. As Bentham and others argued, all psychological facts, in the absence of confession, have to be proved by circumstantial evidence of one sort or another.[29] This implied distance between an unseen thought and discernible evidence of thought, even more than the deliberate concealment pointed to by Stephen, puts a peculiar pressure on inference. (It does not necessarily ensure that an inference will be forthcoming or guarantee its relative force when it comes.) By narrowing his focus on homicide, Stephen made questions of criminal culpability paramount. Since homicide occurs most frequently among parties acquainted with one another, not only the intent of the killer but that of his or her victim must usually be taken into account along with the situation of both. There thus arise distinctions of degree of liability for homicide—murder, manslaughter, accident, or self-defense.[30] Culpability is not measured so with other crimes, and the interactive nature of most murders compels consideration of cause and effect. It is hardly an exaggeration to say that "the jurisprudence of causation is the legacy of the law's persistent effort to determine when a death may be attributed to the conduct of a particular person."[31]

Even if Stephen were writing explicitly on homicide, however, it would not suffice to illustrate relevant facts with five cases of murder. To grasp what has caused him to narrate these five cases and to associate circumstantial evidence with the scene of the human body *willfully*

27. Cf. J. M. Beattie, *Crime and the Courts in England, 1660–1800* (Princeton: Princeton University Press, 1986), 35–139.

28. Leon Radzinowicz dates the "systematic" policing of England from 1861; see his *A History of English Criminal Law and Its Administration from 1750*, 4 vols. (1948–68; rpt. London: Stevens, 1974–76), 4:v.

29. Jeremy Bentham, *Rationale of Judicial Evidence*, ed. John Stuart Mill, 5 vols. (London: Hunt and Clarke, 1827), 3:3–11.

30. George P. Fletcher, *Rethinking Criminal Law* (Boston: Little, Brown, 1978), 350–55, illuminates this quality of homicide. "We are not likely to have learned the principle of graduated culpability from any other offense. It is true that many contemporary statutes recognize degrees of larceny and robbery. But the differentiation in these offences turns on the scale of the wrong, rather than the degree of culpability" (353).

31. Ibid., 358.

deprived of life, we have to search for what he was taught to believe in general about evidence and not merely what he thought was science or logic. In other words, we have to ask why in this particular Victorian culture—as in the detective stories that became popular at this time, of which Stephen was especially contemptuous—circumstantial evidence almost invariably points to murder.

Murder and Natural Religion

An explanation suggests itself in the common grounds of reasoning about evidence in criminal prosecution and in natural religion in England. As previously noted, the legal formulation of the best-evidence rule in the seventeenth century was scarcely distinguishable from its formulation in the argument for natural religion.[32] The two fields sought to legitimize and to sanctify probabilistic thinking, and eagerness for proving crimes by circumstantial evidence in some quarters became no less apparent than eagerness for discovering evidences of Christianity in nature. Needless to say, both disciplines touched on morality and were concerned with punishment or other sanctions; both easily accommodated personal histories to the notion of life as probation—a notion that pervaded the English novel for two centuries and even affected the fortunes of such as Falstaff. What I here propose is that, because of their specialized concerns with death, developments in the fields of religion and law were not only parallel but complementary. The fixation on murder, in discussions of evidence such as Stephen's and myriad fictional counterparts, can be explained by the pursuit in one field of an object deliberately neglected by the other—the brutish evidence of the dead body. That body is regularly seized upon by one form of strong representation—the law's insistence on establishing the cause of death—and blinked at by the other—natural religion's affirmation of a future life. The fulcrum of this complementarity is the corpse featured by a murder trial, or the proof of willful death in this unique instance as against the more difficult task of proving immortality for all.

Though in the course of two centuries a greater sense of connectedness, of chance and inevitability both, perhaps accrued to the word "circumstances," the differences are not important here. What is important, in order to allow for the complementarity of interest in murder, is to realize that enthusiasm for circumstantial evidence, which was

32. See chapter 1, notes 19 and 21.

sustained in the law through the early nineteenth century, runs in tandem with a corresponding enthusiasm inspired by natural religion in the same period. A great many books and essays treat evidence in general in such a way as to serve both applications, and there are frequent cross-references between the two fields. As we have seen, Stephen makes almost no references to reports or treatises of any kind, but Wills's *Circumstantial Evidence,* from which he borrows four of his five illustrations of relevancy, is studded with specific citations to works on evidence such as the following: Butler's *Analogy of Religion* (1736), Thomas Reid's *Intellectual Powers of Man* (1785), William Paley's *Horae Paulinae* (1790) and his *Evidences of Christianity* (1794), James Edward Gambier's *Moral Evidence* (1806), Renn D. Hampden's *Philosophical Evidence of Christianity* (1827), Alexander Crombie's *Natural Theology* (1829), and Henry Brougham's *Discourse on Natural Theology* (1835).[33] Most but not all of these writers were clergymen. Brougham was a popular politician and lord chancellor, perhaps the best known of all the law reformers of his age. Furthermore, Wills himself cannot be thought of as especially partial to natural religion. He makes many more references to case law, at least alludes to the civilian writers on presumptions, and cites Bentham's massive *Rationale of Judicial Evidence* (1827) more than most of his contemporaries in the legal profession. Only one work of natural religion surfaces in Stephen's *Introduction,* when he uses Paley's title, *Evidences of Christianity,* somewhat critically to illustrate the "popular and general" inclusiveness of the word *evidence* itself (6). But he knew many such works at first hand, and his range and output as a Victorian essayist was such that he could not help being familiar with religious questions. His first significant commission as a barrister was to defend, in an ecclesiastical court, one of the contributors to *Essays and Reviews,* the 1860 volume by Benjamin Jowett, Mark Pattison, and five others that took issue with literalist interpretations of the Bible. Stephen argued that interpretation of the Bible had traditionally been guided by critical reasoning, and he thought well enough of his defense that he published the whole of it as a book.[34] He could not have been the son of James Stephen, or as close to the liberal

33. Wills's citations are highly abbreviated. I have listed chronologically the works I have been able to verify and examine.

34. Stephen, *Defence of the Rev. Rowland Williams, D.D., in the Arches Court of Canterbury* (London: Smith, Elder, 1862). "My lord," he addressed the court in the course of quoting from Paley's *Evidences of Christianity,* "that is a book which, when I was at college, was put in my hands as part of my education" (144).

establishment of the day as he was, without being exposed to many different shadings of natural religion.

The question to ask is whether theories of circumstantial evidence, at the most general level, were really separable in law and in religion. The strategy in both fields was to insist on the pragmatic necessity of living with uncertainty. In making their cases, judges and divines drew attention to the nature of probabilistic thinking, as if the main question were the general one of the capacity to decide matters of fact, rather than the immediate fact in issue or belief in God. Their arguments repeatedly took the form of a conditional, as follows: if you can—indeed must—act with uncertainty in everyday concerns, then you can—indeed should—decide that the prisoner is guilty or that Christianity is true. Here is Bishop Butler, adopting the typical stance of natural religion in his *Analogy*:

> Persons who speak of the Evidence of Religion as doubtful, and of this supposed Doubtfulness as a positive Argument against it, should be put upon considering, what That Evidence indeed is, which they act upon with regard to their temporal Interests.[35]

And here is Chief Baron Pollock a century later, charging the jury in *R v. Manning*, a murder trial of 1849:

> If the conclusion to which you are conducted be that there is that degree of certainty in the case that you would act upon it in your own grave and important concerns, that is the degree of certainty which the law requires, and which will justify you in returning a verdict of guilty.[36]

Maria Manning, who was convicted along with her husband, is often said to be the model for Hortense in Dickens's *Bleak House*. Though the publication of *The Origin of Species* in 1859 spelled the beginning of the end for natural religion, and though natural selection gradually

---

35. Joseph Butler, *The Analogy of Religion, Natural and Revealed, to the Constitution and Course of Nature* (London: Knapton, 1736), 315. Subsequent page references are given in parentheses.

36. *The Bermondsey Murder: A Full Report of the Trial of Frederick George and Maria Manning, for the Murder of Patrick O'Connor* (London: Clark, 1849), 62. Pollock continued: "It is not necessary that a crime should be established beyond the possibility of doubt. There are crimes committed in darkness and secrecy which can only be traced and brought to light by a comparison of circumstances, which press upon the mind more and more as they are increased in number. There are doubts more or less involved in every human transaction. We are frequently mistaken as to what we suppose we have seen—still oftener as to what we suppose we have heard."

provided an alternative to the analogy of design in the universe, the standard of proof appealed to by Baron Pollock in *R v. Manning* can still be said to be that of the common law today.[37]

The following argument on the connection between these systems of proof and conviction for murder admittedly depends on the somewhat idiosyncratic contribution of Butler (1692–1752). But the *Analogy of Religion* was, in the first place, an early and popular defense of circumstantial evidence, pursuing almost painfully the general strategy I have noted. It became for many believers a favorite guide to sometimes tortuous paths of induction, from things seen to things not seen: "Suppose the invisible World, and the invisible Dispensations of Providence, to be, in any sort, analogous to what appears," Butler wrote, "or that both together make up one uniform Scheme, the two Parts of which, the Part which we see, and That which is beyond our Observation, are analogous to each other" (89). Arguably, the *Analogy* enjoyed the most lasting influence of all such books. Because it darkly confronted doubt and finally appealed to duty, it proved attractive to many Victorians and was respected by nearly all who knew it.[38] Even Butler's critics seemed drawn to the man, and his particular champion was the great Liberal politician of the age, W. E. Gladstone.[39]

The first thing about the *Analogy* that strikes the student of natural religion is that Butler never bothers to argue the existence of God. So thoroughly does he take that part of the argument of Christianity for granted, that he does not even take note of his assumption until the conclusion of the first part.[40] The *Analogy* begins, rather, with a strongly asserted and strangely blindfold argument on the future life of each human being. From there Butler goes on to a chapter on the government

37. Cohen, *Probable and the Provable,* 49–57, still finds it useful to cite from Pollock's charge to the jury (the sentence given in my text), along with some more sophisticated attempts to characterize a standard of proof. His source in turn is the widely available textbook by Rupert Cross, *Evidence,* 3d ed. (London: Butterworth, 1967), 89n.

38. For example, Stephen, *Defence of the Rev. Rowland Williams,* 126–27, 137–39; also Leslie Stephen, *Life of Sir James Fitzjames Stephen,* 161, 196. As his brother points out, Fitzjames invoked Butler in an argument for avenging the Indian Mutiny in 1857: see "Deus Ultionum," *Saturday Review* 4 (1857): 344–45.

39. In the last years of his life, Gladstone edited *The Works of Joseph Butler* in two volumes and assembled a third volume of his own *Studies Subsidiary to the Works of Bishop Butler* (Oxford: Clarendon, 1896). See especially his reply to those he dubs Butler's "censors"—Walter Bagehot, Sara Hennell, Leslie Stephen, and Matthew Arnold.

40. "That there is an intelligent Author of Nature and natural Governor of the World, is a Principle gone upon in the foregoing Treatise; as proved, and generally known and confessed to be proved" (198).

of God in this world and the next, followed by another on the moral nature of this government. The purpose of the latter is to disabuse anyone who might suppose "the only Character of the Author of Nature to be That of simple absolute Benevolence" (66). Just as, in this life, rewards follow naturally from virtuous behavior and punishment from vice, so in the next life a system of reward and punishment must prevail, and punishment had better be expected rather than false hopes placed in rewards. Having established or hinted this much, Butler can concentrate on "the general Doctrine of Religion, that our present Life is a State of Probation for a future one" (103). This idea of life *as a trial* is very important to the *Analogy,* and the author consciously rejects milder language for the life of moral choice: "The Word *Probation* is more distinctly and particularly expressive of Allurements to Wrong, or Difficulties in adhering uniformly to what is Right, and of the Danger of Miscarrying by such Temptations, than the Words *Moral Government.* A state of probation . . . [implies] trial, difficulties, and danger" (103–4). Space for moral heroism is thus established, as well as preparedness for punishment. The emphasis, in short, is persistently on conduct rather than theology, and this remains true in the second part of the *Analogy,* for "the Design of this Treatise is not to vindicate the Character of God, but to shew the Obligations of Men: It is not to justify His Providence, but to shew what belongs to Us to do" (410). This voice harmonized easily with those of Carlyle, Ruskin, or Arnold in the next age, and it is not hard to see why Butler was popular with Victorians much less certain of the existence of God than he. Leslie Stephen, for example, might scoff at Butler's logic and his style yet bow before the "grandeur" of his moral vision.[41]

Butler by no stretch of the imagination argues strictly on the basis of circumstantial evidence. The *Analogy of Religion* begins by emphatically denying human mortality, and this by resolutely bypassing the one piece of evidence most relevant to the question. Butler's initial chapter takes a long leap forward to what he calls in his introduction, with infinite circularity, "the Foundation of all our Hopes and of all our Fears; all our Hopes and Fears, which are of any Consideration; I mean a future Life" (xvi). The object leaped over and circled round is

---

41. Leslie Stephen, *History of English Thought in the Eighteenth Century,* 2 vols. (1876; rpt. New York: Harcourt, 1962), 1:235–61. Butler "staggers out of Doubting Castle with trembling knees and weary limbs. He puzzles out his track by such guidance as he can find, and that guidance is in substance that, whatever fails, a man must try to do his duty. That belief, if nothing else, is of heavenly origin" (260).

the human body, more especially the dead body. It is curious how abstract the purported foundation of natural religion and the life of probation can be. The best evidence, in this treatise launched in the name of circumstantial evidence, is ignored with a steadfastness that calls the whole enterprise into question. Butler actually proceeds by a series of a priori arguments such as that "since Consciousness is a single and indivisible Power, it should seem that the Subject in which it resides, must be so too" (24–25), or by an a priori rebuttal such as "we cannot argue from *the Reason of the thing,* that Death is the Destruction of living Agents, because we know not at all what Death is in itself; but only some of its Effects, such as the Dissolution of Flesh, Skin, and Bones" (22). The last phrase—"the Dissolution of Flesh, Skin, and Bones"— cliché though it may be, is the single most graphic expression in the entire *Analogy* for the body, the evidence of which tends to prove the termination of individual life. In sum, Butler simply offers a priori arguments about what is and will ever remain unseen, the human soul or no-body. Throughout he seems sincerely oblivious to his desertion of circumstantial evidence in favor of this hearsay of traditional belief, and his brute assertion that phenomenal death is not the end of life lays "the Foundation" of his belief in probation. Gladstone was frankly puzzled by the opening gambit of the *Analogy.* He could not understand why Butler was arguing merely for the survival instead of the immortality of the soul, and therefore he deemed the argument extraneous to that about government here and in the future life.[42] But having noted Butler's suppression of the evidence, we may speculate that survival is indeed the fact in issue.

Now inferences about murder in trials at law welcome the evidence of the body that natural religion rejects. Whereas Butler barely mentions the dissolution of flesh, skin, and bones and is not about to call for an autopsy to determine whether a soul has been injured or an indivisible power divided, the dead human body figures large in testimony in court about unnatural deaths and in the pages of the *State Trials.* "Murders," writes Stephen, "from the nature of the case, leave traces behind them which render it possible to apply the argument from effects to causes with greater force in these than in most other cases." As I shall argue shortly, there is a providential strain to these words, as there is in words describing the probations of natural religion, but at a minimum the "traces" rendering inference possible may be discoverable in the residue

42. Gladstone, *Studies Subsidiary to the Works of Bishop Butler,* 142–43, 151–59.

of the victim's body. The complementarity of law and religion turns on this corpse. Since natural religion contends that there is no death, every indication of the same is in a special sense "unnatural"; the criminal law actually specializes in unnatural death, but from a different, complementary point of view.

The common law—less partial than natural religion to the tenets of Christianity, and despite the elaborate formulas of its traditional indictments—readily supposes that persons die and directs inquiry to the issue of whether and to what degree another person is responsible. The corpus delicti, when the crime is homicide, is literally the body. Has the flesh been attacked, the skin penetrated, or a bone broken? Poisoning is historically the difficult case: there could be grave doubt whether a body had died of poison or of natural causes. Poison attacks the flesh unseen, and some remarkable trials for poisoning were published and incorporated in the *State Trials* because the postmortem testimony was excruciatingly detailed. Every nice question of how someone may have died unnaturally both persuades and distracts the reader curious about death: persuades of death because the dissected body is patently so lifeless, and distracts because this death may have been specially intended but was not yours or mine.

Though Stephen unerringly selects five murder cases, three of them poisonings, from the plentiful literature of the law, he makes relatively little use of the body, or of its remains turned inside out, in introducing the Indian Evidence Act—perhaps because, given the relative valuelessness of scientific evidence in such matters until very recent times, most of it was curiously irrelevant or of indeterminable relevancy. Some typical expert testimony does appear in his ample summary of *R v. Palmer*, from the postmortem of Palmer's friend:

> The heart was contracted and empty. There were numerous small yellowish white spots, about the size of mustard-seed, at the larger end of the stomach. The upper part of the spinal cord was in its natural state; the lower part was not examined till the 25th January [two months subsequently], when certain granules were found. There were many follicles on the tongue, apparently of long standing. The lungs appeared healthy to Dr. Harland, but Mr. Devonshire thought that there was some congestion. (*Introduction*, 102)

Why such details are any more relevant than the testimony of Dr. McDonald about delayed sexual convulsion, which Stephen looks down on as "extraordinary," he does not say, but he might have cited much more expert testimony of the same kind from *Palmer* and from *Donellan* as well, both of which trial transcripts he had studied in full.[43]

It is just because Stephen's narratives of the five trials are so chaste in respect to evidence of the body—as chaste as Butler's *Analogy*, indeed—that a far more casual illustration offered by his argument is both striking and revealing. In this illustration, another body inadvertently supplies the blood and tissue he might have reproduced from his sources and chose not to. The body is apparently his own: a casual example drawn from countless instances of the same kind—the bodies of persons anticipating no unnatural death at all. The passage occurs not in the chapter on relevancy, amid the five murder trials, but earlier, in the chapter on induction, within his definition of facts, which comprise both perceptions and inferences "as to what we should perceive if we were favourably situated for the purpose." Thus Stephen:

> The human body supplies an illustration of this. No one doubts that his own body is composed not only of the external organs which he perceives by his senses, but of numerous internal organs, most of which it is highly improbable that either he nor any one else will ever see or touch, and some of which he never can, from the nature of things, see or touch as long as he lives. When he affirms the existence of these organs, say the brain or the heart, what he means is that he is led to believe from what he has been told by other persons about human bodies, or observed himself in other human bodies, that if his skull and chest were laid open, these organs would be perceived by the senses of persons who might direct their senses towards them. (*Introduction,* 15)

Stephen is not given to symbolism or colorful writing, and the characteristic spareness of this passage makes it all the more moving. Of all the illustrations he might think of for inferring the existence of things unseen—such as the philosopher's cow that has passed out of sight behind the barn—he offers this one of the internal organs of the body, "the brain or the heart." He has already opened himself up on the dissection table, in anticipation of the scene of forensic medicine such as he had read in his sources. No meditated gesture could point more surely to the interest in the body displayed by a general theory of evidence.

Let us envision then, for the sake of argument, a single institution of representing reality in modern England, an institution that changes

43. For *Palmer,* see note 20 above; for *Donellan,* see *History of the Criminal Law,* 3:371n, where Stephen indicates that he has read both shorthand accounts of 1781. Wills's *Circumstantial Evidence,* in the section on the corpus delicti in murder cases (122–63), also

over time, responding to external events and to its own internal forces of habit and instruction, and composed of at least these two great departments of law and natural religion. The two departments evolve in roughly the same era, their theories of evidence intermingle freely, and both are alert to death. One department, however, denies death and the other fixes blame for it. Are natural religion and law opposed on this point, or do they rather hedge each other's bets? Religion, it seems, is a department whose services are more or less continuously open to everyone; law is intermittently adversarial. Religion lays claims to rewards as well as punishments; in law the rewards, if any, are always at someone else's expense. The difference that brings out a symbiotic relation of the two, however, is the difference between death and murder. All persons eventually die, but a few are murdered: the satisfactions of contemplating this inequality are manifold, even if not strictly logical. The main satisfaction would seem to flow from disappointment in one department to vengeance enacted by the other. The essential failure of natural religion to deliver the promised circumstantial proof of a future life is a disappointment that, historically, was never overcome. This inherent disappointment provokes the thought that at least those who intentionally cause death can be sought out and punished. Killing is for these purposes easier to deal with than death, because it always has an agent and sometimes a motive. People would not, should not, do not die, this combined institution protests, and then appears to leap at the possibility that some are killed. One can sometimes prove in the case of homicide what one can never prove about death: one can prove who is to blame. In the special case of murder, a form of scapegoating links "all our Hopes and Fears" of a future life to a specific trial of life and death for the murderer. A *double* ritual of willful death answers to the despair of unwilled death and its specious denial: the murderer obliges by killing someone with malice aforethought, and the law obliges by deliberately hanging the murderer. That this ritual of intended deaths somehow comforts is attested by the deep interest in the trial that negotiates between them. There is a kind of respect and loathing in the community for the pariah who forces a passage between life and death, but the desecration of the body is finally easier to comprehend than the inviolability of the soul.[44] In sum, the intensely concrete, retrospective

---

contains more dissections of the body than necessary to his purposes. That Wills takes a sensible and balanced approach to his subject obviously does not check his interest in reading and passing on such lore.

44. That two of Stephen's five illustrations involved the murder of pregnant women seems to intensify the underlying ritual compensation of his notion of relevancy.

narrative that shapes itself from the trial compensates for the vague prospect of a future life available from natural religion; the satisfaction in representing and proving an unseen crime on the basis of facts and inferences from the facts counters the elusive evidence of Christianity shorn from the testimony of its saints; the trial of somebody who evidently deserves to be tried is easier than the probation natural religion holds in store for all.

If murder thus compensates for death, and trial of a few for the probation of the many, it can further be noted that well into the nineteenth century the sentiments of natural religion were directly supportive of the use of evidence at law. As views of society gradually deserted natural theology for natural history, the providential soundness of circumstantial evidence was still a note frequently heard. The closer the sense of interconnectedness in time as well as space, the greater opportunity of inference from fact to fact in the social organism. This interconnectedness is a blessing, because it ensures that crimes touch on so many minute events in the total scheme of things that they can readily be detected. Thomas Starkie, barrister and later professor of law at Cambridge, writes of "the nature of circumstantial evidence, and of the principles on which it is founded," as follows:

> Fortunately for the existence of society, crimes, especially those of great enormity and violence, can rarely be committed without affording vestiges by which the offender may be traced and ascertained. The very measures which he adopts for his security not unfrequently turn out to be the most cogent arguments of guilt. On the other hand, it is to be recollected that this is a species of evidence which requires the utmost degree of caution and vigilance in its application.

By the time Starkie was writing this (the first edition of his treatise on evidence was published in 1824, a fourth edition posthumously in 1853), the movement of crime prevention and the rise of public opinion had thrown greater emphasis on "the secrecy with which crimes are committed," and an atmosphere of mystery and ritual of detection, such as captured in the novels of Dickens or Balzac, further enhanced the popular faith that murder will out. "Happy it is for the interests of society," Starkie repeats a few pages on, "that forcible injuries can seldom be perpetrated without leaving many and plain vestiges by which the guilty agent may be traced and detected."[45]

45. Thomas Starkie, *A Practical Treatise of the Law of Evidence*, 3d ed., 3 vols. (London: Stevens and Norton, 1842), 1:558–59, 562.

Such doctrine about the nature of reality provides an ample context in which to place Stephen's confidence that murders, though "concealed with as much care as possible," generate enough evidence to hone the edge of induction. The implicit reflection on the providential availability of circumstantial evidence was still more common in the Victorian era, when a natural religionist and a common-law judge might be one and the same person. Jonathan Frederick Pollock, who presided in *R v. Manning*, was a long-lived friend of James Stephen, and the two families were closely connected over several generations.[46] Here are two excerpts from another of Pollock's charges to the jury, in another case of murder, *R v. Kohl* (1865). First the familiar endorsement of the evidence in general:

> Gentlemen, there ought to be as much legal certainty as there can be in any human affairs; and the rule that Lord Tenterden laid down (and I pronounce it in his very words) was "that a jury should be persuaded of the guilt of the prisoner before they found him guilty, to the same extent, and they ought to have the same certainty, that they would require in the transaction of their own most important concerns." This is *my* comment, gentlemen: *They ought to have the highest degree of certainty which the practical business of life admits of. Demonstration is not required; absolute certainty is not required, for it is really unattainable in any case whatever.*

This message about the jury's, or the congregation's, absolution from certainty goes back to the seventeenth century, as we have seen. With no little feeling for his own comment, Pollock goes on to explain that circumstantial evidence is nothing other than "the language of facts," which he then dresses in a regular halo of providential design:

> Gentlemen, this language, as I have called it, "the language of facts," is really that in which God speaks to us in the works and operations of Nature; and by those facts we are told of His goodness, His wisdom, and His power. It is a language understood by infancy; for long before the infant at the breast has learnt to utter an articulate sound by the ordinary forms of speech, that infant at the breast has learnt the language of facts, and before it can speak it understands what is the result of one circumstance occurring and another following, and it knows that there is a connexion between the two circumstances. Indeed, gentlemen, it is

46. See Leslie Stephen, *Life of Sir James Fitzjames Stephen*, 140, 173. Pollock was the grandfather of Frederick Pollock, F. W. Maitland's collaborator and the correspondent of Holmes (note 4 above). Maitland himself wrote *The Life and Letters of Leslie Stephen* (1906).

the language of all intelligent nature—it is the language in which history teaches those who are willing to learn. . . . This sort of evidence, whether you call it "circumstantial evidence," or "inductive testimony," or whatever name you give to it, has this merit—generally speaking, the facts are those which occur in the natural course of things, not created [i.e., by man] for the purpose.

Kohl was duly convicted and hanged, and according to Pollack's grandson and biographer, this "summing up was printed and afterwards circulated to those interested in such matter."[47] To suppose the argument interesting for its own sake is to underscore once again an intimate connection between a system of representation, "the language of facts," and murder.

Despite Stephen's primary identification of reasoning in a court of law with induction in science, his thoughts on the subject exhibit a firm prosecutorial bent and some distant sense of providential outcome. As we have seen, when he offers to explain relevancy he conceives of evidence as if it were solely concerned with murder and likely to result in conviction. He seems to have entered upon adult life with some feeling for natural religion, but always with an agnostic reservation: "What little we have reason to believe about that unseen world is that it exists, that it contains extremes of good and evil, awful and mysterious beyond human conception and that these tremendous possibilities are connected with our conduct here."[48] Like others of his time, he became more and more cautious about ascribing conditions to "that unseen world," though he could not let go of the idea that some form of sanctions was necessary to enforce morality.[49] In Leon Radzinowicz's words, his was "a creed of conduct, not of faith,"[50] and such a position, obviously, was still congruent with Butler's on the one hand and with that of Victorians like George Eliot on the other, who believed that the waning of religion made morality of greater concern than ever. Stephen chose to conclude his *History of the Criminal Law of England* with a paean not to duty but to the sanctions of the law. Since "the religious sanction in particular has been immensely weakened," there was all the more reason to value the "one unquestionable, indisputable sanction" of the

47. Lord Hanworth [Ernest Murray Pollock], *Lord Chief Baron Pollock: A Memoir* (London: Murray, 1929), 182–85.
48. Stephen, "Christian Optimism," *Essays of a Barrister* (London: Smith, Elder, 1862), 121.
49. Leslie Stephen, *Life of Sir James Fitzjames Stephen,* 370–72.
50. Radzinowicz, *Sir James Fitzjames Stephen,* 12.

criminal law.[51] Thus near the close of his life he may have lost what faith he had in religion, but not in the law.

Fitzjames Stephen had neither morality nor natural religion in mind when he wrote the Indian Evidence Act and composed his *Introduction*. He wished to ground the law of evidence in the community's wider need for representations of fact, which were characterized for persons of his class in England more by science than religion. Accordingly, in his chapter on the principles of induction he followed Mill's *System of Logic* and his own sense of scientific investigations. Stephen was too shrewd and open a thinker not to discern important differences between representations in a court of law and in science. Trials must concentrate on a single set of circumstances, arrive at an answer rather quickly, and without the advantage of trained observers. Yet in two respects judicial inquiries seemed to him to have an advantage over science: they need only be "approximate" and, "being limited in extent, the process of reaching as good a conclusion as is to be got out of the materials is far easier than the process of establishing a scientific conclusion with complete certainty" (*Introduction*, 33–34). The turn taken by these last differences might appear calamitous to some litigants or prisoners. All the differences from science, however, reflect the urgency of arriving at a verdict. Stephen's emphasis on the practical and the exigent recalls the observation of natural theologians that the business of life has to be conducted with the knowledge at hand, and in practice the need to reach a verdict reinvests the courts with quasi-divine, because *imper*fectly comprehended, means of arriving at the truth.

These compromises with scientific representation were judicious, so to speak. Stephen might also have stressed the adversary tradition of the common law. In anticipation of a verdict, each side makes strong representations in court, more biased than the investigations of science. But in his third and longest chapter Stephen abandoned science altogether for narrative, and narrative of a very special kind. Again he does not have religion particularly in mind, yet he remystifies the subject of evidence by concentrating exclusively on stories of murder. His examples of relevancy begin to imply that proofs of murder especially warrant the evidence of things not seen. Moreover, his hurried paragraph of explanation suggests that he has just barely become conscious that his five illustrations are murder cases. There are sufficient murders in the *State Trials* and treatises to alert us to the possible connection of

---

51. Stephen, *History of the Criminal Law,* 3:367. Cf. Alexander Welsh, *George Eliot and Blackmail* (Cambridge: Harvard University Press, 1985), 86–87.

the crime with general theories of evidence since the eighteenth century. Attitudes toward death in natural religion and evidence at common law are complementary. Natural religion denies the fact of death; the law seeks to establish it. The prime achievement of an argument from circumstances in one institution is the assurance of a future life; the prime achievement in the other is proof of willful killing. In the construction of evidence at law there is possibly a motive of vengeance that answers to religious hope: thus a person who willfully demonstrates that humans can die ought to be found and convicted. There is also a faith in providential discovery and proof: the murderer will always be found and convicted. This scapegoating is not strictly for the sins of the community, such as the punishment of murderers provides, but for a failure of inference—failure of the argument for a future life conducted by natural religion, also from circumstantial evidence. If that argument, to which all persons are party, fails of conviction, then at least it can be proved that a few persons (not the community and not God) are responsible for willful death. And from the side of the law, specialists in unnatural death can imagine, as if they were all writing detective novels, that murder is the hardest crime to prove—hence a model for inductive reasoning of a particularly stringent kind.

The Extinction of Whole Species

The entire history of science is inseparable from questions of evidence—a consideration that makes it both presumptuous to mention science here and perverse not to. Sometime around the seventeenth century, whether or not with such precipitancy as Ian Hacking suggests, human inquiries in many fields began to depend less and less on the evidence of authority or witnessing and more and more on the evidence of things.[52] Broadly considered, science has not advanced without carefully represented direct *and* indirect evidence, more often than not initially by some strong representation of the same. At a certain point—and this argument was already inherent in Bacon's philosophy—empiricism cannot rest content with evidence immediately available to the senses; the evidence of things on which it rests is thenceforth indirect or circumstantial. John Herschel concedes this necessity for indirection in 1830, when he writes of the verification of scientific theories in these terms:

> the mechanism of nature is for the most part either on too large or too small a scale to be immediately cognizable by our senses; and her agents

52. See chapter 1, note 15.

in like manner elude direct observation, and become known to us only by their effects. It is in vain that we desire to become witnesses to the processes carried on with such means, and to be admitted to the secret recesses and laboratories where they are effected.

Even microscopes, Herschel regrets, do not allow one to see the structure or chemical properties of matter. The study of the planetary system involves the opposite problems of perspective, and "again, the agents employed by nature to act on material structures are invisible, and only to be traced by the effects they produce." From this eloquent concession to things not seen, he moves on to the need for metaphor in theorizing about them.[53]

Two sciences, geology and biology—both widely supported by amateur, untheoretical natural history—strained earlier conceptions of nature and humanity beyond belief; and these two sciences stirred popular as well as professional imaginations in the nineteenth century. What lay concealed in the mechanism of nature for chemistry and physics to discover, in Herschel's terms, was doubly concealed for the historicizing sciences, since most of the effects as well as causes they studied were no longer visible. Evidentially, geology and biology were on a different footing than chemistry and physics because of their dependence on the chance remains of things lost in time. The evidence—merely effects without causes—had to be arranged still more ingeniously, with proportionately far less to go on amid vast stretches of time, than a Morgann could provide for Falstaff or a Jones for Hamlet; and it could be arranged only by constructing such narratives as came to be known as catastrophism, or the story of sudden changes in the earth, and uniformitarianism, or the idea that existing processes could account for past changes (small wonder there were competing narratives). Paleontology required skilled observation like other sciences, but occasions for observation could not be set up at will: studies of past causes and effects were basically deprived of experiment. The relations obtained in the secret recesses of nature mentioned by Herschel but not in laboratories. Thus the closing of Lyell's science to experiment goes a long way to excuse the rhetorical drive of his uniformitarianism. If Lyell was bent on seeing geology as a true "history of nature," a science that would investigate "the successive changes that have taken place in the organic and inorganic kingdoms of nature," then, precisely because history cannot be reproduced in a laboratory, he had to insist on "the undevi-

53. J. F. W. Herschel, *A Preliminary Discourse on the Study of Natural Philosophy* (London: Longman, 1830), 191–93.

ating uniformity of secondary causes" to make the narrative persuasive. If one can simply invent causes, as Lyell implies catastrophists do, then in the absence of experiment anything can be proved. To use the phrase from the subtitle of *Principles of Geology,* only "causes now in operation" provide a rational ground of historical explanation.[54]

Since the strata of the earth's crust are open to observation only in certain locations and the fossil record of earlier forms of life is intermittent at best, paleontology is an art par excellence of constructing narrative from circumstantial evidence, and indeed it was recognized as such by writers on evidence at common law. Some authorities complimented Cuvier, the great French catastrophist, rather than the barrister Lyell for this achievement, even though they might be sowing uniformitarian sentiments in their own fields. Thus Thomas Starkie, barrister, argues that "it is probable that whatever has happened will happen again under similar circumstances, however ignorant we may be of the nature or necessity of the connexion" and appends a footnote on "the extent to which philosophical inferences may be carried" in comparative anatomy: "From a single fossil bone of an animal whose very species is extinct, a skilful anatomist is able to represent the original animal in all its parts. — See Cuvier's Fossil Remains."[55] Cuvier's feat of representation appears again in the edition of William Wills's *Circumstantial Evidence* that, as we have seen, provided four of Stephen's five murder stories:

> A profound knowledge of comparative anatomy enabled the immortal Cuvier, from a single fossil bone, to describe the structure and habits of many of the animals of the antediluvian world. In like manner, an enlightened knowledge of human nature often enables us, on the foundation of apparently slight circumstances, to follow the tortuous windings of crime, and ultimately to discover its guilty author, as infallibly as the hunter is conducted by the track to his game.[56]

That the single fossil bone now points to "many" extinct animals, and by analogy to a singular crime and the hunting down of a still living beast, suggests the loose hagiolatry of science and the popularity of the subject in Victorian times. Stephen himself reminds readers of his *Introduction* that Thomas Huxley compared the "mental process" of de-

---

54. Charles Lyell, *Principles of Geology: Being an Attempt to Explain the Former Changes of the Earth's Surface by Reference to Causes Now in Operation,* 3 vols. (1830–33; rpt. New York: Johnson, 1969), 1:1–2, 76.
55. Starkie, *Practical Treatise of the Law of Evidence,* 1:566–67.
56. Wills, *Essay on the Principles of Circumstantial Evidence,* 27.

tectives to that of Cuvier.[57] In the same decade, Walter Bagehot wrote, "The discovery of a law of nature is very like the discovery of a murder. In the one case you arrest a suspected person, and in the other you isolate a suspected cause." Patently Bagehot has the historically oriented sciences in mind, for he goes on to cite Lyell, in support of his own discussion of business administration.[58]

If theorizing about circumstantial evidence in the law came of age with natural religion in England—and played a complementary role in attitudes toward death, as I have suggested—so most certainly did the new geology and biology come of age. Not only were most natural historians confessed natural religionists, but they amassed the specimens of animals, plants, and minerals, the collections of fossils, the evidence of stunning adaptations on which these sciences relied. Striving to elaborate and thereby to confirm the narrative of God's design, they strengthened the very habits of thinking that would serve a different plot, called natural selection, after 1859.[59] Reassurances from the authors of the Bridgewater Treatises—and from Herschel too, for that matter—prepared a safer atmosphere for Darwin's theory, and enthusiasm for natural religion fueled scientific research much as it had the prosecution of crime. The geologist William Buckland, for example, devoted a chapter of his treatise to showing how bloodshed in the animal kingdom was warranted on both divine and utilitarian principles. Buckland's admiration for sudden death was unstinted:

> By the existing dispensations of sudden destruction and rapid succession, the feeble and disabled are speedily relieved from suffering, and the world is at all times crowded with myriads of sentient and happy beings; and and though to many individuals their allotted share of life be often short, it is usually a period of uninterrupted gratification; whilst the momentary pain of sudden and unexpected death is an evil infinitely small, in comparison with the enjoyments of which it is the termination.

57. Stephen, *Introduction*, 13. For Huxley's comparison of Cuvier to a detective policeman, made on 22 July 1854, see Thomas Huxley, *Lay Sermons, Addresses and Reviews* (London: Macmillan, 1880), 78. Sherlock Holmes subsequently co-opted the idea in "The Five Orange Pips": see Arthur Conan Doyle, *The Adventures of Sherlock Holmes,* 2 vols. (London: Smith, Elder, 1903), 1:158.

58. "The Postulates of English Political Economy," no. 1 (1876), in *The Collected Works of Walter Bagehot,* ed. Norman St. John Stevas, 15 vols. (London: Economist, 1965–86), 11:231–32.

59. See Martin J. S. Rudwick, *The Great Devonian Controversy: The Shaping of Scientific Knowledge among Gentlemanly Specialists* (Chicago: University of Chicago Press, 1985), 17–41; and on natural religion, George Levine, *Darwin and the Novelists: Patterns of Science in Victorian Fiction* (Cambridge: Harvard University Press, 1988), 24–55.

Precisely the sort of deaths that lawyers are constrained to call unnatural, the scientist can celebrate as natural. Of course, Buckland exempts humanity from his observations, because "for moral reasons peculiar to our own species, we depreciate the *sudden* termination of our mortal life"; yet, writing only two years after the New Poor Law, he is also transforming Malthusian pessimism for humanity into exuberant optimism for animals. The carnivorous species he calls, within quotation marks, the "police of Nature," and he remarks that "in absence of carnivora, the uncontrolled herbivora would multiply indefinitely, until the lack of food brought them also to the verge of starvation; and the sea would be crowded with creatures under the endurance of universal pain from hunger, while death by famine would be the termination of ill fed and miserable lives." Neither the personification of these sufferers nor the inverted role of the police (here functioning as systematic killers) seems to strike Buckland as odd; his nature is sanctified by "the dispensations of a creation founded in benevolence, and tending to produce the greatest amount of enjoyment to the greatest number of individuals." Or if these two principles should not suffice, the cycle of nature can be compared to a banking system for depositing bodies and parts of bodies, as follows: "life to each individual is a scene of continuous feasting, in a region of plenty; and when unexpected death arrests its course, it repays with small interest the large debt, which it has contracted to the common fund of animal nutrition, from whence the materials of its body have been derived."[60] Somewhat Panglossian this argument may also be, but it might be urged that such evidently Malthusian conditions of existence had to be embraced enthusiastically by science before natural selection could be realized as a theory—and a theory with the potential of displacing natural religion altogether. Darwin understood his debt to Malthus, but he too was anxious to restrict the application of his thoughts as much as possible at first to life stories other than human. In the nineteenth century, theories of death and extinction were a knife that cut one way if one believed nature included humanity and the other way if not.

Both catastrophists and uniformitarians managed to adhere to natural religion and to take advantage of arguments from circumstantial evidence that it had already provided. Catastrophists like Buckland could be said to be closer to revealed religion because of the story of the flood in Genesis, but they might more usefully be said to read the fossil record

---

60. William Buckland, *Geology and Mineralogy Considered with Reference to Natural Theology*, Bridgewater Treatise 6 (London: Pickering, 1836), 129–34.

differently.[61] Uniformitarians like Lyell were ostensibly more progressive and could even make fun of their opponents' supposedly primitive explanations. Lyell owed his progressive image—his relative secularism and considerable influence—to an alliance with contemporary historiography.[62] His history of the earth was indeed conclusive—a strong representation of gradual changes caused by familiar forces, notable more for its argument than for its confrontation of new evidence. The conclusion was also intended to be reassuring, like that of a historical novel such as *Waverley*: while changes had obviously occurred in the past, nothing untoward or unreasonable need be expected in the present or future. Scott too was a uniformitarian when it came to the consistent causes of history—both his theory and Lyell's were somewhat at odds with their perceived contributions to a particular knowledge of the past.[63] The success of uniformitarianism in establishing geology *as* history nevertheless may have increased the discomfiture, to nearly anyone, of the evidence of past extinctions. Fossils had been lying about for centuries, and people knew more or less how they were formed, but in this era they became evidence for the extinction of whole species[64]— evidence, that is, of something wrong, for what was the need of creating species only to destroy them, and what was the fate of species even now enjoying eating or being eaten? Extinction of species implied a very lopsided universe if only human individuals somehow survived

61. Cf. Gould, *Time's Arrow, Time's Cycle* (note 7 above), 167–79. That Lyell was making a strong representation, in effect, is the point of M. J. S. Rudwick, "The Strategy of Lyell's *Principles of Geology*," *Isis* 61 (1970): 4–33. See also Rudwick's *The Meaning of Fossils: Episodes in the History of Palaeontology*, 2d ed. (New York: Science History Publications, 1976), 164–217.

62. Cf. Roy Porter, "Charles Lyell and the Principles of the History of Geology," *British Journal for the History of Science* 9 (1976): 91–103.

63. While I agree with Gould, *Time's Arrow, Time's Cycle*, that Lyell was writing a brief for a certain "stately" vision of time, I am not sure that this vision can be equated either with the arrow or with the cycle. Gould cites Mircea Eliade on these two ways of viewing time (12–15), but Eliade shrewdly observed that those who think of history as irreversible usually also foresee a stopping of time altogether—such is their terror of time's arrow, as it were. It is this difficulty that I find in Lyell as well as in Scott: in spite of their uniformitarianism, they deeply believe that history is about over with—at least as far as anything truly disruptive is concerned. To believe anything less would be to depreciate the achievement of nature or of civilization. Cf. Eliade, *The Myth of the Eternal Return*, trans. Willard R. Trask (New York: Pantheon, 1954), 147–54.

64. Cf. Ernst Mayr, *The Growth of Biological Thought: Diversity, Evolution, and Inheritance* (Cambridge: Harvard University Press, 1982), 319–20, 347–49, 406. The title page of *Principles of Geology*, vol. 2, features some sentences from John Playfair's *Illustrations of the Huttonian Theory of the Earth* (1802), including, "It is not only the individual that perishes, but whole species."

death. "The reader"—of Lyell's *Principles of Geology*—"has only to reflect on what we have said of the habitations and the stations of organic beings in general, and . . . the igneous and aqueous causes now in action, and he will immediately perceive that, amidst the viscissitudes of the earth's surface, species cannot be immortal, but must perish one after the other, like the individuals which compose them."[65] Construing geology and then biology as immense historical narratives implied the ubiquity and inescapability of natural laws, which were popularized for a time as merely operating rules of Providence.[66] But historical science also meant accepting contingency as part of the rational order of existence, and while history does seek explanations, it often first brutally indicates simply what happened.

How it affected one to think of these matters, to read *Principles of Geology* and weigh the evidence of extinction, are some of the experiences reflected in Tennyson's meticulous poem—for which we have also to thank his melancholic disposition and the pure contingency of his friend's death, with all the other contingencies of life stories. We know so much about Alfred Tennyson (1809–92) that it is scarcely possible to read *In Memoriam* as a fiction. When editors document his deliberate deviations from fact or honest mistakes of memory, it only directs attention to the history of composition of the poem—with glacial slowness, it sometimes seems—from 1833 to its publication in 1850. Indeed, understanding of the poem owes much to A. C. Bradley, whose *Commentary* appeared at the end of the Victorian era.[67] Very briefly, Tennyson composed at different intervals short poems on Arthur Hallam's death and his own experience of loss; he established his particular stanzaic form for this purpose and gradually arranged 131 poems in a narrative sequence. What conventionally might have been an English elegiac poem emerged as a broken story of mourning over a period of ostensibly three years, with an epilogue celebrating the marriage of Tennyson's youngest sister, Cecilia, a full nine years after the death of Hallam—who had been engaged to another sister, Emily. Thus *In Memoriam* tells more about the mourner than the mourned, more about a present threat to the poet's life and to all life than about the death of

---

65. Lyell, *Principles of Geology*, 2:168–69. Graham Hough, "The Natural Theology of *In Memoriam*," *Review of English Studies* 23 (1947): 250, detects "a certain undertone of sombre relish in Lyell's writings on these topics."

66. For example, Robert Chambers, *Vestiges of the Natural History of Creation* (London: Churchill, 1844), 152–64.

67. A. C. Bradley, *A Commentary on Tennyson's "In Memoriam"* (London: Macmillan, 1901).

the friend, which evidences and suggests these things. Tennyson believed that the poem spoke for most people who might read it, and its reception seems to have borne him out. The "I" of the poem, he said, "is not always the author speaking of himself, but the voice of the human race speaking through him." After it was published, Tennyson married Emily Sellwood and was named poet laureate. When he visited Queen Victoria after the death of Prince Albert, in 1862, she apparently told him, "Next to the Bible 'In Memoriam' is my comfort."[68] Much as Stephen Jay Gould has argued that Lyell creatively confused the accepted practices of science with his history of the earth so as to make the latter eminently reasonable, A. Dwight Culler has suggested that Tennyson adopted his verse narrative to his own belief in gradualism.[69] Undoubtedly the uniformitarianism of In Memoriam itself contributed to its popularity; somehow the terrible contingency of things would have a happy resolution.

"Is this the end? Is this the end?"[70] The questions, in an early section of the poem, sequentially seem to complain of the wasting of the poet's love for Hallam and to demand whether death is the end of everything. The complaint, though selfish, is likely to gain a more sympathetic ear today than the demand that begins to mount with the question's repetition. The poet's "wounded narcissism" needs tending, it has been said, for his concern is "not merely the loss of his friend but the threatened survival, in time, of his own selfhood."[71] And Tennyson did very well on that score, since the story of his grief through three Christmases and the wedding of his sister restored him to himself and established his career as a poet. The second meaning of the line, or the general questioning of death by In Memoriam, can seem querulous today, perhaps because in the absence of public debate, belief in a future life has now settled down on one side or the other. Thus that "to have staked his whole theological position on the survival of personality after death marks a limitation in Tennyson's grasp of religion" is another twentieth-century view.[72] But Victorians were more used to talking about death

68. Hallam Tennyson, *Alfred Lord Tennyson: A Memoir*, 2 vols. (London: Macmillan 1897), 1:305, 485.

69. See Gould, *Time's Arrow, Time's Cycle*, 117–32; and A. Dwight Culler, *The Poetry of Tennyson* (New Haven: Yale University Press, 1977), 159–61.

70. *In Memoriam*, 12.16. Quotations are from *The Poems of Tennyson*, ed. Christopher Ricks (see above, note 5), and are cited by section and line numbers in parentheses.

71. Peter M. Sacks, *The English Elegy: Studies in the Genre from Spenser to Yeats* (Baltimore: Johns Hopkins University Press, 1985), 171–72.

72. Paul F. Baum, *Tennyson Sixty Years After* (Chapel Hill: University of North Carolina Press, 1948), 132.

than we are and were prone to believe immortality crucial to morality. Survival beyond death *was* Tennyson's main religious concern, just as it had been Bishop Butler's, and the poem won him great respect. He was prepared if necessary to do without circumstantial proof, and that pronouncement also pleased his readers.

The early sections of *In Memoriam* notably confront the evidence of the dead body. Grieving for Hallam becomes the occasion for sorting out what is not seen from what is seen of human life, what is hoped for from what is felt. The prologue, written in 1849, summarizes in its opening stanzas the position that Tennyson finally prefers to a review of the evidence.

> Strong Son of God, immortal Love,
> Whom we, that have not seen thy face,
> By faith, and faith alone, embrace,
> Believing where we cannot prove;
>
> Thine are these orbs of light and shade;
> Thou madest Life in man and brute;
> Thou madest Death; and lo, thy foot
> Is on the skull which thou hast made.
>
> Thou wilt not leave us in the dust:
> Thou madest man, he knows not why,
> He thinks he was not made to die;
> And thou hast made him: thou art just.

So far from being indebted to natural religion, this prayer that serves instead of a finding on the facts is Pauline, based as it is on the epistles to the Hebrews and to the Corinthians. Tennyson literally returns to Paul's equation of "the evidence of things not seen" with faith and his promise that Christ shall "put all enemies under his feet," including "the last enemy" that is death.[73] At the same time, "the skull" as evidence is present in the foreground, accompanied by the inference that all die—however obliquely stated as a condition wished away ("Thou wilt not leave us in the dust"). The religious issue of death is also framed by the narrative of creation, with traditional allusions to divine responsibility and justice. Though the stanzas reaffirm faith—no questions asked—they are not devoid of logic and the hope of striking a bargain.

---

73. Cf. Hebrews 11:1, "Now faith is the substance of things hoped for, the evidence of things not seen"; and 1 Corinthians 15:25–26, "For he must reign, till he hath put all enemies under his feet. The last enemy that shall be destroyed is death. For he hath put all things under his feet." Ricks, in his note, credits J. Kolb for the allusion to 1 Corinthians.

Since creation is supreme and includes every sentient wish, it would be unjust or inconsistent to deny what man "thinks," and still more can be expected of God's love. The evidence of creation was familiar ground for natural religion, and the poem persists in sampling arguments from design that favor immortality even when they fail. *In Memoriam*—seventeen years in the making—follows in the wake of geology as well as religion, but Tennyson is determinedly outspoken about what he holds to be true a priori.

In those years he read Lyell's *Principles of Geology* (already in its fourth edition by 1835).[74] Yet news of the endlessly changing surface of the earth and the extinction of whole species did not necessarily make the author of *In Memoriam* feel worse about the death of his friend. It does not inform, for example, the lyrics beginning "Old yew" (2.1) and "Dark house" (8.1), which run so movingly to despair. On the contrary, the geology in the poem often underwrites a certain pathetic fallacy, as news of slower changes in the earth braces the mind stoically for the abrupt changes of individual life. In a section that—like the prologue itself—tends to echo the devotional poetry of George Herbert, the voice of uniformitarianism helps to quiet both a macabre murmuring from the grave and love's helplessness. The section begins with testimony about the body again:

> Yet if some voice that man could trust
>   Should murmur from the narrow house,
>   "The cheeks drop in; the body bows;
> Man dies: nor is there hope in dust:"
>
> Might I not say? "Yet even here,
>   But for one hour, O Love, I strive
>   To keep so sweet a thing alive:"
> But I should turn mine ears and hear
>
> The moanings of the homeless sea,
>   The sound of streams that swift or slow
>   Draw down Æonian hills, and sow
> The dust of continents to be;
>
> And Love would answer with a sigh,
>   "The sound of that forgetful shore
>   Will change my sweetness more and more,
> Half-dead to know that I shall die."

74. See Hallam Tennyson, *Memoir*, 1:162; and *Letters of Alfred Lord Tennyson*, 1:145.

The downturn of this section seems to occur with "But" in the eighth line and the poet's hearkening to nature, for in two additional stanzas Tennyson seeks to dismiss the entire conversation as an "idle case," by arguing that "if Death were seen / At first as Death," love would never arise except in gross sensual shapes (35.1–16, 18–19). Minimally, that argument refers simply to the history of his feelings for Hallam, which excluded the idea of death, though as elsewhere in the poem it also turns on desperation: unless one believes in a future life, love cannot be; and love has to be. Yet the turn that ostensibly pains him, from the dust that was a man like Hallam to "the dust of continents to be," is actually constructive in its reference to the slow formation of new land masses. Both the sick mourner, striving to keep Hallam's corpse alive, and love whose "sweetness" is subject to decay may well look to the changes wrought by rivers, wind, and sea, which are satisfyingly concrete but so gradual as not to be badly threatening. To the mourner, the death of Hallam *is* catastrophic; the geology of the poem is not. On reflection, the vast changes of the universe and extinction of whole species make the poet and his readers feel not worse but better.

Three sections of *In Memoriam* confront the scientific news of extinctions head on. In all three the evidence reviewed forces the poet to fall back weakly on his faith: the verb is "trust" in the first two, and the third ends with a refusal to think about the issue — "Behind the veil, behind the veil" (56.28), a double answer to the earlier questions, "Is this the end? Is this the end?" The new doubling suggests both temporal and epistemological veilings, impairment of the senses by death and by ignorance regardless of death one way or the other. Hence these sections are often cited as the bleakest of responses to early Victorian geology. Yet Tennyson's stanzas famously circle about with ends of their own,[75] and in conjunction the three sections manage to use up the evidence of extinction rather than bow to it. The first, though professing only faith, contains its science within an argument of natural religion:

> That nothing walks with aimless feet;
> That not one life shall be destroyed,
> Or cast as rubbish to the void,
> When God hath made the pile complete;
>
> That not a worm is cloven in vain;
> That not a moth with vain desire

75. Cf. Christopher Ricks, *Tennyson* (New York: Macmillan, 1972), 227–30.

Is shriveled in a fruitless fire,
Or but subserves another's gain.
(54.5–12)

The juxtaposition of these two stanzas at first seems to parody the argument from design—though no more so than the solemn assurance of William Buckland that "while each suffering individual is soon relieved from pain, it contributes its enfeebled carcase to the support of its carnivorous benefactor."[76] Tennyson is far from intending parody, since he instances the whole argument as an article of faith. His point is that worms are cloven willy-nilly, and moths fly into flames without being crazy, because they are creatures of nature. No more than Buckland will he allow that humanity and nature are the same, though he broaches this subject in the section that follows:

The wish, that of the living whole
No life may fail beyond the grave,
Derives it not from what we have
The likest God within the soul?

Are God and Nature then at strife,
That Nature lends such evil dreams?
So careful of the type she seems,
So careless of the single life;

That I, considering everywhere
Her secret meaning in her deeds,
And finding that of fifty seeds
She often brings but one to bear,

I falter where I firmly trod,
And falling with my weight of cares
Upon the great world's altar-stairs
That slope through darkness up to God,

I stretch lame hands of faith, and grope,
And gather dust and chaff, and call
To what I feel is Lord of all,
And faintly trust the larger hope.
(55.1–20)

76. Buckland, *Geology and Mineralogy,* 132.

Here the task posed for natural religion—why the evidence points only to the survival of species and never of individuals—is so strenuous that Tennyson soft-pedals it as the difference between "careful" and "careless," in two lines that have nonetheless resonated ever since *In Memoriam* was published. Except to put the question, he will modestly have none of it: modesty is the keynote of the entire section, for even the dramatic falling beneath the altar of God is framed by a "wish" and a "hope" first and last. Logically the poet is not positioned between Nature and God, as the drama on the altar stair begins to suggest, but still on the side of God against Nature and the study of nature, as in the first two stanzas. "Are God and Nature then at strife"—perhaps the most famous question in a poem of nearly as many questions as *Hamlet*[77]—is thus a partial substitution for the question, Are Tennyson and science utterly opposed? As with "careful" and "careless," the locution sidesteps the issue of individual survival after death. Both God and Nature, after all, are constructs that help keep people and poets out of the fray, away from the need to decide this issue on the evidence.

Rhetorically, Tennyson holds the issue of extinction in reserve for the section that follows, where it is introduced with great effect, as if in dire answer to the argument above:

> "So careful of the type?" but no.
>   From scarpèd cliff and quarried stone
>   She cries, "A thousand types are gone:
> I care for nothing, all shall go."
>
>   (56.1–4)

The female pronoun identifies this voice as Nature's, and the poet pulls out all the stops from his reading of Lyell and other up-to-date science.[78] Yet the foot of this cliff and bottom of the quarry, sites where the evidence of extinction of whole species has been exposed, are not the nadir of the poem. For one thing, the evidence of extinction contravenes—as the voice states—the lines of the previous section, in which the poet felt he was approaching a nearly insurmountable problem for religion. But further, with extinction geology has introduced something worse than death, which operates as murder does on the imagination

77. Cf. Harry Levin, *The Question of Hamlet* (1959; rpt. New York: Viking, 1961), 17–43.

78. With a nice sense of history, Eleanor B. Mattes, *"In Memoriam": The Way of a Soul* (New York: Exposition, 1951), 58–59, suggests that section 55 derives from Butler's writings but section 56 from Lyell's.

of Hamlet. In grieving, as Hamlet grieves for his father and Tennyson for his friend, the mind seems to want to dwell on worse and worst cases—and of course I have argued above that dwelling on the evidence for murder was a way of compensating for natural religion's inadequate assurances of a future life. If anyone ever complained of that inadequacy in a poem—or poem after poem strung together as *In Memoriam*—it was Tennyson, and in these sections we find him engaged in the strategy of contemplating worse and worst cases. There is his personal loss, which is the occasion of the poem and of the feelings he struggles with. There is the evidence of biology that every individual perishes and only species survive in any meaningful sense, which is intellectually worse news. And there is the truth of geology that species have become extinct, the worst news. But these horrors, which are also progressively remote, are strangely satisfying to anyone who has suffered a unique loss: that is why the poet touches on them the way he does.

Thus Queen Victoria was not an unperceptive reader of the poem. Everyone notices that the narrative of *In Memoriam* is melioristic: the poet's mood lightens, the episodes of mourning reflect increasing confidence, a few sections recast earlier ones in more optimistic language. The epitome of the poem's geology lessons is usually said to be the section beginning "Contemplate all this work of Time," and obviously Tennyson would not extend this invitation so unguardedly were not time to be viewed confidently at this point. Based on the idea that "The solid earth whereon we tread / In tracts of fluent heat began," the section transforms the underlying volcanic stuff into a forge for life, which is conceived in Carlylean spirit as a tool "To shape and use"—no "idle ore,"

> But iron dug from central gloom,
> And heated hot with burning fears,
> And dipt in baths of hissing tears,
> And battered with the shocks of doom.
> (118.8–9, 20–25)

The argument of the section is technically catastrophic, and human history seems bound to change for the better over time. Tennyson then superimposes the belief that humanity can imitate or "type this work of time" by self-improvement. Thus his invitation to contemplate time leads unabashedly, if a little unexpectedly, to his concluding exhortation, "Arise and fly / The reeling Faun, the sensual feast; / Move upward, working out the beast, / And let the ape and tiger die" (118.16, 25–

191

28). Though this exhortation no doubt primarily intends to subdue the animals within us, its last line may also be comfortably misread: Let apes and tigers die but not us.

For many readers the sections toward the end of *In Memoriam* brake or throw into reverse the dark emotions of the early sections. The most serene invocation of evidence of the earth's change, for example, is this:

> There rolls the deep where grew the tree.
>   O earth, what changes hast thou seen!
>   There where the long street roars, hath been
> The stillness of the central sea.
>
> The hills are shadows, and they flow
>   From form to form, and nothing stands;
>   They melt like mist, the solid lands,
> Like clouds they shape themselves and go.
>
> But in my spirit will I dwell,
>   And dream my dream, and hold it true;
>   For though my lips may breathe adieu,
> I cannot think the thing farewell.
>
>   (123.1–12)

The lyric is joyous; and its imagery, except for "the long street," is strictly speaking not available to the eye. The motions of the hills, which Tennyson renders visible only by collapsing eons of time, depend on inference from a few facts and are no more subject to direct observation than any of the other things that, according to Herschel, are of most interest to science. The argument—if the last stanza can be called that—merely claims that moving hills and all are material as opposed to spiritual things, and very sweetly the poet concedes that his lips are material too. Modestly he stipulates only belief and will "hold" his dream true—a stipulation that, amplified and frequently repeated, is typical of *In Memoriam*. But the deployment of geology here in no way logically differs from that of the earlier sections, where it similarly provides the poet with a bad state of things with which to compare his own case. The hills and the deep, with the myriad forms of life they have contained, have suffered a worse beating than he has.

That Tennyson provides a tale of increasing hope and lifted spirits by the end of *In Memoriam* need not mean that he accepts progressive evolution as descriptive of the actual course of events beyond his own or anyone else's experience. Famously, and vaguely, the poem concludes with "one far-off divine event, / To which the whole creation moves"—

words of Christian prophecy rather than scientific theory. The apocalyptic note might sound more congenially in catastrophic than in uniformitarian ears, but if truth were told no one geology of the time could free itself of all the others. In the last editions of his *Principles,* Lyell himself was forced to acknowledge "the possibility of a law of evolution and progress," simply because his earlier theory could not accommodate all the evidence.[79] In general, Tennyson's scientific leaning was uniformitarian, but uniformitarianism—precisely because it was conservative and treated everything as predictable even when it was not—was a distinctly calming doctrine. The doctrine is broadly about history, and Tennyson's allegiance to it emerges unmistakably in opposition to the metaphors of this political section of his poem:

> But ill for him that wears a crown,
>   And him, the lazar, in his rags:
>   They tremble, the sustaining crags;
> The spires of ice are toppled down,
>
> And molten up, and roar in flood;
>   The fortress crashes from on high,
>   The brute earth lightens to the sky,
> And the great Æon sinks in blood.
>   (127.9–16)

Since the section begins and ends with the words "all is well," it is easy to see how uniformitarianism rejects political catastrophism—"even though thrice again," in the poet's words, "The red fool-fury of the Seine / Should pile her barricades with dead" (127.6–8). To gloss Tennyson's repeated "all is well," Christopher Ricks prints Lyell's argument that "the general tendency of subterranean movements, when their effects are considered for a sufficient lapse of ages, is eminently beneficial, and that they constitute an essential part of that mechanism by which the integrity of the habitable surface is preserved, and the very existence and perpetuation of dry land secured." Moreover, "causes acting in the interior of the earth . . . although so often the source of death and terror to the inhabitants of the globe . . . are, nevertheless, the agents of a conservative principle above all others essential to the stability of the system."[80]

79. See Gould, *Time's Arrow, Time's Cycle,* 167–73. Lyell's words are quoted from the eleventh edition of *Principles of Geology* (1872), 1:171.

80. See *Poems of Tennyson,* 2:446–47n. Ricks quotes from the fourth edition of *Principles of Geology* (1835), 2:290–91, 403.

While choosing hypotheses as they suit him, Tennyson searches this way and that for evidence of a future life. Some of the inferences he entertains amount to hardly more than saying that he could never be comfortable with or make sense of life that ends in death.

> My own dim life should teach me this,
>> That life shall live for evermore,
>> Else earth is darkness at the core,
> And dust and ashes all that is.
>
> (34.1–4)

Without continuance in a future life, he would have no use for God, or choice, or patience, and this particular section closes with the wholly unreasonable thought that if he really is going to die, he might as well die right away. Typically he argues that none of the higher instincts of love and morality are consistent with death, which he therefore associates with bestiality and scorns all the more. Occasionally the observations brought to bear on some possible evidence seem especially promising:

> The baby new to earth and sky,
>> What time his tender palm is prest
>> Against the circle of the breast,
> Has never thought that "this is I:"
>
> But as he grows he gathers much,
>> And learns the use of "I", and "me",
>> And finds "I am not what I see,
> And other than the things I touch."

But what follows from this description of the growth of an individual's sense of identity? Only an inference that the effort would be wasted "Had man to learn himself anew" (45.1–8, 15) after death: that is, if there is a future life, the principle of economy would suggest that it be fully adult and provided with memory. The inference is merely whimsical, but so it is with most of the gestures toward proving something in the poem. Contrast the strong feeling in a section that subordinates proof altogether and dismisses outright the evidence of the dead body:

> I wage not any feud with Death
>> For changes wrought on form and face;
>> No lower life that earth's embrace
> May breed with him, can fright my faith.

194

> Eternal process moving on,
>   From state to state the spirit walks;
>   And these are but the shattered stalks,
> Or ruined chrysalis of one. . . .
>
> For this alone on Death I wreak
>   The wrath that garners in my heart;
>   He put our lives so far apart
> We cannot hear each other speak.
>   (82.1–8, 13–16)

Even so the poet stops to assert his faith that "the spirit walks," while "shattered stalks" and "ruined chrysalis" in the second stanza are figures that help to distance the evidence of the body, here unmistakably devoured by "lower life." But anger, not inference, controls the last stanza, with its modern statement that separation is more painful than just the facts of death.

It seems that whenever Tennyson attempts a strong representation he is weak, but that when he tries to tell how he feels he is strong—especially when he is feeling bad. His considered position, at the close of *In Memoriam* and frequently expressed elsewhere, is that the question of a future life "never can be proved" (131.10). For that matter, he makes it clear that he does not really believe in natural religion: "I found Him not in world or sun, / Or eagle's wing, or insect's eye." Rather, as he says, unbelief angered him, and "I have felt" (124.5–6, 16). Yet the writer of *In Memoriam* roves past and around so many proofs and sciences of his day that one may be forgiven for thinking that his strict adherence to faith as the substance of things hoped for is only his fallback position.[81] In the words of the prologue, "We have but faith: we cannot know; / For knowledge is of things we see"; yet Tennyson had read Herschel and the others, the best scientists of the day, and he understood that science also constructed stories of things not seen. In short, he protests so much that one comes away from his great poem of grief thinking that here was a man who felt he ought to be making strong representations but could only tell of his experience.

---

81. Cf. Culler, *Poetry of Tennyson,* 175: "Such is Tennyson's effort, based upon the psychology, the physiology, the pneumatology, the philosophy, and above all the astronomy of his day, to construct a science of immortality. It is not very successful and he felt that it was not."

5

Stories of Experience

Oh Cardinal, those lithe live necks of ours!
Here go the vertebrae, here's *Atlas,* here
Axis, and here the symphyses stop short,
So wisely and well, —as, o'er a corpse, we cant, —
And here's the silver cord which . . . what's our word?
Depends from the gold bowl, which loosed (not "lost")
Lets us from heaven to hell, —one chop, we're loose!
"And not much pain i' the process," quoth the sage:
Who told him? Not Felice's ghost, I think!
                              —Guido Franceschini, 1869

O good *Horatio,* Ile take the Ghosts word
for a thousand pound.
                              —A Prince, 1604

ONE OF THE MEASURES OF modernism in the arts is undoubtedly a new respect for testimony. It is not that artists think any less well of their own voices, but that their subject matter has changed. In narrative, the need to establish the facts and draw the appropriate conclusions—the very atmosphere of proof and trial and sanctions—gives way to a renewed interest in experience that can be captured only from testimony. It now seems ironic—or possibly just mistaken—that Hosea M. Knowlton, attempting to validate the use of circumstantial evidence to condemn Lizzie Borden in 1892, should hark back to Defoe's *Robinson Crusoe* just when James, Conrad, Woolf, and Joyce were about to surrender the prerogatives of narrative to the supposed voice or consciousness of certain characters. Of course, Knowlton was partly engaged in the same maneuver as these literary artists; by insinuating to the Massachusetts jury that Crusoe "had no lawyer to tell him" what was evidence, he only pretended to disparage the professionalization of narrative. Similarly, James's heroine in *The Golden Bowl* needed no lawyer to discover the facts and manage her own fate, while at the same time her side was amply supported by James's own intelligence (as both sides in *Commonwealth v. Borden* were well represented). The Jamesian method collapses the distance between the management and the character without surrendering all the gains realized for narrative from circumstantial evidence. Literary history never repeats itself exactly any more than other histories do; and stories of things not seen can *be* stories of experience when they are told from a certain point of view.

In speaking of "stories of experience" or even "testimony," I am conscious of evading the very problems of representation that narrative once more manages to overcome. But for present purposes I mainly want to contrast such stories with the historic devotion of narrative to proofs from circumstantial evidence.[1] Thus the difference can be ex-

1. "Stories of experience" is meant to recall Robert Langbaum's *The Poetry of Experience*

pressed as that between stories of things not seen and stories of something seen, heard, sensed, or experienced—a difference played out in literary history by the general loosening of claims to objectivity and rising interest in subjectivity at the end of the nineteenth century. In the terms of this book, experience is not evidence or ever aimed at objectivity. Commonly "experience" means to us something prior to representation that nonetheless still gets represented somehow. Indeed, one does not have to employ a lawyer *or* a novelist to have an experience and, what is more, to tell of the experience: people do it all the time. Lawyers, doctors, priests, and other professionals make a business of advising what lies behind or ahead of an experience, but of itself experience should be narratable without assistance and without consequences—or at least without sanctions. The Latinate word conveys such meanings as risk and trial—compare "experiment"—but generally without any forensic suggestion: to write of experience should need only weak, not strong, representation. This is what happened and this is how someone felt about it: no need to prove that something was the case, that someone was innocent or otherwise.

Testimony in this sense has to have been a still more ancient practice than proof. Stories of experience also overlap and intertwine with strong representations in the eighteenth and nineteenth centuries. Even Tom Jones has experiences, in Fielding's narrative, that are not strictly required to establish his innocence and good nature, though after the romantic revival such stories of experience may seem woefully understated. Thus the story of Waverley makes it seem that Jones has no subjective life worth worrying about, even though Scott also makes a strong representation of his hero's sociability. *The Prelude* is a still more remarkable example of a narrative of experience, and Wordsworth set a new standard of subjectivity for writers in English. Yet the poem was not published until 1850: in that year the two great competing narratives in prose were Thackeray's *Pendennis* and Dickens's *David Copperfield*—also about experience, also autobiographical, but possibly even stronger representations of innocence and sociability than Scott's *Waverley*. In 1850 middle-class life was still very commonly regarded as a trial, and those novels were still very much about the ends of life, still written in the tradition of managed circumstantial evidence.[2]

(see chapter 3, note 1), since the dramatic monologues of Browning and others importantly compromised strong representations.

2. Cf. Alexander Welsh, *The City of Dickens* (1971; rpt. Cambridge: Harvard University Press, 1986), 213–28.

The same year saw the publication of *In Memoriam,* at once respectful of the strong representations of science and natural religion and stubbornly opposed to accepting them as equivalent to what the poet felt about death. In short order, as we have seen, Tennyson sampled so many arguments for a future life that his poem can hardly be appreciated outside the tradition presided over by Butler's *Analogy of Religion;* yet he finally elected to throw over those arguments, and the debate with himself about them is subordinated to a story of experience. From any critical perspective, *In Memoriam* was far more a narrative of its author's life—and exemplary to fellow living beings—than a conventional elegy for the dead. It was a poem composed largely of witnessing, and of witnessing to the writer's own feelings rather than to the qualities of his friend. Tennyson, who was already a formidable exponent of the dramatic monologue, said of his poem in memory of Hallam that "the different moods of sorrow as in a drama are dramatically given."[3] Like Dickens and Thackeray and other established Victorian writers, he also thought of life as a trial; but the trial in the poem was that of grief, not of innocence or guilt.

My purpose in this chapter is first of all to examine the continued erosion of strong representation in two of the most modern texts of high Victorianism, *The Ring and the Book* and *The Moonstone.* Both works, by a suitable coincidence of literary history, were published in 1868 (though Collins's novel appeared some months earlier, Browning's poem had been much longer in the making). Both directly confronted and even appropriated the managed narrative of circumstantial evidence in an attempt to create a story of experience (though their championing of experience was also compromised, by Browning's fierce belief in life as a trial and by Collins's routine submission to the property conventions of the English novel). For a culmination of such adaptation and protest, then, I shall turn to James's *The Golden Bowl,* in which the vestiges of life as a trial have pretty well disappeared and the property motive is surpassed in the first chapter. This last completed novel by James, published in 1904, was in effect the last in the series of English novels that began with Fielding as well as a contribution to modernism on both sides of the Atlantic. In all three literary works—by Browning, Collins, and James—testimony has come back into use as a primary means of representation. Personal responses to an event take precedence

---

3. Hallam Tennyson, *Alfred Lord Tennyson: A Memoir,* 2 vols. (London: Macmillan, 1897), 1:304.

over the event: individual points of view, not some pending verdict, become the ostensible stopping place for the argument; the writers press into service a variety of points of view without seeming to adjudicate among them. Even this strategy was not strictly new, for eighteenth-century epistolary novels took advantage of similar means. The first letter in Smollett's *Humphry Clinker* began, "Doctor, the pills are good for nothing—I might as well swallow snow-balls to cool my reins."[4] It cannot be an accident that a story published by James in 1882, also epistolary in form and entitled "The Point of View," begins, "My dear child, the bromide of sodium (if that's what you call it) proved perfectly useless."[5] But neither James nor Browning nor Collins actually returns to writing narrative construed *as* testimony in any case. The new stories do not merely report experience, they also investigate it, and their spirit of investigation owes something to the narratives of circumstantial evidence that they appropriate. These stories suggest that there may be still more sides to the truth than can fairly be represented. While they are not strong representations, they often show characters making such representations, usually in vain. They are typically concerned with the experience of knowing rather than the question of what has occurred—and thus may have forfeited one strong claim to realism.

As their titles suggest, *The Ring and the Book, The Moonstone,* and *The Golden Bowl* partly aspire to a symbolic representation of events. The objects named—the ring and book, the moonstone, the bowl—either appear in a story or signify its very making, but the story is not about any of these objects; it is about the characters' experience. Instead the symbols make expanding reference, in a process of comprehension. Each has some immediate evidentiary significance, but this is transformed in the course of the narrative. In the case of the two novels, the moonstone and bowl (both flawed, it is said) eventually cease to function as evidence: the strong representations of crime they have begun to invite are no longer viable. These stories are distinctly not murder mysteries: Browning's poem is about a murder, but the identity and evildoing of the murderer are never in doubt; the two novels feint

---

4. Tobias Smollett, *The Expedition of Humphry Clinker,* ed. Lewis M. Knapp and Paul-Gabriel Boucé (New York: Oxford University Press, 1984), 5. The allusion of the second clause is to a line of Falstaff's in *The Merry Wives of Windsor* (3.5.20–21).

5. Henry James, "The Point of View," in *The Complete Tales of Henry James,* ed. Leon Edel, vol. 4 (London: Hart-Davis, 1962), 467. A. Dwight Culler, *The Poetry of Tennyson* (New Haven: Yale University Press, 1977), 155–56, ventures a comparison of *In Memoriam* to epistolary novels and recalls the poet's fondness for Richardson.

toward murder, perhaps, but they settle for curiously positive versions of theft and of adultery. All three stories have as much to do with trust as with finding out the truth. The evidence they implicitly accept is that of death because, together with birth, death after all delimits experience.

Browning's Ring around a Murder

"Do you see this Ring?" "Do you see this square old yellow Book?" With these abrupt allusions to its artistry and source, already mirrored in its title, the poem begins.[6] The Ring—or at least the first of four volumes of the long Victorian poem—is in the reader's hands; the Book—some contemporary records of a late seventeenth-century Roman murder trial—is thrust only figuratively in the reader's face. These twin gestures of present and absent making, not identical but related, are characteristic of *The Ring and the Book,* as is the insistence on the reader's seeing, if not the historical events themselves, at least the recounting of them. In the first and twelfth parts, Browning speaks for himself; in between are ten dramatic monologues—"voices we call evidence" (1.833)—of real and supposed participants in the murder trial of 1698. Both the frame and the form of the poem demand binocular vision of "pure crude fact" (1.35, 86) and what can be made of it.[7]

The accident of stumbling upon the old yellow book in 1860 no doubt enhanced the poet's sensation of holding facts in his hand—"real summed-up circumstance / Adduced in proof of these on either side" (1.146–47). The Book was actually a set of pamphlets bound together with some manuscript reporting of the case: the separate documents and partiality of the pleadings supplied two prominent features of the Ring, or the poem itself. Robert Browning (1812–89) was well known as a poet by this time and had already published some of his best short

6. Robert Browning, *The Ring and the Book,* ed. Richard D. Altick (1971; rpt. New Haven: Yale University Press, 1981), bk. 1, lines 1, 33. Further citations from this edition are given by book and line numbers in parentheses.

7. *The Ring and the Book* was first published in four volumes—three books each, a total of 21,116 lines of blank verse—from 21 November 1868 to 27 February 1869. The sequence of the monologues is as follows: (1) The Ring and the Book; (2) Half-Rome; (3) The Other Half-Rome; (4) Tertium Quid; (5) Count Guido Franceschini; (6) Giuseppe Caponsacchi; (7) Pompilia; (8) Dominus Hyacinthus de Archangelis, Pauperum Procurator; (9) Juris Doctor Johannes-Baptista Bottinius, Fisci et Rev. Cam Apostol. Advocatus; (10) The Pope; (11) Guido; (12) The Book and the Ring. See William Clyde DeVane, *A Browning Handbook,* 2d ed. (New York: Appleton, 1955), 318–48.

monologues. A year after the discovery of the yellow book Elizabeth Barrett Browning died, and Browning did not begin writing his poem until 1864. After that he worked at it regularly, though it took four years to bring to completion. That *The Ring and the Book* was his first long poem of this period contributed to its fame, but it also held a fortunate combination of things for him. Ten dramatic monologues devoted to the same concrete historical event brought out ineluctably what the form could accomplish—namely, provide a representation *of* points of view. At the same time, the wrangling of a law case chimed well with the kind of noises Browning's characters often made.

In his version of the story, of what Browning refers to as the Ring, three composite onlookers—called Half-Rome, the Other Half-Rome, and Tertium Quid—and four principal characters—Count Guido Franceschini, Giuseppe Caponsacchi, Pompilia, and the pope—in their respective monologues tell as many times over again the facts: the thirteen-year-old Pompilia's marriage to the count; the discovery that she was not the child of her supposed parents, who arranged the marriage; the cruelty of Guido and Pompilia's flight with Caponsacchi, a young priest; the legal separation and temporary settlement of the conflict; the surprise stabbing of Pompilia and her stepparents by Guido and four hirelings a few weeks after she had given birth to a child. The reader soon makes out that each monologue's time of telling falls in regular sequence, between 2 January, the day of the murder, and 22 February 1698, the day of Guido's execution. That Pompilia managed to survive twenty-two wounds for four days allows her monologue to be one in the sequence even though she is the murder victim. Because Guido, after his legal conviction, pleaded that he was of the minor clergy, Pope Innocent XII entered the case to sustain the conviction: his—or rather Browning's pope's—impressive monologue comes next to last in the completed poem, before Guido's second, unpleasant revelation of himself in the knowledge that he is about to lose his head (a euphemism he does not fail to examine closely). Browning, obviously, is still very much managing the evidence for this multiple story of experience; it is all testimony, but he has himself composed the testimony (or here and there simply translated some Latin or Italian prose into English blank verse). He so idealizes three of his characters—Pompilia, Caponsacchi, and the pope—that a reader has little difficulty deciding where the truth lies. Caponsacchi on his part regards Pompilia as an angel of truth, and the pope several times over commends them both—"each / Champion of truth, the priest and wife I praise" (10.682–83). There seems almost a conspiracy of truth telling among these good characters, whose speaking parts were nearly pure inventions of the poet.[8]

Nevertheless, in all the monologues the interest of the tale is subordinate to the telling. No one can read the poem merely to discover the outcome, for Browning promptly destroys the suspense when he translates the title of the old yellow book at the beginning:

> A Roman murder-case:
> Position of the entire criminal cause
> Of Guido Franceschini, nobleman,
> With certain Four the cutthroats in his pay,
> Tried, all five, and found guilty and put to death
> By heading or hanging as befitted ranks.
>
> (1.121–26)

Rather, this story is of the murder case as experienced by the principals and others at the time, and problems of knowing and of trust are featured large in it. As in *Tom Jones*,[9] the first way of knowing featured is gossip: the reader, in effect, is held at the edge of the crowd that gathered a couple of centuries ago while Browning shows how shocking news spreads.

> First, the world's outcry
> Around the rush and ripple of any fact
> Fallen stonewise, plumb on the smooth face of things;
> The world's guess, as it crowds the bank o' the pool,
> At what were figure and substance, by their splash:
> Then, by vibrations in the general mind,
> At depth of deed already out of reach.
>
> (1.839–45)

Representations then begin to be made on every side, for even Half-Rome, the Other Half-Rome, and Tertium Quid have their distinct opinions of the facts. The principal characters, with much more at stake, inevitably have sharply divided and conclusive stories to tell. Capon-

---

8. The source of the poem still survives in the Balliol College library at Oxford and was translated by C. W. Hodell as *The Old Yellow Book* (1908; rpt. London: Everyman, 1911).

9. Unlike Fielding's repeated introductions in his novel, however, Browning's are all packed into the first book in order to keep the subsequent monologues clear of his own voice.

sacchi, in particular, is adroit at drawing inferences from the facts. Guido lies as it suits him, until with his last breath he craves favor—"my first true word"—by denying everything he has said previously (11.2418). The pope wisely awaits the full story and makes up his mind as a judge or jury should: "Truth, nowhere, lies yet everywhere in these— / Not absolutely in a portion, yet / Evolvable from the whole: evolved at last / Painfully, held tenaciously by me" (10.228–31). Thus strong representations are made by all the male principals, but Browning directs attention to how they are made and why. It is not just a matter of adding up truths and falsehoods, for everywhere the poem highlights trusting, knowing, and deciding. Its skepticism demands to know not only "Who shall say how, who shall say why," but how anyone can accurately see, given "The instinctive theorizing whence a fact / Looks to the eye as the eye likes the look" (1.862–64).

Browning never confuses his story of experience with the experience that preceded it in time, and in the introductory book of his poem he aggressively takes up questions of epistemology, both perceptual and evidentiary. Since *The Ring and the Book* comprises a series of dramatic monologues, he compares it to a stage play: "Let this old woe step on the stage again! / Act itself o'er anew for men to judge." But such representation does not occur "by the very sense and sight" in either print or a play, and if it did our knowledge would be "at best imperfect cognizance, / Since, how heart moves brain, and how both move hand, / What mortal ever in entirety saw?" Eyewitnessing cannot penetrate to things not seen, such as motives; and besides, neither a poet nor a historian can possibly administer to the reader a "dose of purer truth than man digests," but only the usual mixture, "truth with falsehood, milk that feeds him now." Therefore this particular poet-historian will inform the reader as best he can, at once depreciating testimony and acknowledging that it is all we have to go on:

> To-wit, by voices we call evidence,
> Uproar in the echo, live fact deadened down,
> Talked over, bruited abroad, whispered away,
> Yet helping us to all we seem to hear:
> For how else know we save by worth of word?
> (1.824–37)

The marked sense of both the limitations and the use of language—"worth of word"—differs considerably from the many reassurances of the exponents of circumstantial evidence that high probability (or violent presumption, as the law used to say) would do for certainty.[10] Browning's belief verges on relativism and is equally modern in its conscious admission of fiction:

> Well, now; there's nothing in nor out o' the world
> Good except truth: yet this, the something else,
> What's this then, which proves good yet seems untrue?
> This that I mixed with truth, motions of mine . . .
> Are means to the end, themselves in part the end?
> Is fiction which makes fact alive, fact too?
> The somehow may be thishow.
>
> (1.698–707)

Thus the very limitations of knowing lead to this cogent appeal for heuristic fictions and eventually come to justify aestheticism—for "Art may tell a truth / Obliquely" (12.855–56).

Given Browning's recurrent attention to the difficulty of making any representations at all, it is fair to ask what he thinks the law can do in this line. In this book I have argued that a trial based on circumstantial evidence became a dominant model for English narrative by the end of the eighteenth century: Browning not only elevates testimony over managed circumstantial evidence but kicks the model of a trial as hard as he can. Though he is writing, in part, about an actual murder trial, and one that reached a verdict he thoroughly approves, he still kicks away. There is just as much satire of the law and of lawyers in *Tom Jones* as here, but the trials and mock trials that Fielding made fun of usually got the facts all wrong: not so in *The Ring and the Book,* where the facts are got right but are not what is in question. Precisely in the respect that trials are an institution for finding the truth, Browning despises them. Consider the remarks of Tertium Quid on the popularity of trials with the mob:

> "Now for the Trial!" they roar: "the Trial to test
> The truth, weigh husband and weigh wife alike
> I' the scales of the law, make one scale kick the beam!"
> Law's a machine from which, to please the mob,
> Truth the divinity must needs descend
> And clear things at the play's fifth act—aha!

10. For Browning's poem and some dilemmas of deconstruction, see W. David Shaw, *Victorians and Mystery: Crises of Representation* (Ithaca: Cornell University Press, 1990), 300–21.

> Hammer into their noddles who was who
> And what was what.
>
> (4.12–19)

The mob (but only the mob) needs a trial to sort out facts, show who was who and what was what. The voice, of course, is only that of Tertium Quid getting started on its (his and her) monologue. But compare the heavy sarcasm and the figure of the law as stage machinery to the sarcasm and machinery of an earlier passage from Browning's introductory book:

> Then, since a Trial ensued, a touch o' the same
> To sober us, flustered with frothy talk,
> And teach our common sense its helplessness.
> For why deal simply with divining-rod,
> Scrape where we fancy secret sources flow,
> And ignore law, the recognized machine,
> Elaborate display of pipe and wheel
> Framed to unchoak, pump up and pour apace
> Truth in a flowery foam shall wash the world?
> The patent truth-extracting process, —ha?
> Let us make all that mystery turn one wheel,
> Give you a single grind of law at least!
>
> (1.1105–16)

Elsewhere Browning shows he is aware of the differences between an Italian trial of the seventeeth century and an English jury trial, but that does not seem to be the point here. Neither the affront to common sense nor the display of machinery is associated with some particular system of law, and while the metaphor is first introduced with a suggestion of harmless mystery, the plumbing of "the patent truth-extracting process" tends to sink toward groundpipes, and "a single grind of law" implies a very slow turning.

Virtually no character in *The Ring and the Book* has anything kind to say about the law except Guido—who imagines he can beguile the prosecution—and the two lawyers, Arcangeli and Bottini. The dramatic irony of their four monologues—two for the villain and one each for the lawyers—is generally the heaviest of the entire poem. Neither Arcangeli, who has the job of defending Guido, nor Bottini the prosecutor, who in effect is the official representative of Pompilia's side, understands or much cares about the moral nature of the man and child-wife as reflected elsewhere. For one thing, the lawyers are mercenaries: "Now, how good God is!" Arcangeli exclaims, "How falls plumb to point / This murder, gives me Guido to defend" (8.75–76); and Bottini's last words about the case and his profession are, "Still, it pays" (9.1577). But Browning's truly clever point about the lawyers and their marshaling of the evidence is made by having them not narrate the facts but rehearse their narrative for the trial. Their monologues differ in this respect from those of the other characters, each of whom tells the story of Guido and Pompilia from a certain point of view, in the design that justifies regarding *The Ring and the Book* as one long narrative poem. Arcangeli is preparing his brief, "Explaining matters, not denying them!" (8.315). For a defense he need not tell a story so much as guard against any that tells against his client—though wistfully he relates how Caponsacchi might have been said to commit the murder if only Guido had not already confessed to it. Bottini's monologue does give the facts from the prosecution's point of view, but this narrative is deliberately framed as another rehearsal: also regretful of lost opportunities, Bottini delivers the story as the oration he is *not* allowed to make, since the pleadings in this Roman trial are in writing. By thus presenting their arguments as rehearsals, Browning demolishes the pretense of lawyers to give a true account of what has happened. The professional managers of evidence he portrays as strictly rhetoricians.

Though Guido's pretensions occasionally move a reader to gusts of indignation something like laughter, Browning's villain is on the whole far more outrageous than comic. What is playfully absurd about the character and his defense can better be enacted through Arcangeli, whose monologue is genuinely entertaining. Arcangeli's routine is a triumph of the poetry of experience. Not only does Browning expose the working lawyer to satire, he sets off the man's career from his domestic life—though far more attractively than Dickens treats the lawyer Vholes and his family concerns in *Bleak House*. The relative daring of this conception is worth noting. Elsewhere in the poem, and most notably at the end of Caponsacchi's monologue, a Victorian celebration of the "small experiences of every day, / Concerns of the particular hearth and home" (6.2092–93), is manifest, even as it is in Tennyson's contemporaneous narrative of Arthurian times, *Idylls of the King*. But Arcangeli the lawyer treasures home life too, though he is the mercenary defender of a moral monster. Arcangeli has taken on Guido's defense for bread and butter—and thanked God for it. Eating bread and butter is just what he relishes most, as long as he can enjoy the repast with his family:

> Commend me to home-joy, the family board,
> Altar and hearth! These, with a brisk career,
> A source of honest profit and good fame,
> Just so much work as keeps the brain from rust,
> Just so much play as lets the heart expand,
> Honouring God and serving man, —I say,
> These are reality, and all else, —fluff,
> Nutshell and naught.
>
> (8.51–58)

Thus Browning puts a weak representation of life—"These are reality"—in competition with the strong representations being prepared for the trial—which are reduced to "fluff, / Nutshell and naught"; and he dramatizes the ascendancy of the former over the latter by allowing Arcangeli constantly to be distracted, either by fond thoughts of his eight-year-old son—Browning had a son not much older—or by thoughts of his dinner. The boy has the same name as his father, Giacinto, and is destined for the same career, but he appears in the monologue as a bewildering series of diminutives—Cinone, Cinozzo, Cinocello, Cinuolo, Cinicello, Cinino, Ciniccino, Cinucciatolo, Cinoncino, Cinarello, Cinotto, Giacintino, Cinuccino, Cintino, Cineruggiolo, Cinuccio—only one of which is twice repeated. It is such comic precision that causes the allusions to daily life to compete so successfully with the strong representations Arcangeli is composing all the while. His mind wanders again and again toward dinner, and not without highly specific designs:

> May Gigia have remembered, nothing stings
> Fried liver out of its monotony
> Of richness like a root of fennel, chopped
> Fine with the parsley: parsley-sprigs, I said—
> Was there need I should say "and fennel too?"
> But no, she cannot have been so obtuse!
> To our argument! The fennel will be chopped.
>
> (8.541–47)

With this reassurance, he forces himself back to the matter of Guido and wife killing. Toward the end of the task, as dinner approaches, the weak representations overtake the strong and mix metaphorically in Arcangeli's plan of defense: "I spare that bone to Spreti"—his assistant in the case—"and reserve / Myself the juicier breast of argument— /

Flinging the breast-blade i' the face o' the Fisc"—his opponent, Bottini—
"Who furnished me the tid-bit" (8.1575–78).

For all Browning's attack on trials at law as a way of establishing
truth and his mischievous portrayal of lawyers, he nevertheless chose
to write his long poem about a criminal trial, with lawyers on both
sides and even an opportunity for the murder victim to speak her piece.
There can be no question that the case history and pleadings of the old
yellow book presented materials for the study of evidence and an institution for arriving at truth. In the poem also, Arcangeli and Bottini,
Guido and Caponsacchi, and the pope—to say nothing of the other
monologuists—sift the available evidence and use inference to make
their representations, while Browning invites the reader to follow their
construction of "truth." The word abounds in *The Ring and the Book,*
though it is often spoken with scorn. "The triumph of truth!" Half-
Rome scoffs at the trial of Guido (2.1087); the poet apparently nurses
similar feelings throughout, for he designs a resounding reply to all
such false or dubious truths in Pompilia's allegorical triumph at the end,
when she confidently announces, "I rise" (7.1845). Browning also associated both Pompilia's triumph of truth and the composition of the
Ring with his own deceased wife Elizabeth.[11]

The method of the dramatic monologue itself, however, depends
intimately on inference of just that kind that Maurice Morgann celebrated in the plays of Shakespeare. Morgann, remember, treated *Henry
IV* purely as reading text and extolled the strains of narrative that could
be inferred from the dialogue; dramatic character already meant, for
him, some fragments of biography shored against defeat. The monologue form is itself designed as a text for reading, and the rules of the
genre do not admit any evidence from which inferences can be drawn
except the single voice. This constraint obviously puts more pressure
on inference: the work of representation done by an actor on the stage,
and normally shared with other actors, devolves upon the reader's
capacity to make out what is going on, as well as what has happened
already and is likely to happen thereafter: in short, the monologue can
be still another art of telling things not seen. Morgann credited Shakespeare with deliberately planting the obscure evidence from which ample
histories could be unfolded: Browning carefully crafted the monologues

---

11. For the association of the Ring and the poet's inspiration with his own marriage
to Elizabeth Barrett Browning, see 1.1390–1416 and 12.864–70. J. E. Shaw, "The 'Donna
Angelicata' in *The Ring and the Book,*" *PMLA* 41 (1926): 55–81, demonstrates the ide-
alization of Pompilia by comparison with the yellow book and then takes up the literary
model of Dante's Beatrice.

of *The Ring and the Book* to induce inferences in the reading—for "Fancy with fact is just one fact the more" (1.464), both in composing the poem and in interpreting it. Moreover, writing and reading of dramatic monologues presupposes a hermeneutics of suspicion: it is doubtful that the form could have evolved without the suspicion directed at testimony, over a period of about a hundred years, by the vogue of circumstantial evidence. In some respects Browning's monologues hark back to the confessional narratives of Defoe; at the same time, writing and reading them demands not only a variety of responses from amusement to contempt but above all a studied analysis of what people say or even know about their own motives.

The strenuous philosophy expressed in much of Browning's poetry owes something to the lasting persuasion—wholly consistent with his upbringing in English Dissent—that life itself is a trial. So despite the manifest mockery of trials at law in *The Ring and the Book*, the poem—or more especially its pope—vigorously presents a moral trial. As has long been recognized, the pope's monologue speaks more of Browning than of Innocent XII. Though Innocent did intervene when the historical Guido pleaded a clerical privilege, the sources no more than informed Browning that the pope refused to delay the execution. In the poem, the pope argues the case at length, and his overview surmounts the uncertainties arising from the previous monologues. Partly his voice is attractive because of his frank self-examination in the course of his decision. The pope's own impending death enforces choices that are nothing if not Browningesque:

> shall I too lack courage? —leave
> I, too, the post of me, like those I blame?
> Refuse, with kindred inconsistency,
> Grapple with danger whereby souls grow strong?
> I am near the end; but still not at the end;
> All till the very end is trial in life . . .
> Shall I dare try the doubt now, or not dare?
> (10.1298–1306)

If some persons do not recognize that "Life is probation and this earth no goal / But starting-point," that is because each individual is free to strive or not to strive: otherwise, "Why institute that race, his life, at all?" (10.1435–38). This crossing of two metaphors for life, a trial and a race, puts a premium on deciding the truth and applying it.

Browning's pope reviews the evidence in Guido's case and finds reasons only for hurrying the criminal's death. Noticeably, he decides as if it were mainly for himself rather than the public weal: his last lines are, "I may die this very night / And how should I dare die, this man let live?" (10.2132–33). The pope's determination, and not solely his judgment, dominates the poem. It is a very personalized finding of the truth, not unrelated to the intuitionism of Pompilia and Caponsacchi, the two actors in the affair whom the pope says he admires.[12] Though his position is an exalted one—nearly as much so, given the constraints of the form, as that of the narrator in *Tom Jones*—his superior grasp of the evidence comes down to his confidence in himself: comparable, no doubt, to godlike wisdom. Though *The Ring and the Book* tells of experience by adopting the mode of direct evidence or testimony, this privileged vision sweeps aside others' testimony as effectively as a preponderance of circumstantial evidence might—except that this is not circumstantial evidence and Browning's pope is not Fielding. Testimony is both human and fallible, the pope argues:

> when man walks the garden of this world
> For his own solace, and, unchecked by law,
> Speaks or keeps silence as himself sees fit,
> Without the least incumbency to lie,
> —Why, can he tell you what a rose is like,
> Or how the birds fly, and not slip to false
> Though truth serve better? Man must tell his mate
> Of you, me and himself, knowing he lies,
> Knowing his fellow knows the same.

This dimmest view of testimony sees it as wholly inadequate to experience (expressed in words as "what a rose is like, / Or how the birds fly") and, upon consideration, inevitably and knowingly a lie. The pope therefore does not call for a return to testimony in narrative but despairs of its value far more than any enthusiast of circumstantial evidence would. Testimony, he continues, will always be denied, and denials denied in turn: "Therefore this filthy rags of speech, this coil / Of statement, comment, query and response, / Tatters all too contaminate for use, / Have no renewing." From this truly despairing position Browning's pope cannot find his way back except by faith and personal convictions that are simply unargued:

---

12. Cf. Caponsacchi's account of how he and Pompilia trusted one another: "As I / Recognized her, at potency of truth, / So she, by the crystalline soul, knew me, / Never mistook the signs" (6.931–34).

> He, the Truth, is, too,
> The Word. We men, in our degree, may know
> There, simply, instantaneously, as here
> After long time and amid many lies,
> Whatever we dare think we know indeed
> —That I am I, as He is He, —what else?
>
> (10.360–80)

If everyone needing to know the truth and to act upon it had power of life and death such as the pope's, this means of knowing things would be rather frightening. In my own view, though intuition may be the property of the three most deserving characters in the poem—the pope, Pompilia, and Caponsacchi—it is finally no more satisfactory guide to truth than Tennyson's hopes for immortality.[13] The value of Browning's re-representation of an old murder case lies in his brilliant invention and his critique of testimony. He does much more than turn false testimony to account—as is frequently done elsewhere in the management of circumstantial evidence—because the monologues are not wholly dedicated to proving some fact at issue. They represent personality at a given moment, and from that moment, over time. They tell casually rather than causally of lives that are stories of experience. No wonder Browning could exult, as he reports, in the discovery of the old yellow book:

> A book in shape but, really, pure crude fact
> Secreted from man's life when hearts beat hard,
> And brains, high-blooded, ticked two centuries since.
> Give it me back! The thing's restorative
> I' the touch and sight.
>
> (1.86–90)

His exultation is romantic: the uncanny chance survival of the documents renders the past suddenly concrete. But above that, the story these documents told was of two solemnly connected deaths, a murder and the execution of the murderer. Such double rituals of willed death, I have suggested, at once distract and reassure one. Death most certainly limits everyone's experience, and it therefore has special poignancy for

---

13. Browning and Tennyson were far from alone, of course, in worrying the grounds of belief. *The Ring and the Book* was nearly contemporaneous with John Henry Newman's *An Essay in Aid of a Grammar of Assent* (1870), to cite only the most striking Victorian discourse on belief.

any celebration of experience. "What a rose is like, / Or how the birds fly" can have no interest to one after death. Difficult as it is to tell what a rose or bird flight is like, the urgency of telling is soon past—is already past for brains that "ticked two centuries since." Romantic stories of the past relish this pastness; but perhaps more important for Browning, death argues by negation that some things we do know, without saying how. His problem with testimony—or my problem with intuitionism, for that matter—can be got round by reflecting on the shortness of opportunity. Knowing and acting on the truth is what one does while one can; hence the stopping point of the pope's monologue becomes "how should I dare die, this man let live?"

Though Browning cannot finally argue this position successfully, he dramatizes it relentlessly. There are two dread moments in his poem of experience, the murder of Pompilia with her stepparents and the execution of Guido. Each monologuist is occupied with the first of these moments from the start, and of course their stories overlap and repeat one another. Pompilia herself typically recalls only a sort of tranquility followed by the murderers' tap on her door. Thus in her testimony the killing becomes, with abridged syntax, "The night and the tap" (7.1695). But that same hushed evasion of the sufferer leads with scarcely the necessity of proof to the second moment of violence, the beheading of Guido that is anticipated by nearly all. As the poem first gets under way, and Pompilia is dying, Half-Rome describes the bodies of the other victims, her stepparents; as the poem ends, well after her death, Guido grotesquely cries out as he is led off, "Pompilia, will you let them murder me?" (11.2425). Guido's equation of his punishment with murder, of course, shows that he still comprehends nothing of his guilt. But the paired "murders," or unnatural deaths, frame the experience told in *The Ring and the Book*.

Except, of course, for the experiences of contriving the Ring: the first and last books of the poem Browning reserved to himself. If we understand intuitionism as a confession of failure in knowing, however, and willful death as a highly dramatic definition of experience that partly compensates for this failure, Browning's theory of representation has a certain logic. For he thinks of mimesis as a process of resuscitation— "Creates, no, but resuscitates, perhaps" (1.719). His own life as an artist is thus in delicate balance with the violent deaths on which he lavished such care.

> Why, all the while, —how could it be otherwise? —
> The life in me abolished the death of things,

Deep calling unto deep: as then and there
Acted itself over again once more
The tragic piece.

(1.519–23)

For some readers the intuitionism may seem more acceptable when Browning returns, at the end of *The Ring and the Book,* to the subject of his art. Once again he puts down even testimony, as he urges his "British Public" to "learn one lesson" from the poem: "that our human speech is naught, / Our human testimony false, our fame / And human estimation words and wind." Now, however, it is art rather than faith that finally overtakes the failure, since "Art remains the one way possible / Of speaking truth, to mouths like mine, at least" (12.831–40). Other readers may feel that Browning here mystifies art as thoroughly as the pope mystifies being and God.

Collins's Setting for a Moonstone

The Moonstone, a novel exactly contemporaneous with Browning's long poem and bristling with similar contentions about point of view, can scarcely be called tragic. True, a threat of sudden death hangs over any character who comes in proximity to the moonstone, since three fanatical Brahmins will stop at nothing in their mission to return the stone to its proper setting, the forehead of the idol in India. But unless one counts the murder of one well-deserving thief who has paid little attention to the Indians anyway, the threat proves entirely anticlimactic. As far as characters one cares about are concerned, the Indian plot in the novel, while thrilling and mysterious, devolves to a rite of initiation. Initiations may be fraught with seeming danger and death, but only as rites of passage into some new phase of life. In *The Moonstone* this passage turns out to be one of the most conventional in the English novel after Scott, and as such it entails both a large inheritance of property and a strong representation of the hero's innocence. Whether Collins could fall back on this convention and still advance a story of experience is the question here.

A friend and sometime collaborator of Dickens, Wilkie Collins (1824–89) was one of the chief originators of so-called sensation novels in the 1860s. *The Woman in White,* serialized at the end of 1859, helped set a fashion for hidden danger and mystery beneath the facade of everyday life, or gothic terrors updated for sophisticated modern be-

215

ings.[14] In 1865 the young Henry James ceded Collins "the credit of having introduced into fiction those most mysterious of mysteries, the mysteries which are at our own doors," and correctly pointed out that sensation novels relied for their construction on "a happy choice of probable circumstances."[15] *The Moonstone,* Collins's foremost contribution to detective fiction, first appeared in Dickens's weekly *All the Year Round* from 4 January to 8 August 1868. Its division into several independent narratives bearing on the same action, as in *The Ring and the Book,* can be regarded a significant coincidence of literary history, since Browning's poem was nearly complete by that time. The design is not quite so radical as Browning's, and of course Collins's narrators supposedly produce written prose rather than spoken verse. A principle of economy in the novel distributes the action strictly sequentially among the several narrators; and far from telling the outcome of the story at the beginning, Collins maintains suspense to the very end by unveiling the mystery—how the diamond was stolen—one bit at a time. Both economy and suspense compromise the degree to which *The Moonstone* can succeed as a story of experience, since the reader's attention is directed relentlessly to the solution of the mystery. But the livelier narratives, by the house steward Gabriel Betteredge and the evangelist Miss Clack, receive the same sort of attention to fixed attitudes and everyday activities that Browning lavishes on the lawyer Arcangeli. Prejudices and cross-purposes abound; and as Miss Clack protests, though she longs to "improve"—that is, improve her fellow characters, her readers, and her facts—she is "condemned to narrate."[16] If Browning, after all, expresses the problem of recording experience as a rather hackneyed one of telling "what a rose is like," Collins's famous detective in this novel is notoriously more interested in cultivating roses than in anything else, and the great Cuff explains why this is so. " 'If you will look about you (which most people won't do),'

14. See Winifred Hughes, *The Maniac in the Cellar: Sensation Novels of the 1860s* (Princeton: Princeton University Press, 1980); Patrick Brantlinger, "What Is 'Sensational' about the 'Sensation Novel'?" *Nineteenth-Century Fiction* 37 (1982): 1–18; and Jenny Bourne Taylor, *In the Secret Theatre of Home: Wilkie Collins, Sensation Narrative, and Nineteenth-Century Psychology* (London: Routledge, 1988), 1–26.

15. Henry James, *Literary Criticism: Essays on Literature, American Writers, English Writers* (New York: Library of America, 1984), 742–43. In this review of Mary Elizabeth Braddon's *Aurora Floyd,* James was almost certainly guided by Henry Mansel's review of novels by Collins and others in the *Quarterly Review* 113 (1863): 482–514.

16. Wilkie Collins, *The Moonstone,* ed. J. I. M. Stewart (Harmondsworth: Penguin, 1966), 2.1.241. Subsequent references to this edition are given in parentheses, by narrative number, chapter, and page for passages in the Second Period (as here) or chapter and page for passages in the First Period (exclusively devoted to Betteredge's narrative).

says Sergeant Cuff, 'you will see that the nature of a man's tastes is, most times, as opposite as possible to the nature of a man's business' " (12.134–35).

Here we have Cuff quoted in Betteredge's narrative; later will come a brief narrative by the sergeant himself. Individual testimony is as important to *The Moonstone* as it is to *The Ring and the Book,* because of the insistence on different points of view and on the difficulty of representation. Betteredge explains at the outset that the narratives have all been commissioned by Franklin Blake (who is also the hero of this "Romance," as the subtitle of the novel has it). At the end of his contribution, the house steward spells out the plan of the book and its evidentiary justification:

> I can only state that I am acting under orders, and that those orders have been given to me (as I understand) in the interests of truth. I am forbidden to tell more in this narrative than I knew myself at the time. Or, to put it plainer, I am to keep strictly within the limits of my own experience, and am not to inform you of what other persons told me—for the very sufficient reason that you are to have the information from those other persons themselves, at first hand. In this matter of the Moonstone the plan is, not to present reports, but to produce witnesses.

By this point, of course, Betteredge has repeatedly narrated what other witnesses have told him. The underlying model for the novel is an investigation rather than a trial at common law, but we know that Collins had studied law briefly and that he was partly inspired by the evidence in the Road murder case of 1860.[17] Betteredge's next sentence shows that some idea of the rules of evidence—at least the rule against hearsay—governs the design. "A member of the family reading these pages fifty years hence," he says, will "be asked to take nothing on hearsay, and . . . treated in all respects like a judge on the bench" (23.233)—or more precisely a jury. In a footnote to the next narrative, Franklin Blake promises as editor of the volume that none of the testimony—"endorsed by the attestations of witnesses who can speak to the facts"—has been altered (1.1.235–36).

The narratives are by no means evenly distributed in the novel. Though Betteredge and Clack may have earned greater space than other

---

17. For the Road murder and other background of *The Moonstone,* see Sue Lonoff, *Wilkie Collins and His Victorian Readers* (New York: AMS, 1982), esp. 174–88, 261–64. Unlike Browning, obviously, Collins had a considerable respect for the model of the English trial: see also his preamble to *The Woman in White* (Harmondsworth: Penguin, 1974), 33.

witnesses owing to their capacity to entertain, the main purpose of the arrangements seems to be managing evidence after all, and especially managing the pace of concealment and revelation—that is, the suspense. A prologue and epilogue to *The Moonstone* document how the fabulous diamond was seized in a deed of violence, by one John Herncastle at the storming of Seringapatam in 1799, and eventually returned to the temple by the descendants of the three guardian priests.[18] How the diamond was maliciously designed as a birthday gift for Rachel Verinder—the heroine and innocent niece of the outcast thief—is left for Betteredge to tell. His narrative, about two-fifths of the total pages of the novel, constitutes the entire "First Period," which—from the stone's disappearance again on the night of its presentation—is called "The Loss of the Diamond." Only the "Second Period," called "The Discovery of the Truth," is further subdivided—into eight narratives in all, of very uneven length. The longest, in the second period, are by Drusilla Clack and Franklin Blake, whose contributions total about as many pages as Betteredge's. Of course Collins, who has written all the parts, has refrained from writing still others. This novel that is ostensibly about a crime not seen quietly omits the testimony of an actual eyewitness, the heroine herself.[19] Still, these narratives that are so obviously (to the critic) drawn up to create a single impression also make their pitch *against* a managed narrative of circumstantial evidence.

Collins first spars with circumstantial evidence—and with Sergeant Cuff—in Betteredge's narrative. He subdues a strong representation of the facts as Browning does, by refracting it through an eccentric point of view; but in this case the point of view is not that of the person

18. The anonymous narrator of the prologue to *The Moonstone,* who was present at Seringapatam in 1799, is another amateur of the law of evidence like Betteredge. Thus he never exposed his cousin Herncastle (they are all cousins in this novel) because "I have no evidence but moral evidence to bring forward. I have not only no proof that he killed the two men at the door; I cannot even declare that he killed the third man inside—for I cannot say that my own eyes saw the deed committed." By "moral evidence" he means that he has only a presumption, but ironically, since he has seen Herncastle standing over the one Indian with "a dagger dripping with blood" and the warm bodies of two others close by, the scene enacts precisely the example of violent presumption in Coke's maxim and therefore might be regarded as full proof (see chapter 1, note 34). Needless to say, Collins's purpose is not to punish this criminal in any event, but to establish an unpunished secret crime of the past that can threaten the tranquility of the present—to identify the moonstone, in short, with more potential violence and guilt.

19. By tactfully not requiring any narrative from Rachel Verinder, Collins not only maintains suspense until near the end but protects the heroine's delicacy. Her story would give away the show; and although her frank love for the hero is testified to by others and warmly endorsed by the writer, it would threaten the male prerogative if she just announced it in her own voice.

making the representation. Cuff enters the scene only about halfway through Betteredge's narrative, after the local police have demonstrated their incompetence (as they do over and over again in detective novels still to be written). Therefore the detective encounters not only a crime to solve but a head gardener with contrary ideas of rose cultivation and a house steward who has the advantage of narrating the affair. By conscripting the services of a prejudiced and skeptical Betteredge as his first narrator, Collins can examine the detective's strong representation of the facts from one side and also initiate a game of guessing what he is thinking. There are in fact not two narratives unfolding from one, as in most detective novels,[20] but three: the story of what happened to the diamond, which has not been seen since the night of Rachel Verinder's birthday; the story of the investigation, or of what Cuff is up to; and the story of Betteredge's understanding of the case. (Still a fourth movement of this narrative can be thought of as Cervantine, though it is hard to say how successful it is. From his opening sentence to his last, Betteredge repeatedly consults and often quotes from *Robinson Crusoe*. The joke is that he regards Defoe's novel as a sacred text, not as a representation of unique events, for he can open it at any page and find wisdom or prophecy appropriate to his present situation. Collins's simultaneous buildup and put-down of *Robinson Crusoe* in this part are obviously ironic but never quite result in any distinct claim for the contrasting narrative form of *The Moonstone*.)

On the basis of circumstantial evidence—no eyewitness to any crime has come forward—Sergeant Cuff concludes that Rachel has only pretended to miss the diamond and that she intends to raise money on it, to pay debts such as "young ladies of rank . . . dare not acknowledge to their nearest relatives and friends." That conclusion is probably not believed by most readers, however, since it is confined and controlled by the first narrative perspective, which is Betteredge's. It is immediately challenged, both by the narrator and by the heroine's mother. "It was downright frightful to hear him piling up proof after proof against Miss Rachel," and Betteredge confesses himself to be "(thank God!) constitutionally superior to reason." Lady Verinder, similarly, knows her daughter, and firmly lectures Cuff that "the circumstances have misled you" (21.205–8). She then performs a simple psychological test on Rachel, as suggested by the detective, and reports once again "that the circumstances, in this case, have fatally misled him." Thereupon,

20. Cf. Tzvetan Todorov, *The Poetics of Prose*, trans. Richard Howard (Ithaca: Cornell University Press, 1977), 45–46. See also Shaw, *Victorians and Mystery*, 288–99.

crossed by Lady Verinder and fought to a draw over roses by the gardener, Sergeant Cuff takes his pay and goes off on the refrain, "Why not say, the circumstances have fatally misled me?" (22.218–9).[21]

Within this period there originates another line of argument from circumstantial evidence that Cuff can only partly master, since its full unraveling awaits the return of Franklin Blake to the scene in the novel's second half. The inferences necessary are heroic in more than one sense, for they expand in epic proportions from a mere smudge in a fanciful design on the boudoir door, newly painted by the hero and heroine in person on the afternoon of the birthday dinner. Whoever smeared the paint later that night could have taken the moonstone from the Indian cabinet, and consequently a search begins for the article of clothing that touched the paint. (Cuff assumes that the paint has been brushed by a petticoat, because of either his ready hypothesis about "ladies of rank" or his general convictions about women.) Around the tiny smear of paint—apparently the only physical trace of the crime—must be reconstructed all the other facts of the case, including the movements of everyone in the house. When the local police superintendent scoffs at such a trifling circumstance as this, Sergeant Cuff counters with his experience in a recent murder case.

> At one end of the inquiry there was a murder, and at the other there was a spot of ink on a tablecloth that nobody could account for. In all my experience along the dirtiest ways of this dirty little world, I have never met with such a thing as a trifle yet. Before we go a step further in this business we must see the petticoat that made the smear, and we must know for certain when that paint was wet. (12.136)

In his example of the spot of ink, notice, the key to successful inference is the qualification, "nobody could account for." If there were in that murder case tablecloth and ink, after all, there were presumably thousands of other objects in the vicinity of the crime, any one of which might (or might not) be evidence of some untoward activity. In order even to perceive a trifling disruption in the usual state of things, it is

---

21. In many ways my reading of *The Moonstone* coincides with that of D. A. Miller, *The Novel and the Police* (Berkeley: University of California Press, 1988), 33–57. I certainly agree that Cuff's powers are cast aside, and that the novel ultimately supports "things as they are." On the other hand, I read the detective's powers as descending upon another professional, Ezra Jennings, rather than being dispersed everywhere in the community, and the community as involving exclusively persons with income from property and their servants.

essential to assume a closed universe of tidy cause and effect, no matter how small; and once something out of order has been perceived, or not accounted for, the detective can only pray that a discoverable cause will have some bearing on the crime, or on events that in turn bear on the crime, and so forth.

To amplify a single telltale circumstance like smeared paint, much work is needed, therefore, and other skills of investigation besides a sharp eye. Among these skills, rapid elimination of innocent causes of trifling evidence ranks high, for the secure inference must be drawn to *one* possible cause. Numerous hypotheses have to be constructed only to be torn down. At the same time, a detective in the field may have to anticipate the countermoves of a detection-conscious thief or murderer—whose moves, when made, may also be evidence of guilt. This elaborate scenario for proof, already a prospective narrative of crime and detection, is precisely what guides Sergeant Cuff as he follows up his single clue to the missing diamond. If no one can be found with paint on his or her clothes, or no clothes with paint can be found and traced to an owner, then possibly evidence can be uncovered showing that someone has hidden or destroyed the clothes. He therefore calls for the laundry book of this large Yorkshire house:

> The stained article of dress may be an article of linen. If the search leads to nothing, I want to be able to account next for all the linen in the house, and for all the linen sent to the wash. If there is an article missing, there will be at least a presumption that it has got the paint-stain on it, and that it has been purposely made away with, yesterday or to-day, by the person owning it.

Note the need to "account" for everything, as in the example of the ink stain. Given the remote conditional bearing of the evidence in hand, and the additional evidence he is seeking, on the crime to be solved, the detective needs to work with the speed of a calculating machine if he is to complete any successful inference before the criminal conceals more traces or slips away entirely. Collins's famous detective, however, is up to the task: "the great Cuff opened the washing-book, understood it perfectly in half a minute, and shut it up again" (13.146–47).

From interrogating the servants and inquiring in the village Cuff learns that one maid, Rosanna Spearman, has indeed suspiciously gone off and purchased enough new linen to make a nightgown. He decides, therefore, that Spearman must have assisted Rachel Verinder in spiriting away the diamond:

Between twelve and three, on the Thursday morning, she must have slipped down to your young lady's room, to settle the hiding of the Moonstone while all the rest of you were in bed. In going back to her own room, her nightgown must have brushed the wet paint on the door. She couldn't wash out the stain; and she couldn't safely destroy the nightgown without first providing another like it, to make the inventory of her linen complete. (18.189)

Notice the extraordinary acuteness and capacity for inference that the detective attributes to the maidservant in this line of reasoning. She is, to be sure, a convicted thief: but if her level of awareness were very much lower than that of the detective, *his* inference about her actions would not hold up. He also depends on that "inventory." There has to be a way of accounting for all the linen in the house, for otherwise the absence of a single piece of it could not be known, let alone signify. Finally, Cuff is downright lucky in his reasoning, that some outsider's overcoat—worn by one of the mysterious Indians perhaps—did not smear the paint. It is no accident that, inspired by Collins's example, so many detective novels find their proper setting in the English country house. This quintessentially Victorian place has room for all the suspects, while its strict economy and bookkeeping permit inferences from the slightest ink or paint stain.[22]

Now Sergeant Cuff is partly right about Rosanna Spearman's activities but wholly wrong about her motives, because his train of circumstances derails completely at the point of intersection with his other, false, conclusion that the heroine and daughter of the house still possesses the diamond. He correctly guesses that if there is a smear there may be a corresponding stain, and that someone might have a motive to conceal the stain. But from this point on this line of inference—or strong representation—may as well be, and more accurately can be, identified with Spearman's thinking. As the reader learns in the second period of *The Moonstone*, with Cuff gone from the scene and after Spearman has abandoned herself to the Shivering Sands, she *has* sequestered a nightgown with paint on it and replaced it with a new one: but the nightgown in question belongs to Franklin Blake. As the latter remarks, upon discovering this months later, "The paint on the nightgown, and the name on the nightgown are facts" (3.4.361), and the facts point to him as the person who passed through the door of Verinder's boudoir at about the time the diamond was taken. Spearman has had both the wit to comprehend the evidence and a motive to conceal it without de-

22. Cf. Miller, *Novel and the Police,* 33–34.

stroying it. She was in love with the handsome hero, and he must either be grateful to her for concealing the evidence of his guilt, as she thought, or threatened by her knowledge and possession of it. Her subsequent suicide, in despair of his ever loving her, shows that she has rejected the latter idea—of sexual blackmail—if she ever entertained it. Rosanna has finally to be judged both clever and good, though a little bit crazy about Mr. Franklin Blake. Her reasoning is a match for Sergeant Cuff's, and she makes no such egregious error as he. Both her detective work and Cuff's lead to parallel conclusions, however, in that each attributes the disappearance of the moonstone to one of the novel's protagonists. The circumstantial evidence in the first period (trust the sergeant, though he may be wrong) points to Rachel Verinder and in the second (trust Rosanna, though she may be acting) to Franklin Blake. Thus far Collins, in his roundabout way with narrative points of view, has still replicated a conventional novel plot in which the evidence at first implicates the hero or heroine but will finally show them both innocent.[23]

Set a thief to catch a thief. The woman from the reformatory, making a difficult way back as a housemaid and shaken by a hopeless infatuation for one of the gentry, reads the evidence of the stained nightgown well, and her care to deed the nightgown to the hero before her suicide enables "The Discovery of the Truth" of the novel's second period: Franklin Blake was the man. But neither Cuff nor Spearman, expert in circumstantial evidence as they are, has any conception of the unconscious mind, the intermittence of human memory, or the effects of opium. To conjecture and then to demonstrate how Blake may have taken the diamond without knowing it requires advanced psychology and an even more modern kind of detective, the medical assistant Ezra Jennings. And here Collins shows himself very up-to-date indeed, and not content with writing a detective story as such. More than three decades before any of Freud's psychoanalytic writings, he has studied the writing of the Victorian physiologists William Carpenter and John Elliotson on the workings of the unconscious mind.[24] Once Spearman's evidence has been recovered and the heroine of the novel has finally confessed

23. In his preface to the first edition, Collins claimed he had "reversed" the procedure of his earlier novels, which traced "the influence of circumstances upon character," by tracing in *The Moonstone* "the influence of character on circumstances." In this assertion he undoubtedly has in mind Rachel Verinder's decision to remain silent about what she saw on the night of her birthday, yet his reference in the next sentence to "the conduct pursued, under a sudden emergency, by a young girl" might also apply to Rosanna Spearman's actions.

24. For Collins's sources here, see Ira Bruce Nadel, "Science and *The Moonstone*," *Dickens Studies Annual* 11 (1983): 251–52. A wider exploration of contemporary theories

that she saw Blake remove the diamond from the Indian cabinet, Ezra Jennings is able to quote directly both these authorities, as well as Thomas De Quincey's *Confessions of an English Opium Eater,* in order to persuade the hero that he may have taken the diamond while in an opium trance and to suggest how they can conduct an experiment to test the hypothesis.[25]

The affinities between this last episode of *The Moonstone* and psychoanalysis should not be altogether surprising. Collins's novel packed in a combination of themes from nineteenth-century science and social science—mostly advanced by arguments from circumstantial evidence—from which psychoanalysis eventually emerged: criminal investigation, the importance of personal histories, concealment of information, searching of the memory by means of association, consideration of sexual motives, psychology of drug effects, and a theory of the unconscious—to which I would add a manifest interest in innocent forms of guilt. Jennings could not begin to guess that the hero had been drugged without his knowledge had he not pieced together his predecessor Candy's broken recollection of what happened at the birthday dinner. Initially Blake resists telling the medical assistant why he so urgently needs to know what happened that night—that he has been shamefully accused of taking the diamond himself; but there is a fraternity of guilt between the two, and Jennings is enabled to help by having previously analyzed his own case. "I have mentioned an accusation which has rested upon me for years. There are circumstances in connexion with it that tell against me. I cannot bring myself to acknowledge what the accusation is. And I am incapable, perfectly incapable, of proving my innocence" (3.9.428). This predicament, which in outline was also Edward Waverley's and is now Franklin Blake's as well, hovers on the verge of transformation from the political and social sphere to the personal and psychological.[26] Some thought needs to be given, therefore, to the resemblances between Jennings's

---

of personal identity and the unconscious is provided by Taylor, *In the Secret Theatre of Home,* 27–70, 174–206.

25. It should be said that Ezra Jennings's experiment, since so many things might go wrong with it, is as lucky in its success as Sergeant Cuff's conjectures about the paint smear. In Jennings's words, to recreate with Blake "the physical and moral conditions of last year . . . was the next thing to a downright impossibility" (4.480). Collins makes sure that the unlikely experiment succeeds.

26. For two psychoanalytic readings of *The Moonstone,* see Charles Rycroft, "A Detective Story: Psychoanalytic Observations," *Psychoanalytic Quarterly* 26 (1957): 229–45; and Albert D. Hutter, "Dreams, Transformations, and Literature: The Implications of Detective Fiction," *Victorian Studies* 19 (1975): 181–209.

means of recovering his client's past and psychoanalysis, to the sexual symbolism and relations in the novel, and to the whole question of whether Collins breaks free of English novel conventions or simply gives them a new dimension.

It is not as if at this point anyone had actually charged Franklin Blake with theft or threatened his disgrace. Rather, he needs to square his relationship with Rachel Verinder if possible and to reconcile her evidence and that of Rosanna Spearman with his own utter bafflement and inner denial of the experience. Before, Sergeant Cuff lectured his hearers on the importance of trifles in criminal investigation; now, in the hero's narrative of his interview with Verinder, who still loves him, the emphasis on circumstantial evidence has shifted to his personal case. He can only hope that "she might have overlooked something in the chain of evidence—some mere trifle, perhaps, which might nevertheless, under careful investigation, be made the means of vindicating my innocence in the end" (3.7.394). The family lawyer, Bruff, who also plays a part in the second period, advises Blake to concentrate on what lies ahead and how the diamond may still be traced: "let us look to what we *can* discover in the future, instead of to what we can *not* discover in the past." But the hero replies, as if anticipating the thrust of all psychoanalytic investigations, that surely "the whole thing is essentially a matter of the past—so far as I am concerned" (3.8.405). Thus he is far more prepared for Jennings's sympathetic intervention in the case than Bruff's. By the time of his writing, at least, he has been convinced that "the slow and toilsome journey from the darkness to the light" (3.5.380) is preferable to living with half-knowledge.

From the moment the moonstone disappeared the hero has placed himself in the forefront of the investigation—though it cannot be said that he accomplishes much without the assistance of Cuff, Bruff, and others. When he recovers Rosanna Spearman's cache containing his own nightgown, he makes a discovery like that of Oedipus of old: "I had penetrated the secret which the quicksand had kept from every other living creature. And, on the unanswerable evidence of the paint-stain, I had discovered Myself as the Thief" (3.3.359). But to attain a full understanding, he requires the step-by-step reenactment of the past under Ezra Jennings's direction, a reenactment to which he himself cannot be witness as the principal actor. The actual experiment, tending to confirm that the hero took the diamond unconsciously while under the influence of opium, is narrated by Jennings day by day and hour by hour in his diary but would hardly stand as proof of innocence in a criminal trial. With circumstantial and eyewitness evidence against him, a defendant at law would be rightly suspected in this experiment (suspected by the police, prosecution, judge, and jury) of faking the opium trance that is supposed to show how he might have behaved unconsciously on the night of the birthday. The routine thought up by Jennings makes sense as proof only if the reader is persuaded that Blake, a good patient, is sincerely trying to discover the truth for his own sake; and even so, unconscious wish fulfillment might be propelling the hero through the necessary motions, which have already been discussed many times with his doctor as warranting his innocence. In fairness to Collins, it should be said that psychoanalysis is open to a similar objection.

As soon as the reader accepts that the hero took the moonstone while unconscious, the sexual symbolism of the novel appears transparent — at least to twentieth-century readers versed in Freud. It is as if Franklin Blake that night had rudely anticipated his marriage to Rachel Verinder. They are in love, but "the loss of her jewel" — to such a cool lover at such an hour of the night — "seems almost to have turned her brain" (11.118). That is the testimony of her mother, as quoted by Betteredge; well before the end of *The Moonstone* it becomes clear to the reader that the daughter has been at once deeply offended by Blake's act and anxious to protect him, and only the conflict of those feelings has prevented some earlier clarification from occurring. But meanwhile reports of her reaction to "the loss of her Diamond" (12.139) and of "her secret" (23.223) connote an intimacy that cannot publicly be expressed without marriage. On the man's side, the symbolism of the novel suggests determined violation of the woman. Blake's going in and out of doors in an opium trance seems cool enough, but his getting into this situation in the first place trails with it the violation of the temple and theft of the same diamond at Seringapatam.[27] The bad man on that occasion, now deceased, is the relative of both the hero and the heroine. By deeding the diamond to Rachel, her uncle as good as intended her death, and as the novel gets under way it falls to Franklin's lot to "put my cousin's legacy into my cousin's hands" (6.73) — in which clause the first "cousin" refers to the monster and the second to the maiden. No sooner has he undertaken this embassy than "a shabby, dark-complexioned man" begins to follow him about, and in the oriental fantasy of this novel the dark Brahmins symbolize something like the id.[28] An

27. Cf. John R. Reed, "English Imperialism and the Unacknowledged Crime of *The Moonstone*," *Clio* 2 (1973): 281–90.

28. The analyst of the novel, Ezra Jennings, is also dark and of so extraordinary an appearance that it is difficult for Franklin Blake to look at him. Collins seems to have

aside in Miss Clack's narrative hits this interpretation exactly: "how soon," she remarks, "may our own evil passions prove to be Oriental noblemen who pounce on us unawares" (1.1.241). By the time Blake has conveyed the diamond to Yorkshire and placed it in his fair cousin's hands, he and Betteredge have become pretty well aware of the danger posed by three Indians lurking about the house. Yet on the night of the birthday the Indians manage to come out from the shrubbery disguised as jugglers and to confront the dinner guests directly. Few readers can fail to register the sense of exposure and even violation of the heroine in Betteredge's telling of this moment: "there she stood, innocent of all knowledge of the truth, showing the Indians the Diamond in the bosom of her dress!" (10.106). A similar meaning resides beneath the diamond, in a gift from the well-meaning hero worn under the same dress, for later that night Betteredge has seen Miss Rachel "slyly slipping the locket which Mr. Franklin had given to her, out of the bosom of her dress, and showing it to him for a moment, with a smile which certainly meant something out of the common, before she tripped off to bed" (11.113). And probably there is more sexual symbolism that I have failed to note.

Yet though Collins certainly anticipated Freud, and psychoanalysis owes much to nineteenth-century novel making, the symbolism of *The Moonstone* does not point exclusively or even primarily to sexuality as the principal theme. More than most Victorian writers, Collins took sexual attraction for granted, and his theme is more like truthfulness: to recall the order of the titles of the two periods, it is "the discovery of the truth" after "the loss of the diamond." But "truth" in English means more than a true representation; the word has to serve also (as it need not in other European languages) for loyalty and trust. One has only to recall what truthfulness means for Pompilia, Caponsacchi, and the pope in *The Ring and the Book* to sense the important moral dimension of the theme. Collins's novel is about the estrangement of two lovers brought about by representations of the truth in the first place—that is, by the evidence of the heroine's own eyes and by circumstantial evidence on several accounts (even Rachel has learned enough about Franklin's financial debts to infer a motive for his taking the diamond; otherwise she might not believe her own eyes). Thereafter, the main action turns on how trust—truthfulness in the full sense—can be re-

---

felt he needed an Indian (Jennings is apparently half Indian) to cope with the mystery surrounding the other Indians, much as in the last pages of *The Woman in White* he introduced a fresh Italian, backed by a secret society, to cope with Count Fosco.

stored. The book is utterly conventional in this respect, and a good reminder of the conventions necessary to keep in mind in reading *The Golden Bowl*. But since the conditions for trusting differ somewhat according to gender, it is best to consider the heroine's and hero's roles separately.[29]

Rachel Verinder can be typed as a favorite English heroine, spirited and independent but absolutely truthful; and this novel enacts a favorite English plot, a test of the heroine's truth. Since such heroines are committed both to truth telling and to being true, a double bind can easily be tied by putting the two commitments at odds, and this is exactly what Collins does in *The Moonstone*. His Rachel is an utterly frank and truthful person, but she comes into knowledge of an act that threatens to disgrace the man she has set her heart on. She passes the test on several scores: the position she is in nearly makes her ill; she several times allows suspicion to be directed at herself rather than implicate her lover or innocent persons; and above all she continues to be true to the hero in spite of everything. Collins is partly critical of these conventions. His reservations about submitting personal relations to proof are something like Browning's, for among the right sort of persons faith in one another counts most. But Rachel is nevertheless tested, and she has no narrative voice of her own in the novel. Until her confession of loyalty, to judge her truthfulness the reader must depend on the testimony of those who know her. Betteredge clearly testifies to both her truth telling and her loyalty when he states that "there was not so much as a shadow of anything false in her," and that he can "never remember her breaking her word" (8.87). And Lady Verinder asserts, in opposition to Sergeant Cuff, that her daughter "is *absolutely incapable* of doing what you suppose her to have done" (21.205). The assertion that Rachel Verinder is a heroine of truth who can defy even evidence at law comes from the third of her older admirers, the lawyer Bruff himself, who states, "If the plainest evidence in the world pointed one way, and nothing but Rachel's word of honour pointed the other, I would take her word before the evidence, lawyer as I am!" (1.3.262). Not unlike Browning's pope, Bruff believes that a heroine's testimony is always the best evidence. *The Moonstone* is largely a case of Bruff versus Cuff: faith in personal acquaintance rather than chains of circumstance. Collins thus deploys a highly conventional novel plot, the test of the heroine's truth,

29. Cf. Alexander Welsh, "The Allegory of Truth in English Fiction," *Victorian Studies* 9 (1965): 7–28. This article did not deal explicitly with Collins, but some pages on *The Golden Bowl* anticipate what I say about that novel below.

to criticize and finally override the business of detection. Paradoxically, his model work is an antidetective novel.[30]

Franklin Blake's role is that of a hero. He falls under the same cloud of suspicion as the heroine, and to a certain extent their estrangement casts them in parallel roles. When Bruff puts it to him that Rachel "believes you have stolen the diamond," the hero wails, "What right has she to suspect Me, on any evidence, of being a thief?" (3.6.383,385). In short, their mutual trust ought to support his truthfulness. Yet hero and heroine are not strictly parallel. A test of truth—even a martyrdom, as for Cordelia—is common for English heroines, and often it comes down to a loyalty test. Victorian novels make much less an issue of the truthfulness of a hero—either his truth telling, which is taken for granted, or his loyalty, which can be bestowed more widely than a woman's. While the two women in *The Moonstone* who love Franklin Blake suffer their doubts silently, the hero stands before the reader— as the chief suspect of a crime, no less—without having his truthfulness ever really come into question. His innocence has to be seen as even more total than Waverley's, since his involvement with anything anti- social is strictly unconscious. Collins's innovation was the test of the hero's *consciousness* of the truth, which provided a new depth-psycho- logical frame for innocent guilt like Waverley's. The very convention that the reader can take Blake's sincerity for granted lays the groundwork for Ezra Jennings's experiment—though the power of unconscious memory to reproduce the character's past *actions* may be doubted.[31]

Again, while two protagonists may be as necessary to love and marriage as they are to an action of estrangement, the rite of initiation in *The Moonstone* is ultimately the hero's. One should not be misled by the emblem of virginity presented by Rachel Verinder on her birthday, with the moonstone between her breasts and dark men staring. Of course it is her birthday, her openness to violation, her rite of passage too—and death threatens anyone who possesses the moonstone. But she stands there as the object of male desire, and the enactment of the

30. Cf. Miller, *Novel and the Police*, 44. I do not, however, agree that the detective function is "agentless."

31. If Collins had any doubts, he overcame them in this fashion: "Having first ascer- tained, not only from books, but from living authorities as well, what the result of that experiment would really have been, I have declined to avail myself of the novelist's privilege of supposing something which might have happened, and have so shaped the story as to make it grow out of what actually would have happened—which, I beg to inform my readers, is also what actually does happen, in these pages" (from the preface to the first book publication of *The Moonstone*, 1868). Compare Browning's more tem- perate line, "The somehow may be thishow."

rite is the responsibility—though unconscious—of the hero later that night. The intercalation of sexual mating with the celebration of birth and the threat of death marks this as a rite of initiation, for such rites typically invoke several passages of life at once.[32] As in a fairy tale, however, the active role on this occasion is that of the honored birthday guest, the hero. And nothing happens: no real theft takes place except for another cousin's privately removing the diamond to London; no one is murdered or violated. Collins has very cleverly let this prospective rite take the place of the usual climax in so many English novels, a proposal scene. Franklin Blake is never made to ask for Rachel's hand; he just goes in and picks up her diamond and—just as unconsciously—turns it over to cousin Godfrey Ablewhite. The only proposal scene as such in *The Moonstone* is another matter, a lampoon: Godfrey down on his knees before Rachel while Miss Clack, who has her heart set on him and who narrates, peers from behind a curtain.

Collins ensures that the initiation will be the hero's story in two ways. First, the burden of explaining it falls upon the hero, and the accomplishment of this with Jennings's guidance provides the denouement of the novel. But second, the heroine needs no urging or shy awakening to love but has apparently already accepted the situation. Here is another way Collins seems ahead of his time: without compromising the principle of male initiative, he quite likes to portray women as frankly desiring beings—more obviously so than men perhaps. A little like Freud and others at the end of the Victorian era, he reinstates the venerable idea that women are always interested. In *The Moonstone* all the women except Lady Verinder want men (and she, whatever her quotient of desire may have been, was patently the dominant partner in her marriage). Dickens and Thackeray might be capable of satirizing Miss Clack's lusting for a man, but they would not be comfortable with either Rosanna Spearman's or Rachel Verinder's open confession of love. The latter breaks the ordinary rule for heroines by showing right away where her interest lies. Furthermore, she "confessed to her mother that she loved cousin Franklin," according to Bruff, "and her mother . . . trusted cousin Franklin with the secret" (1.3.265). She confesses her love for Franklin again as Godfrey Ablewhite proposes to her, and she tentatively accepts Godfrey on that occasion, as heroines are not supposed to do. The only unpleasant side to Collins's reporting of her passion is the superiority ceded to the hero, who positively exults

32. Cf. Mircea Eliade, *The Sacred and the Profane: The Nature of Religion,* trans. Willard R. Trask (New York: Harcourt, 1959), 184–97.

in his narrative of their interview, "While her hand lay in mine I was her master still!" (3.7.393).

The midnight pantomime of stealing a diamond prefigures the hero's conventional marriage to an heiress rather than a love relation that was already his. Indeed, sayings about "the family jewels" have always yoked sex and property, and even unconsciously—the reader is to believe—Franklin Blake only wants to take the jewel for safekeeping. The significance of the heroine's birthday for him is its sign of her inheritance; the sleepwalking takes place before he has realized his own inheritance, and the passage is therefore one to fortune. Custom and law, furthermore, give the husband and not the wife the right to property.[33] Thus even legally the rite of passage is the hero's and not the heroine's. At the climax of their interview—a second or third alternative in *The Moonstone* to the usual proposal scene—Rachel Verinder angrily breaks out, "*You villain, I saw you take the Diamond with my own eyes!*" (3.7.393). It is like a confirmation of Proudhon's radical definition of property as theft. Though the hero registers a "humiliation" in his narrative of this moment, neither he nor Collins seems to appreciate the crudity of his sexual triumph—"I was her master still"—in the moments following. It is as if women shudderingly enjoyed having their property taken away—all at once, in the first and only important surrender.

Whereas the hero's unconscious motive in removing the diamond is to safeguard it, every proven or supposed motive for stealing it put forward in the novel involves the payment of debts. The true "villain" Godfrey Ablewhite—every syllable of whose name is ironic or opposed to Collins's own values—is so entirely subject to debt that the lawyer Bruff can easily chart his tacking back and forth amid the London loan sharks. Notoriously, Sergeant Cuff concludes that Verinder has stolen her own diamond because he has wide experience of ladies of rank and their private, sometimes secret, debts: she must urgently need to raise money on the diamond. But she herself has every reason to suspect Blake, because she has overheard the demands of a French lawyer who has followed him as far as Yorkshire in pursuit of money owed and finds that her mother has paid Blake's debt for him. The hero's private account of the matter to Bruff tells all: he was foolish "to accept" a loan from a small restaurateur and "found" that he could not pay it back; but such is the experience of "thousands of other honest men" (3.6.386)—that is, of gentlemen. Thus every conscious motive or need

33. See Lee Holcombe, "Victorian Wives and Property: Reform of the Married Women's Property Law, 1857–1882," in *A Widening Sphere: Changing Roles of Victorian Women*, ed. Martha Vicinus (Bloomington: Indiana University Press, 1977), 3–28.

for money entertained in *The Moonstone* is attributed to pressing private debts. An economy that totally ignores production and consumption but respects debt is perhaps as near as one can come to a pure fiction: the idea seems to be of a world inhabited solely by rentiers and their servants. But that is the world of most memorable English novels from Fielding to James, and Collins's attention to detection and individual testimony, to a rite of passage and of property, and to the preservation of a good conscience under damnable circumstances seems only to have made this literary history less ambiguous. What is really astonishing is that English novels should for so long a time have successfully persuaded readers of all classes to identify with such rentiers as Franklin Blake and Rachel Verinder.

The hero and heroine of *The Moonstone* lead charmed lives—he even more than she—and merely their luck is attractive; hence their accession to property may hardly be noticed by readers congratulating them on escaping with their lives. The handling and brief possession of the diamond surround them with death—with Indians, for whom "the sacrifice of life is nothing at all" (10.109)—but happily they do not die. This privilege, which is distinct from mere wealth and power but associated with them, is obviously enhanced in the novel by the deaths of five other characters: Ablewhite, who falls victim to the Indians; Spearman, the victim of suicide; Jennings, prey to a painful disease; and Lady Verinder and Blake Senior, the parents. In the human sacrifice department, therefore, the novelist scores well ahead of the three Indians, who sacrifice only Ablewhite. Though it might be supposed that these deaths of others celebrate the readiness of Rachel Verinder and Franklin Blake to live, they look suspiciously to be about property rather than experience.

The sacrifice of the parents passes without much comment, as if merely incidental to the property plot. Still, while many novelists would be content to leave the inheritances in the offing, Collins chooses to establish the independence of both protagonists well before the denouement. That even before inheriting a vast property each has only the one same-sex parent enhances personal freedom as well as fortune. Franklin Blake's father never directly appears in any of the narratives, and still in the background, he dies. A black-edged letter reaches the hero while he is "wandering in the East" between the novel's two periods, and "it informed me that my father was dead, and that I was heir to his great fortune" (3.1.339). The event opportunely changes the hero's status from that of someone needing a fortune—hence possibly a thief—to that of one possessing a fortune—hence ready for an éclair-

cissement with the heroine on equal terms. The offstage event also gives
authority to Blake's narrative, which begins on this page, with this
news. So the hero's thoughtful arrangement of the several narratives
comprising *The Moonstone* is not without its freight of property.

The deaths of the three other characters—from the same generation
as the protagonists—signify differently according to the alternative lives
they suggest. In the character Ablewhite are deposited all such materialist
motives as might be suspected of the hero. Ablewhite regards only the
diamond's cash value; he is the real thief and real hypocrite, the cousin
whose debts have infected his morals, who actually wants money and
women. He may be the idol of charitable ladies in London, but he has
a villa and mistress in the suburbs. In a novel the hedonist is a marked
man, because unlike a hero he actually believes in pleasure.[34] The two
deformed characters, Spearman and Jennings, have rightly been judged
Collins's more original creations, but getting rid of them is satisfying
too. Rosanna Spearman reduplicates the frank sexuality of the novel's
heroine and is punished for it, so that in the poetic justice of the thing
the heroine need not be punished. Spearman's rather Amazonian name
is refreshing but finally a reminder that aggression from her sex is
unwanted. Her unrequited love, so inconceivable to the hero, is a drag.
She is also a thief and a sore reminder of the theft of the diamond. The
elimination of Ezra Jennings is a little harder to understand except in
conjunction with Spearman's. Even more than she, he is a person capable
of penetrating secrets—a matter he himself is sensitive about in his own
past and in his treatment of Mr. Candy. But it is mainly their suffering
and hopelessness, the miserable lives they lead, that are best brought
to a close. Both are deformed, unattractive, difficult for the hero to
turn his eyes upon; and their survival beyond the end of the novel would
only disturb our identification with the beautiful people.

Though Collins prudently limits their life spans, he is often given
credit for taking notice of such as Rosanna Spearman and Ezra Jennings.
He perhaps had a genuine sympathy for, and questions in his mind
about, stigmatized persons and women he deemed too ugly for love
(Marian Halcombe in *The Woman in White* is his most conspicuous
portrait of the latter). Spearman and Jennings, however, have two other
associations that distinguish them: poverty and homoeroticism. Rosanna herself breaks out with uncontrollable passion for Franklin Blake,

34. Though Dickens, in his forties, may have learned personally of the Bohemian life
from Collins, the latter's Godfrey Ablewhite very likely owes something to Carker the
manager in *Dombey and Son*.

but her passion and deformity appeal to another crippled person, Limping Lucy, who loves her and hopes to live with her in London, where they might comfort and support each other. This plan is upset by Rosanna's infatuation with Blake and destroyed altogether by her suicide, and thereafter Lucy regards the novel's hero as a murderer. It is she who radically draws a line between rich and poor in *The Moonstone* and longs for a French Revolution in England: "Ha, Mr. Betteredge, the day is not far off when the poor will rise against the rich. I pray Heaven they may begin with *him*. I pray Heaven they may begin with *him*" (23.227). Similarly, Jennings's lowly position in life is not due to his organic disease, the pain from which he bears silently, but to his appearance, his mixed race, and the stigma of some "horrible accusation." His experience briefly doubles that of the hero, just as Spearman's overt passion reflects the heroine's, since Blake is also under a cloud when they meet. But Jennings is different: "physiology says, and says truly, that some men are born with female constitutions—and I am one of them!" (3.9.428, 422). Thus he can bond with the hero as they work together to clear away suspicion of what Blake has done. Rachel Verinder, who attends the successful experiment, affectionately recognizes Jennings's kinship with her own sex in this relation; and he just as warmly goes out of his way, in his narrative, to report coming upon her kissing his sleeping patient: "She looked back at me with a bright smile, and a charming colour in her face. 'You would have done it,' she whispered, 'in my place!' " (4.483). Then why should Ezra Jennings die? Besides the reasons of delicacy and convenience already mentioned, the eroticism evoked from Jennings's role and invoked on Spearman's behalf by Lucy runs counter to the conventional novel plot that Collins still insists on perpetuating. Theirs is a love without any bearing on property, and they themselves are very poor. Poverty and homoeroticism, then, are experiences that receive sympathetic interest only before being swept aside.[35]

"You villain, I saw you take the Diamond with my own eyes!" an angry woman has addressed Franklin Blake. Though he can report her asking forgiveness at the end of that interview, it is not clear that *he* ever asks forgiveness or that he has ever done anything wrong. "He's a murderer! he's a murderer! he's a murderer! He has been the death of Rosanna Spearman!" are Limping Lucy's words (23.226). But the charges will not stick. No matter what anyone thinks—Lucy, Rachel,

---

35. Homoeroticism is not remarked by Miller in connection with *The Moonstone*, but it is central to his interpretation of *The Woman in White*; see *Novel and the Police*, 146–91.

or reader—Franklin Blake is innocent, though his own faith might easily be shaken by the evidence. Just before the interview with Rachel, he admits to experiencing a sense of shame and annoyance but not to guilt:

> Innocent as I knew myself to be, certain as I was that the abominable imputation which rested on me must sooner or later be cleared off, there was nevertheless a sense of self-abasement in my mind which instinctively disinclined me to see any of my friends. We often hear (almost invariably, however, from superficial observers) that guilt can look like innocence. I believe it to be infinitely the truer axiom of the two that innocence can look like guilt. (3.6.388)

From this testimony it may be judged that the novel, or at least this hero, has moved still further into the defensive mode since Waverley's time (once again 'tis sixty years since). Blake has not been arrested or at this point even been confronted by Verinder. He has not suffered from opinion as Jennings has. Nor will he be arrested or maligned later—so charmed is his life. With fewer grounds for distress by far than Waverley, Collins's hero generalizes that innocence looks like guilt and implies that guilt is a fiction to be treated accordingly. This "axiom" of late nineteenth-century man—countered only momentarily by the two women—marks another anticipation of Freud's thought. Once readers were thoroughly accustomed to having innocence look like guilt, psychological guilt could be accepted as commonplace.

The Moonstone, I believe, shows how difficult it is to shake off the habit of making strong representations of innocence in the English novel after Fielding and Scott. In his attention to testimony and use of multiple narratives, Collins thought to represent the process and thereby the experience of discovering the truth. But he sequenced the narratives rather than allowing them to pile up as Browning did in *The Ring and the Book*; and he revised the model of a trial, which he claimed to be using, only as far as a suspenseful investigation of the crime, in which the discovery of the truth would be equivalent to a verdict. In his allowance for the possibility of unconscious behavior, he may have advanced a poetry of happening instead of experience, since he necessarily had to resort, as psychoanalysis would, to indirect evidence of the unconscious. Perhaps he made readers ponder what it might mean to perform an act unconsciously, and in Betteredge's narrative he certainly captured some sense of a communal experience.[36] But while

---

36. Cf. Miller, *Novel and the Police,* 37–41. Betteredge's "comical intuitions . . . embody community norms" (40).

driving so hard the usual bargain of sex and property and thinking women spoke only in anger, he let "the discovery of the truth" wag the dog once again.

Breaking the Golden Bowl

The narrative strategies of Henry James's late novels—and the famous style itself—are far more varied and tactical than literary histories often allow. Even the brilliant exposition in his prefaces to the New York Edition of 1907–9 consists largely of second-guessing of his own intentions and ad hoc reasoning about his compositions. The strategy I am concerned with here is that generally known as "Jamesian" point of view: narrating a story in the third person about some first person's consciousness of events. The first Jamesian critic, Percy Lubbock, rightly pointed to the rich investiture in authorial language and knowledge of the characters supposedly undergoing the experience and even admitted that this combined narrative of author and character was a trick possible only in a novel.[37] But Lubbock cheapened the method by steadily implying that its purpose was to sustain dramatic illusion. James designed to explore in this way experience, which he mainly thought of as apprehension rather than doing in any case.[38] It can readily be shown that James exploited the strengths of both direct testimony and managed indirect evidence in his work of representation, and that he drew on more than one kind of narrative in the English and European novel traditions that he knew so well. Others—most notably Austen and Flaubert—had experimented with confining narratives to a limited point of view, just as some—Hawthorne and Brontë, for example— had explored what would come to be called the international theme in

37. Percy Lubbock, *The Craft of Fiction* (New York: Viking, 1957), 156–71, 251–64. First published in 1921.

38. James's reasons for narrating a specific point of view, implicit nearly everywhere in his later fiction, are succinctly stated in his preface to *The Princess Casamassima* (the prefaces all date from 1907 to 1909). He begins with the assumption that consciousness is what needs to be communicated: "the figures in any picture, the agents in any drama, are interesting only in proportion as they feel their respective situations; since the consciousness, on their part, of the complication exhibited forms for us their link of connexion with it." Second, granting this much, one must concede "the unreality of the sharp distinction, where the interest of observation is at stake, between doing and feeling." And from this point of indifference, feeling emerges as more important: "what a man thinks and what he feels are the history and the character of what he does." James further insists that "the great chroniclers"—except for purely epic writers—have usually recognized this principle. See *Literary Criticism: French Writers, Other European Writers, the Prefaces to the New York Edition* (New York: Library of America, 1984), 1088–93.

the novel. Yet in his lifetime (1843–1916) James achieved so much in both these lines that they are justly identified with his name.

The very first sentence of the preface to *The Golden Bowl* reflects the competition of direct and indirect evidence that has so often been the subject of the present book. "What perhaps most stands out for me," James wrote, "is the still marked inveteracy of a certain indirect and oblique view of my presented action." This "mode of treatment," however, may well be "the very straightest and closest possible," for it has emerged from a compromise or combination of strategies. To get closer to the represented action would require confession or eyewitness testimony, with their inherent limitations and untrustworthiness; but to manage the narrative from afar, as a mere author, has always seemed to him hopelessly removed from experience:

> Anything, in short, I now reflect, must always have seemed to me better — better for the process and the effect of representation, my irrepressible ideal — than the mere muffled majesty of irresponsible "authorship." Beset constantly with the sense that the painter of the picture or the chanter of the ballad (whatever we may call him) can never be responsible *enough,* and for every inch of his surface and note of his song, I track my uncontrollable footsteps, right and left, after the fact, while they take their quick turn, even on stealthiest tiptoe, toward the point of view that, within the compass, will give me most instead of least to answer for.[39]

It may be remembered that, for the young James, the first "irresponsible" novel was Scott's *Waverley,* which was also like a ballad and curiously "undertook to prove nothing but facts."[40] In that early and accurate perception of literary history, he played with the idea of irresponsibility to characterize the transition from didacticism to realism. The playfulness, to be sure, tugged at the practice of strong representation, doubted a little the demise of the didactic novel, even as it praised Scott. Now at the end of his career, James embraces representation as his own "irrepressible ideal" and from his renowned seniority in the profession, as it were, rules on the responsibility of novelists to track experience. He follows "after the fact" still, because he has by no means thrown over the tradition of Fielding and Scott, Balzac and Dickens; but he marches with "uncontrollable footsteps" because the same tra-

---

39. Henry James, *The Golden Bowl,* 2 vols. (1909; rpt. New York: Kelley, 1971), v–vi. Further references to this reissue of the New York Edition of the novel will be given by book, chapter, and page numbers in parentheses; books 1–3 comprise the first volume and books 4–6, the second.

40. See chapter 2, note 73.

dition—at its best it was scarcely "muffled"—managed narrative for the wrong ends. By uncontrollable steps James does not mean some new form of irresponsibility, but he rejects plotting in advance what ought to happen in favor of empathy with the characters. The choice of a point of view, finally, will fall to the one that gives most "to answer for," since—as with Browning—the work of art, or heightened apprehension, is also an epitome of experience.[41]

Reading a late James novel is nonetheless dictated by what the author permits one to know, even if the parameters have been fixed by this ideal of his submission to one or more characters. Since, presumably, to work out the prince's thoughts at the beginning of *The Golden Bowl* will give the author most to answer for, he follows that character's footsteps into Bond Street in London. The shops and passersby are conducive to a young nobleman's free association and begin to curb the restlessness that brought him here; but that consequence is only a sign that the author has directed each footstep after all—and in thus beginning has made a thousand other choices, mostly of omission. Rapidly it becomes apparent that all sights and sounds give way in this first chapter to reverie and recollection by the character. As James focuses the prince's consciousness on some necessary exposition of events that have gone before, only his management of the verb tense (the rest of the chapter reverts to the past perfect) keeps any sense of the present moment before the reader. So while Amerigo is being agreeably used in this way—not wholly different from the way he is used by Maggie Verver and her father in the novel—ironies that even James may not be fully aware of dance about the narrative. But in the main he is as firmly in control of the design as Fielding could wish to be. Within a few more chapters, the screen of dramatic irony that colors any reading of this novel has been set in place. The reader quickly learns something the Ververs do not know: namely, that the prince and Charlotte Stant were acquainted before he met Maggie. The Ververs are aware that Charlotte has suddenly turned up for Maggie's wedding to the prince, but they are not privileged to know, as the reader is, anything of the first major scene—

41. Like Collins in the preface to *The Moonstone,* but far more persuasively, James treated the priority of character in his preface to *The Portrait of a Lady.* For warranting this stance he cited Turgenev at some length but was quick to bring forward his own habit of "investing some conceived or encountered individual, some brace or group of individuals, with the germinal property and authority" of his fictions (*Literary Criticism . . . Prefaces,* 1071–74). For James's attitude toward Browning, see Ross Posnock, *Henry James and the Problem of Robert Browning* (Athens: University of Georgia Press, 1985); also James, "The Novel in *The Ring and the Book*" (1912), in *Literary Criticism: Essays,* 791–811.

in their own novel, so to speak, or at least Maggie's novel. Walking by private appointment in Bloomsbury this time, the prince and Charlotte discover the shop with the golden bowl, a piece of flawed crystal that would appear to be as deadly a gift for anyone as Collins's flawed diamond. Though Amerigo dissuades Charlotte from purchasing the bowl as a gift for either Maggie or himself, the reader has now necessarily been alerted to the discovery of their past and of this scene—since a golden bowl, after all, has been trumpeted in the novel's title.

The precise history of the prince and Charlotte is never clear. Notoriously, shortly after this expedition to Bloomsbury, Colonel and Mrs. Assingham discuss whether the two friends had "time" for an affair in their previous relations. By deliberately querying the relationship but leaving the answer ambiguous, James ensures that its discovery by Maggie in the second volume cannot be reduced to a strong representation of the facts; rather, he intends to represent her experience of knowing and living with the knowledge. Yet since the reader has been told of it, the mere concealment of the past and the shopping trip put discovery in suspense; and after Maggie's marriage to the prince and her father's quite more extraordinary marriage to Charlotte go forward (and James needs the better part of his first volume just to make the second marriage plausible),[42] the dramatic irony is nothing less than melodramatic—or if the style would permit, sensational. Needless to say, such an achievement depends on the closest supervision of the prince's point of view while following him about London. For what would be more natural for Amerigo, when he hears of Charlotte's return, than to think quite precisely on what their former relationship had been? Charlotte also possesses much useful knowledge of the past and knows her own motives for coming to the wedding. But so wary is James of Charlotte that he virtually excludes her consciousness from the novel, quite as Maggie excludes her from knowledge in the final episodes.[43]

42. For the donnée of the novel, see *The Notebooks of Henry James,* ed. F. O. Matthiessen and Kenneth B. Murdock (New York: Braziller, 1955), 130–31, 187–88.

43. Charlotte's point of view is briefly accommodated by the opening chapter of book 3, as she verges on speaking to Fanny Assingham about her position. From then on the privacy of her thoughts is never violated again, so that the question of her potential availability is as enticing to the reader, perhaps, as it is to Prince Amerigo. In not narrating the thoughts of the false and sexually forward woman, James has ample precedent in Thackeray, to cite but one novelist. The reader learns just as little of the thoughts of Becky Sharp in *Vanity Fair,* Beatrix in *Henry Esmond,* or Blanche Amory in *Pendennis* as of Charlotte's. Their deceptions are thus left to be discovered by events, and the reader is thereby encouraged to identify with the protagonist and better-behaved characters who

In his preface to *The Golden Bowl,* James tried to make out that the novel's two volumes, entitled "The Prince" and "The Princess," reflected the points of view of the two characters. Such was his design, no doubt; but the footsteps led right and left, this way and that, and consequently he can claim no more than a carefully qualified "manner in which the whole thing remains subject to the register, ever so closely kept, of the consciousness of but two of the characters" (vi). In practice, not only was he very selective of the consciousness of those two characters over time—as their entire histories might be construed by a Morgann or a Bradley, say—but his apportionment of pages to them varies markedly. The prince's consciousness is forced to share the first volume with dialogues between the Assinghams, with Adam Verver's thoughts, and with some few pages of Charlotte's; much of the time the prince is simply not around in the volume named for him. The second volume is given over more consistently to Maggie's consciousness, but far from absolutely. And of course in both volumes, in accordance with the method, the author is as ubiquitous in his way as Fielding was in his unmuffled majesty.

In his preface James also half suggested that, in assigning points of view, he had made less of detached observers and more of participants in the action of *The Golden Bowl.* But in the writing he depended heavily on Fanny and Bob Assingham as observers—at least one of them detached. He was stringent of characters in any case: there are only the four principals—their odd personal relations like a square with two love triangles overlying it—and the two Assinghams off to one side. The dialogues of the last two not only serve the reader well, by taking the measure of the square and calculating triangles, but almost surely helped the writer in conceiving of the action and its denouement. Because Fanny Assingham—an American married to her colonel and now permanently resident in England—is the matchmaker of the novel, her role within the fiction is congruent with James's outside it.[44] Though James,

---

are similarly in the dark. At least since F. O. Matthiessen, *Henry James: The Major Phase* (1944; rpt. New York: Oxford University Press, 1963), 96–104, in fact, the novelist has received a bad press for his treatment—or Maggie's treatment—of Charlotte Verver in the last books of *The Golden Bowl.* But the charge of cruelty, I suggest, is easily brought against James because he describes—through Maggie's consciousness—so much more of the antiheroine's suffering than is customary.

44. My view of the Assinghams' role in the novel corresponds to that of Ruth Bernard Yeazell, *Language and Knowledge in the Late Novels of Henry James* (Chicago: University of Chicago Press, 1976), 87–99. Though Yeazell writes of Fanny as "a parody of the Jamesian artist" (97), this remark is not offered as a dismissal. For the contrary notion that the Assinghams' perceptions are superficial, see R. B. J. Wilson, *Henry James's Ultimate*

as the aloof Flaubertian artist, can permit himself no visible interest in the outcome of the story, Fanny has a social stake in the marriages she helped arrange. The far more detached Bob can keep his valuable critical distance from the action merely with husbandlike questions, such as "why keep meddling?" (1.4.86). Fanny's apprehension of the principal characters is limited, since James feels that even his own power of composition is the reward of putting questions that give him most to answer for, and not an absolute power of authorship. But this very limitation makes the business of knowing easy to dramatize, accessible to the reader, and the place to start when reviewing what the novel does with evidence.

The typical dialogues of the Assinghams—scenes in their own right in *The Golden Bowl*—commence with close speculation and inference from slight evidence, then range from hopeful forecasting to outright prophecy on Fanny's side. Once Charlotte, as Mrs. Verver, finds herself in a position to consummate her friendship with her son-in-law, she naturally begins to deny Mrs. Assingham access to more knowledge of her attitudes and activities. But when the adultery has taken place, Fanny no less than Maggie herself senses a difference in the air. Her dialogue with the colonel in the last two chapters of the novel's first volume is thus more sober and more daring than earlier talks. In the first of these chapters Fanny pushes her inferences in a direction parallel to the adulterers' own sense of their position, which she of course can only surmise. They have not returned from Matcham, she supposes, in order to demonstrate "good faith" behind "their false position. It comes to the same thing" (3.10.376). But just when the reader judges that this time Fanny has altogether surrendered to wishful thinking, she bursts into tears that show she well understands the thinness of her argument. Then in the following chapter she looks to the future once more and to Maggie, as the heroine and wise fool who will save the others: so far does Fanny regain her authority from this upswing of the dialogue that she can once more look back, in language reminiscent of the Master, at "the beautiful symmetry of my plan" (3.11.389).

The authority earned within the second volume, "The Princess," is of course Maggie's: her awakening—still partly disguised as anxious concern for her father—her inferences, and her wisdom dominate the

---

Narrative: "The Golden Bowl" (Saint Lucia: University of Queensland Press, 1981), 169–81. Wilson consequently reads Fanny's breaking of the bowl as self-serving and "a reversion, under pressure, to old discredited means of dealing with newly ramifying difficulties" (179).

upswing of the novel as a whole.[45] Yet because of the overt dialogue and the degree of detachment in the part played by the two Assinghams, their contribution comes closest to a study of the evidence as such. At times the discussion resembles a debate in some armchair courtroom, with the colonel in cross-examination. At the opening of the same long dialogue, which so rapidly descends to wishful thinking only to rise again to heights of inspiration, Bob Assingham has patiently waited for his wife to begin, sensing that her thoughts that night are somewhere in proverbial "deep waters." In *The Golden Bowl* such elaborate metaphors as this confirm the seriousness with which James regards the character, though—as with Browning's two lawyers in *The Ring and the Book*—he permits more humor in the performances by the Assinghams than he does elsewhere in the novel. It is also one of the rare times that James "goes behind" the colonel's thoughts.

> She had been out there on these waters for him, visibly; and his tribute to the fact had been his keeping her, even if without a word, well in sight. He hadn't quitted for an hour, during her adventure, the shore of the mystic lake; he had on the contrary stationed himself where she could signal to him at need. Her need would have arisen if the planks of her bark had parted—*then* some sort of plunge would have been his immediate duty. His present position, clearly, was that of seeing her in the centre of her sheet of dark water, and of wondering if her actual mute gaze at him didn't perhaps mean that her planks *were* now parting. He held himself so ready that it was quite as if the inward man had pulled off coat and waistcoat. Before he had plunged, however—that is before he had uttered a question—he saw, not without relief, that she was making for land. He

45. The most recent interpretation I have seen, Sharon Cameron's *Thinking in Henry James* (Chicago: University of Chicago Press, 1989), 83–121, by insisting on the novel's "problematic" of reference rather than the dramatic action, denies that an upswing occurs. But Cameron never adequately locates this problematic in the novel, though she believes that the second volume "exists to contest" (95) the notion of "shared reference" that is "dominant" in the first (107). A great many pages of James's writings focus on attempts by one person to reach the consciousness of another, and he shows how this is possible through the use of inference (Fanny and Maggie, from different starting points, most obviously master the process in this novel). I take Cameron at her word that she believes "when you see into another's mind, what you see is the difference from yours" (102), and "to look into another's mind is to be blocked by its impenetrability" (108), but as the history of circumstantial evidence from criminal prosecution to psychoanalysis shows, it is not necessary to stop short with this difference or impenetrability. Cameron notes that "characters in *The Golden Bowl* are not concerned with what can be known but rather with what can be done" (84), and she eventually demurs that "the novel's problematic, which I have been developing, and the novel's subject have curiously little to do with each other" (119).

watched her steadily paddle, always a little nearer, and at last he felt her boat bump. The bump was distinct, and in fact she stepped ashore. "We were all wrong. There's nothing."

"Nothing—?" It was like giving her his hand up the bank.

"Between Charlotte Verver and the Prince. I was uneasy—but I'm satisfied now. I was in fact quite mistaken. There's nothing."

"But I thought," said Bob Assingham, "that that was just what you did persistently asseverate. You've guaranteed their straightness from the first."

"No—I've never till now guaranteed anything but my own disposition to worry. I've never till now," Fanny went on gravely from her chair, "had such a chance to see and to judge. I had it at that place—if I had, in my infatuation and my folly," she added with expression, "nothing else. So I did see—I *have* seen. And now I know." Her emphasis, as she repeated the word, made her head, in her seat of infallibility, rise higher. "I know."

The Colonel took it—but took it at first in silence. "Do you mean they've *told* you—?"

"No—I mean nothing so absurd. For in the first place I haven't asked them, and in the second their word in such a matter wouldn't count."

"Oh," said the Colonel with all his oddity, "they'd tell *us*."

It made her face him an instant as with her old impatience of his short cuts, always across her finest flower-beds; but she felt none the less that she kept her irony down. "Then when they've told you, you'll be perhaps so good as to let me know."

He jerked up his chin, testing the growth of his beard with the back of his hand while he fixed her with a single eye. "Ah I don't say that they'd necessarily tell me that they *are* over the traces." (3.10.366–67)

Beneath such distinctions between boating and lifesaving, flowerbeds and beards—the Assinghams have strictly gendered comic roles in the novel—lie differences in weighing evidence throughout. Though Fanny—in order to get up courage, it seems—speaks here with papal "infallibility," her ordinary mode is endless inference from close observation. Her husband as usual would rather have direct evidence, while his irony in this instance shows precisely why direct evidence would not do. When he points out that the prince and Charlotte would be likely to testify truly only if they were innocent, he points up a notorious weakness of testimony in criminal cases and also the weakness of his own general position. Still, he would value their denial, whereas Fanny's training is not to expect words one way or the other but to put two and two together for herself, as she narrates her boat across deep waters. Her weaker half, or husband, plays straight man to her authorial intelligence and hence plays repeatedly to her hand, as here. "Do you mean they've *told* you?" The question should stop inference in midstream, since Fanny is wrong about the facts this time, and in that sense the planks of her boat are certainly falling apart. And she will exacerbate her wrong in the second volume, by tampering with the evidence. Yet the novel still underwrites her position.

The Golden Bowl resembles *The Moonstone* in other ways besides the headlining of a flawed symbol. Though they differ radically in style, both novels offer several points of view of the action, as well as heroines who can absolutely be depended on. When Fanny Assingham allows herself to believe in the technical innocence of Charlotte and the prince, the novel enacts another mistaken conclusion from circumstantial evidence. "This isn't murder," Fanny will exclaim; but neither was Collins concerned with murder, and both novels in their different ways finally come to represent initiations. Undoubtedly James adopts certain routines of the Victorian sensation novel and transforms them in his last great work. Bob and Fanny Assingham study as closely as detectives the question of what Charlotte and the prince may have done on the afternoon following their stay at Matcham. "They got it clear," Fanny says of the evident opportunity, "inasmuch as they didn't become traceable again, as we know, till late in the evening." James then comments on the dialogue as it proceeds:

> On this historic circumstance Mrs. Assingham was always ready afresh to brood; but she was no less ready, after her brooding, devoutly to add: "Only we know nothing whatever else—for which all our stars be thanked!"
>
> The Colonel's gratitude was apt to be less marked. "What did they do for themselves, anyway, from the moment they got that free hand to the moment (long after dinner-time, haven't you told me?) of their turning up at their respective homes?"
>
> "Well, it's none of your business!"
>
> "I don't speak of it as mine, but it's only too much theirs. People are always traceable, in England, when tracings are required. Something sooner or later happens; somebody sooner or later breaks the holy calm. Murder will out."

But this very colloquy about a fact in issue and the traces it leaves for discovery is the cue for Mrs. Assingham's sharp rejoinder, "Murder will—but this isn't murder" (4.7.134). Her resistance to an inference she herself is fully able to draw is something like Lady Verinder's resistance to Sergeant Cuff's finding on the basis of circumstantial evidence, with this difference: in *The Moonstone* Lady Verinder proves to be right on the facts and all innocence is strictly preserved, whereas in *The Golden Bowl* Mrs. Assingham is prepared to back a solution that overrides the facts if necessary. The latter's denial, "this isn't murder," becomes an affirmation of life; her heroine, Maggie, is already busy picking up similar cues, and not merely clues, from the behavior of the others. James's superior irony can meanwhile be felt in the phrase "this historic circumstance"—a fact in issue that might easily have been the object of a strong representation like a murder (a poisoning case, say) but in this novel is a fact so subdued that readers have been known to miss it altogether. Instead of asking what happened or magnifying the secret of the past, or aiming at "the discovery of the truth," the novelist and his two closest deputies, Fanny Assingham and the princess, concentrate on the salvageable present and future.[46]

The princess's consciousness, obviously—and not only her sexual awakening, mediated by the prince's adultery, but her quickening intelligence and assertiveness—is the study of the second volume. But insofar as I am claiming that James not only was capable of ironizing the "historic circumstance" of his own novel but was placing in perspective a certain historic narrative from circumstances, it is necessary to follow a little further the footsteps of Fanny Assingham. She is the only character besides the heroine, in the second volume, to be ceded briefly her point of view; she is summoned to the scene by the heroine precisely when the golden bowl makes its reappearance in the novel; and she is summoned by the novelist to shatter the bowl against the polished floor, in the house in Portland Place. That action catches Maggie a little by surprise, to be sure, but a character in a novel is never so bold as to destroy what is named in the very title of the book without tacit direction from the author—the one who "can never be responsible *enough.*" In a novel with as few visible actions as this—merely its two

---

46. Mark Seltzer, *Henry James and the Art of Power* (Ithaca: Cornell University Press, 1984), 59–95, treats *The Golden Bowl* somewhat the way D. A. Miller treats *The Moonstone* (note 21 above—their common ground is the notion of power derived from Michel Foucault). But of course *The Golden Bowl* is not a sensation novel—it is significantly about adultery rather than bigamy, for example—and though Seltzer makes some important points, he has no substantial grounds for adducing the "criminal" continuity of love and power (66, 80, 94). He is certainly stretching a point when he ascribes "people are always traceable" to Fanny, the more authoritative of the two Assinghams, rather than to the colonel (63). As I have indicated, it is Fanny who corrects this apprehension in the novel.

prodigious kisses have caused remark—the bowl breaks with unforgettable violence, the more so because its breaker steps out of the passive role of providing interpretation. It is a memorable moment in James's fiction and, I would argue, a last rite of circumstantial evidence.[47]

How the piece of flawed crystal turns up again in the story must strain most readers' belief, but as the part titles "The Prince" and "The Princess" suggest, *The Golden Bowl* is also something of a fairy tale. Rejected four years earlier by the prince in his private shopping trip with Charlotte, the bowl has remained in the Bloomsbury shop until Maggie, seeking a birthday gift for her father, purchases it at a price that would be justified only if it were not flawed. The shopkeeper supposedly has a twinge of conscience and comes around to the house, where he sees pictures of the two who visited his shop before and tells Maggie the story. James partially succeeds in veiling the coincidence by making the shopkeeper more and more mysterious, as if in a fairy tale he had come to haunt or help the prince and princess. The discovery, however, mentally pulls together for Maggie everything she has felt since the night her husband returned late from Matcham. That he was privately, if not secretly, with Charlotte shortly before her marriage supplies a last link to her surmises that they had some relationship besides what was known to her. She thereupon summons Fanny Assingham so as to confront her with the evidence and find out what she knows. But despite Fanny's partial connivance in concealing the old friendship of Charlotte and Amerigo and the anxious measure of her own responsibility, she is firmly allied with the heroine in the scene that follows. Maggie essentially wishes to learn, and neither to prove nor to condemn; and she is now in possession of "the proof," as she calls it— the bowl that has conveyed to her a specific history. The bowl on the mantlepiece is a fact, as Collins's Franklin Blake might say; or as Maggie declares to Mrs. Assingham, "That cup there has turned witness."

---

47. This argument is at least congruent with recent philosophical approaches to *The Golden Bowl* by Paul B. Armstrong and Martha Craven Nussbaum. In *The Phenomenology of Henry James* (Chapel Hill: University of North Carolina Press, 1983), 136–86, Armstrong enlists Husserl, Sartre, Merleau-Ponty, and Heidegger to delineate the epistemology, and especially the problem of "the opacity of others," that James works with in the novel. I suggest that a native vocabulary of circumstantial evidence enabled James to drive home the very same points; it is possible to cope indirectly with the opacity of others, that is, but *The Golden Bowl* does not endorse coping that is professionally managed or morally conclusive. In a series of articles, Nussbaum has perceptively argued that James's novel, by affording a "sustained exploration of particular lives," describes a complexity of understanding and response that eludes moral theory or scientific knowledge. See especially her "Flawed Crystals: James's *The Golden Bowl* and Literature as Moral Philosophy," *New Literary History* 15 (1983): 39–47.

Fanny, though she is the witness called for cross-examination in the scene, dodges the point and asks how Maggie and her husband will get through dinner at the ambassador's that evening with this new difficulty "unexplained"; but Maggie replies that the story told by the bowl is "fully, intensely, admirably explained" without her personally confronting Amerigo at all. "I've plenty to go upon and to do with as it is," she believes, and she is determined to wait for him to speak.

> Mrs. Assingham turned it over. "Then it all depends on that object that you regard, for your reasons, as evidence?"
>
> "I think I may say that *I* depend upon it. I can't," said Maggie, "treat it as nothing now."
>
> Mrs. Assingham, at this, went closer to the cup on the chimney . . . "Then it all depends on the bowl? I mean your future does? For that's what it comes to, I judge."
>
> "What it comes to," Maggie presently returned, "is what that thing has put me, so almost miraculously, in the way of learning: how far they had originally gone together. If there was so much between them before, there can't—with all the other appearances—not be a great deal more now." And she went on and on; she steadily made her points. (4.9.161–68)

For the heroine, in short, the introduction of the bowl completes her case, an argument scrupulously developed from the circumstantial evidence—or a strong representation if she chose to make it more conclusive and stressed knowing rather than learning.

In this scene Fanny Assingham's own far-reaching capacity for inference is more than matched by Maggie's, as indeed the princess's intelligence steers the long denouement that fills the second half of the novel. Though the heroine is somewhat crossly, and understandably so, completing her case with respect to the past and present, she does not really need the reminder that the future is what any such discovery "comes to." Since Matcham and the midpoint of the novel she has shown signs of tending to the future; moreover, *The Golden Bowl* itself, viewed as the last in the series of James's novels—or even as the last English novel of an epoch—takes the same turn.[48] For James in *The*

---

48. One may recall Bruff's advice in *The Moonstone* to tend to the future, which the hero overrides with his quasi-psychoanalytic insistence on uncovering the past. Though Collins's novel also turns aside from this advice, James's aggressively takes it up, led by the rather steely determination of the princess to ignore what has occurred. Cf. Gabriel Pearson, "The Novel to End All Novels: *The Golden Bowl*," in *New Essays on Henry James*, ed. John Goode (London: Methuen, 1972), 360: "every subsequent novel can be

Portrait of a Lady and elsewhere had addressed the future only with instances of heroic renunciation; and even in *The Ambassadors* and *The Wings of the Dove,* which in some respects form a trilogy with his last novel, the results wrested from moving accessions of consciousness are at best comically, at worst tragically belated.[49] Maggie Verver, though she may be princess only of volume 2, sees her way in time and seizes the future like the heroine of a comedy that she is, though this is a comedy so sobered with detection and experience that it has probably never brought many readers to smile. Fanny Assingham draws the smiles and also delivers the novel's one audible shock, by abruptly and deliberately destroying the evidence of the past.

> And Fanny Assingham, who had been casting about her and whose inspiration decidedly had come, raised the cup in her two hands, raised it positively above her head and from under it solemnly smiled at the Princess as a signal of intention. So for an instant, full of her thought and of her act, she held the precious vessel, and then with due note taken of the margin of the polished floor, bare fine and hard in the embrasure of her window, dashed it boldly to the ground, where she had the thrill of seeing it lie shattered with the violence of the crash. (4.9.178–79)

Though the act startles Maggie as much as the reader, Fanny's "signal of intention" sufficiently invites the heroine to intervene if she pleases. As to their intentions, the older and younger women see pretty much alike. The fate of strong representation in the novel, a representation of adultery and duplicity, is decided by their conniving destruction of the evidence.[50]

If there is also duplicity in mistreating evidence this way, that is a responsibility Maggie accepts in the remaining action. She is to begin with in *The Golden Bowl* a heroine of truth like Rachel Verinder, but

---

viewed as in some way post-novelistic—parasitic, parodic, nostalgic, ironic—or in some more or less posthumous relationship to the great classical nineteenth-century novel, whose last paradoxical example is *The Golden Bowl.*"

49. Cf. the very last gesture permitted Maria Gostrey: "she sighed it at last all comically, all tragically, away." Henry James, *The Ambassadors,* 2 vols. (1909; rpt. New York: Kelley, 1971), 2:327.

50. Armstrong essentially makes the same point as I do about evidence in the novel. While he writes that the Bloomsbury shopkeeper "provides Maggie with a point of entry into the hermeneutic circle," noting Maggie's "interpretation of the bowl," her "hermeneutic abilities," and "her hermeneutic encounter with the bowl" (*Phenomenology of Henry James,* 164–67), however, I have been arguing that in the guise of circumstantial evidence a hermeneutics of suspicion antedates nineteenth- and twentieth-century philosophy.

with still more in common with Dickens's Amy Dorrit and Florence Dombey, or Scott's Jeanie Deans: that is, not only a heroine who undergoes a test of truth but one who is to save the others of her family or immediate community. "It will be *she* who'll see us through," in the typical promise of Mrs. Assingham (3.3.280). Maggie herself fully accepts this role in the end, as she thinks of the powerful "temptation" of her accrual of knowledge but realizes that the others rely on her to assume "the whole complexity of their peril," and indeed "because she was there, and there just *as* she was, to lift it off them and take it; to charge herself with it as the scapegoat of old." But as she immediately also recognizes, modern heroine that she is, she is not to die—like Browning's Pompilia—but to live: "live on somehow for their benefit, and even as much as possible in their company, to keep proving to them that they had truly escaped and that she was still there to simplify" (5.2.233–35). So many nineteenth-century Beatrices or Cordelias live, and—not to put too fine a point on it—live happily ever after, that Maggie cannot claim originality on this score.[51] Far more surprisingly, she has begun to identify living with lying. Even the sexual awakening she appears to experience in the second volume owes something to duplicity, and not merely to mediation. More precisely, it is not sex she is learning about (she is after all the mother of a Principino) but intimacy, and that she learns from her own exclusion from a part of her husband's life.[52] She learns that intimacy *means* exclusion, and she begins to exclude Charlotte and, still more gingerly, her father from her life. She breaks up the square with two triangles, and to do this requires more than a few family and social lies. Almost immediately in volume 2—and so much is unprecedented for a heroine, unless a figure of falsehood like Becky Sharp—she feels herself to be an actress: "she went—she felt herself going; she reminded herself of an actress" (4.2.33); "she felt not unlike some young woman of the theatre" (5.1.208). Thus as she takes on the sins of the others as the scapegoat of old, she will not be a martyr to truth but more likely will project different truths for different members of the audience. She breaks out

51. The denouement of *The Golden Bowl*, as Armstrong rightly argues (182–84), has Charlotte rather than Maggie serving as the scapegoat in the accepted uses of this term. Still, Maggie herself notes the anomaly of performing as a living scapegoat, and her observation touches some of the principal contradictions of the heroine's special role in English novels—contradictions most evident in the high Victorian pedestal erected beneath an Agnes Wickfield, say, but not fully to be comprehended without study of Rose Bradwardines and Sophia Westerns as well.

52. " 'What one considers intimate? Well, I know what I consider intimate now. Too intimate,' said Maggie, 'to let me know anything about it' " (4.9.161).

of the double bind of truth for heroines by accepting the condition of loyalty and at the same time learning to lie. She will be as loyal to her husband and father as Cordelia but will not tell them unfortunate truths that would disable both them and herself. And to her rival, the splendid Charlotte out of her cage in the interlude of the bridge game—one of James's great dramatic scenes—she will lie outright. When Charlotte asks for satisfaction, in effect, by demanding to know how she has offended, Maggie is prepared for her. "It was only a question of not by a hair's breadth deflecting into the truth," and James's heroine swears on her honor that she has not been offended (5.2.250–51).

Thus Maggie Verver both is and is not the conventional figure of truth of English allegory: the novel inexorably moves toward a sustained and glorious triumph of truth, not without its splendid animal dragged beneath the chariot wheels, yet the awakened heroine seals her victory by conscious lying. Likewise *The Golden Bowl* both is and is not a highly conventional novel, and it ought to be more widely recognized for its literary historical iconoclasm. It was written, after Hardy and Conrad had entered their contributions, by an adopted Englishman who was possibly more familiar with the European novel than any novelist since Scott, and whose novels on the international theme had already left behind the most common plot—the courtship plot—of English fiction. Yet *The Golden Bowl,* though it rapidly stands convention on its head,[53] tracks this conventional plot more closely than *The Ambassadors* or *The Wings of the Dove.* It begins instead of ends with the principal marriage, and names like "Amerigo," "Adam," and "American City"—to say nothing of peopling the novel with a prince and princess—are modishly unrealistic and also poke fun at James's own favorite themes and characters. To be thus raucously conventional is to write about the novel as it had previously been conceived. English novels were not about adultery, as James well knew, but about courtship as a prelude to marriage; they nevertheless often made it their business to sort out a triangle, but typically one of father, daughter, and hero.[54] The daughter, in the usual plot, has somehow to form a marriage without seeming to break with her father or other male guardian, and this is the action that James

---

53. James virtually eradicates the significance of property in the plot by heaping up wealth for the hero and heroine to begin with. "I haven't the least idea . . . what you cost," Maggie says to Amerigo, who on his part is very much aware that "all about him, was money, was power, the power of the rich peoples" (1.1.12, 17–18). They have done nothing and will do nothing to deserve all this.

54. Cf. Ruth Bernard Yeazell, "Podsnappery, Sexuality, and the English Novel," *Critical Inquiry* 9 (1982): 339–57.

imitates in his last novel, though with an outlandish twist.[55] Maggie, who has lived and traveled about with Adam Verver as her sole parent since she was ten, for all intents and purposes goes right on living with him after her marriage to Amerigo. To that triangle, prompted by his witty little donnée, James added the extraordinary second marriage of the father and the adulterous triangle. The solving of the latter, or Continental, triangle leads to the solving of the former, and *The Golden Bowl* concludes quite conventionally with the true marriage of hero and heroine—the same with which it began.[56]

One has only to recall how unusual for James that happy ending really is. For this celebration of intimacy he determined on a plot that externally went nowhere, in respect either to its beginning or to the English novel convention: by hedging his heroine's coming of age, however, he made sure of his novel's revisionary status, as a representation not of innocence but of experience. The main puzzle left dangling was the unfortunate father. In *The Golden Bowl* even the Assinghams cannot figure out Adam Verver, and he seems to be left to the reader's free imagination.[57] "Charlotte's too inconceivably funny husband," as Fanny calls him (4.7.135), is partly comic, no doubt, because he is the cuckold; though in a novel with a sublime "fool" as heroine, we are sometimes asked to accept Adam's sublimity too, without being given any glimpse of his consciousness that would confirm it. Maggie's anxiety to protect her father and Fanny's cautions on the subject become a little precious, to say the least.[58] But perhaps the best way to understand

55. Virginia Fowler, *Henry James's American Girl: The Embroidery on the Canvas* (Madison: University of Wisconsin Press, 1984), 107–40, provides the most complete account of *The Golden Bowl* as an assertion of the heroine's independence from her father.

56. Dickens, Thackeray, and George Eliot all wrote major novels about first marriages that were unsatisfactory, but the best known of these concluded with a second, happy marriage in the usual form. *The Golden Bowl,* in contrast, represents continuously the original marriage and the risks it is exposed to.

57. On Adam Verver, see John Bayley, *The Characters of Love* (London: Constable, 1960), 248–53. That Verver does not quite succeed as "a fantasy figure," according to Bayley, reflects Matthiessen's earlier judgment that, oddly, "James seems to take Mr. Verver at his own estimate" (*Henry James,* 89).

58. With an unsparing examination of Maggie's line, "only sad and strange and not caused by our fault" (6.1.333), Philip M. Weinstein, *Henry James and the Requirements of the Imagination* (Cambridge: Harvard University Press, 1971), 191–94, produces the most damaging moral criticism of the father-daughter relation as James conceived it. The problem seems to go back to James's mere sketch of the plot in 1892, when he characterized the relation as "exceptional" but not even remotely wrong or incestuous: "a necessary basis for all this," he conjectured then, "must have been an intense and exceptional degree of attachment between the father and the daughter—he peculiarly paternal, she passionately filial." But the reason this idea for "a little tale" (*Notebooks,* 130–31) emerged as so

the tenderness and solicitude expressed for the man is again to recall the basis of the plot, the delicate withdrawal from the side of her father to that of her husband—the story of Adam and Eve with three actors. In his other novels James is not solicitous of fathers; in this one he writes of fathers as Dickens might. For Maggie to be so assiduously careful of her parent, of course, enables her to pursue her own ends with apparent modesty: her maneuvering toward the novel's denouement is for Adam Verver's sake, she feels. The modesty is also conventional[59]—yet she sends her father packing, with Charlotte, back to American City. The implication, perhaps, is that only the American girl—the true hero of the international theme—can fully assimilate the European experience. *The Golden Bowl* is James's stirrup cup and burial urn for America, that is, as well as for the English novel.

That children may survive them is the solace of parents, but the solace at the same time bears the tidings of death. A daughter born or a daughter awakened to life marks the beginning of the end for the father she is expected to care for, in the male-centered myths and realities of our culture. No wonder the Cordelias and Maggies are expected to save men, if they likewise inexorably point to departures and passings. The quizzical marriage arrangements in the donnée for *The Golden Bowl* enabled the author to underscore this lesson. Adam Verver's marriage to a younger woman was to square his daughter's marriage and his loss; it later permits an awakening on Maggie's part that could scarcely exclude tender care for him. But it is of course not sex that Adam is deprived of by his daughter's marriage to a prince and her giving birth to a Principino, but life; and life Charlotte cannot restore to him any more than Maggie can. The golden bowl that becomes the evidence of intimacy is also Adam's and everyman's life; breaking the bowl symbolizes not only putting an end to the kind of proof expected hitherto of novels but the inevitable unmaking of the triangles of generation

---

bold a statement in James's last completed novel, I suggest, is that "he peculiarly paternal, she passionately filial" was already a standard formula for the English courtship novel's plot (triangularly driven by the rule of male inheritance). Thus the donnée presented a challenge that James could not refuse, more especially when the mediation of the Charlotte character allowed him to double the triangle and the conventional definition of desire, as the love of father and son-in-law for the same woman. The geometry of the plot was both mythic and metacritical.

59. For this inescapable convention and its many contraventions, see Ruth Bernard Yeazell, *Fictions of Modesty: Women and Courtship in the English Novel* (Chicago: University of Chicago Press, 1991).

conventionally defended in English novels. The bowl breaks in three pieces, but when "under Amerigo's eyes she picked up the shining pieces," Maggie finds "that she could carry but two of the fragments at once" (4.10.182). The piece left on the floor has to be Adam's. Latterly the entire object was to have been Adam's, a birthday gift for the man who already has collected most of the other things in the world for his museum in American City; but the bowl will not be so collected. Quite without James's novel a golden bowl symbolizes life, because of the familiar lines of the preacher in the Bible: "or ever the silver cord be loosed, or the golden bowl be broken."[60] Again a rite of passage is enacted in *The Golden Bowl*, as at the end of most English novels. A birthday celebration that was to have been and a symbolic death of Adam Verver coincide with Maggie's initiation.

As in *The Ring and the Book*, death defines experience as well as the passing of generations. For death is also present in "the open bloom of the day" for the prince and Charlotte, when they seize their "bright minute" from grim Matcham. "So therefore while the minute lasted it passed between them that their cup was full; which cup their very eyes, holding it fast, carried and steadied and began, as they tasted it, to praise." James does not fail to connect this cup, which appears to come spontaneously to mind, with his bowl symbolism,[61] as the two friends prepare for their excursion to "Glo'ster, Glo'ster, Glo'ster":

> "We must see the old king; we must 'do' the cathedral," he said; "we must know all about it. If we could but take," he exhaled, "the full opportunity!" And then while, for all they seemed to give him, he sounded again her eyes: "I feel the day like a great gold cup that we must somehow drain together."
>
> "I feel it, as you know you always make me feel everything, just as you do; so that I know ten miles off how you feel! But do you remember,"

60. Ecclesiastes 12:5–7. "Also when they shall be afraid of that which is nigh and fears shall be in the way, and the almond tree shall flourish, and the grasshopper shall be a burden, and desire shall fail: because man goeth to his long home, and the mourners go about the streets: Or ever the silver cord be loosed, or the golden bowl be broken at the fountain, or the wheel broken at the cistern. Then shall the dust return to the earth as it was; and the spirit shall return unto God who gave it."

61. Matthiessen, *Henry James*, 83, may have been the first to wonder whether James had in mind Blake's lines in *The Book of Thel*, "Can wisdom be kept in a silver rod, / Or love in a golden bowl?" Obviously Blake's symbolism too is based on Ecclesiastes, while Thel's refusal of experience might have some inverse bearing on Maggie's triumphant coming of age. Cameron, *Thinking in Henry James*, 114–18 and 189, weighs Blake against Ecclesiastes as guides to interpreting James's golden bowl.

she asked, "apropos of great gold cups, the beautiful one, the real one, that I offered you so long ago and that you wouldn't have? Just before your marriage"—she brought it back to him: "the gilded crystal bowl in the little Bloomsbury shop."

Though Amerigo shuns this memory and hopes that the present occasion is not "cracked," Charlotte replies, "Don't you think too much of 'cracks' and aren't you too afraid of them? I risk the cracks" (3.9.356–59). That they are false to their trust and doubly bound to adultery that afternoon is wholly consistent with James's theme. Falsehood is never inconsistent with experience—as Maggie learns and Amerigo, as a man and a European, has known all along.[62] James showed in *The Golden Bowl* that unless protagonists as well as others were permitted to tell lies a novel could not really represent experience. That English novels for about 150 years were most often about some fact in issue and its truth or falsehood, he understood, prevented them from being about experience even when they tried—as *The Moonstone,* say, tried. In this last novel, he preached the lesson of the dramatic monologues that had profoundly influenced his modernism—the lesson that experience involves distortions of reality and only rarely shares the same ideal aim as the finding of a fact.

James nevertheless felt, with Browning, that art somehow reconciled truth and experience and fended against time. The writing of narrative, for one thing, is continuous with every other phase of experience, as the concluding paragraph of his preface to *The Golden Bowl* states—and all the prefaces to the New York Edition, remember, conclude rather than commence the arguments of the fiction:

> All of which amounts doubtless but to saying that as the whole conduct of life consists of things done, which do other things in their turn, just so our behaviour and its fruits are essentially one and continuous and persistent and unquenchable, so the act has its way of abiding and showing and testifying, and so, among our innumerable acts, are no arbitrary, no senseless separations. The more we are capable of acting the less gropingly we plead such differences; whereby, with any capability, we recognize betimes that to "put" things is very exactly and responsibly and interminably to do them. (xxiv)

---

62. Cf. Amerigo's thoughts at the time of his engagement: "He had noticed it before: it was the English, the American sign that duplicity, like 'love,' had to be joked about. It couldn't be 'gone into' " (1.1.15).

It can be seen that, with its Arnoldian stress on "conduct," this is a moral defense of narrative, while things "which do other things in their turn" are such as are usually accounted for by circumstantial evidence.[63]

But in the act of elaborating his claims for art and its relative permanence, James throws over the notion so popular with early Victorians and even with George Eliot—not to say with Freud—that all experience fits together and is potentially recoverable as evidence of the past. "Our literary deeds," he contends, do not altogether "lose themselves," though the vaster part of experience *is* lost. In life,

> We are condemned, in other words, whether we will or no, to abandon and outlive, to forget and disown and hand over to desolation, many vital or social performances—if only because the traces, records, connexions, the very memorials we would fain preserve, are practically impossible to rescue for that purpose from the general mixture. We give them up even when we wouldn't—it is not a question of choice.

One recalls Bob Assingham's contention that "people are always traceable, in England, when tracings are required," and Fanny's prompt objection that "this isn't murder." While it would be foolish to suggest that James had in mind Victorian authors of treatises on evidence, on the threshold of modernism he simply denies their major assumption that the needed facts can always be rescued, that the evidence always or ever suffices. Art turns away from preoccupation with strong representations; if traces are wanted, one's art is still "essentially traceable, and in that fact abides, we feel, the incomparable luxury of the artist" (xxv)—a luxury not afforded by life. Much like Browning, in short, James cast his lot with art.

In *The Golden Bowl,* however, James also challenged the conclusive aspect of literary realism. For about 150 years, in the English novel after Fielding, what the evidence proved was as important as the disparagement of testimony. A strong representation, it seems, fixes blame and therefore in the wider sense assures of freedom from blame. *The Golden Bowl* does not fix blame or provide that assurance, and critics who have most trouble with the last chapters may be reading them— just because of the novel's engagement with a conventional action— from too great anticipation of a usual representation to those effects.

---

63. On the last paragraph in James's preface, see J. Hillis Miller, *The Ethics of Reading: Kant, de Man, Eliot, Trollope, James, and Benjamin* (New York: Columbia University Press, 1987), 105–9.

James's novel is not so different, in this way, from Woolf's *Orlando* or Joyce's *Ulysses*; and in its entertainment and rejection of proof from circumstantial evidence, it is quite like Forster's *A Passage to India*. But no one even begins to study those works as strong representations.

Index

257

Index

Knights, L. C., 113n.
Knowlton, Hosea M., 2–6, 8, 18, 198

Langbaum, Robert, 103–4, 109, 116n.,
  198n.
Langbein, John H., 10n., 18, 19n., 24n.,
  33n., 47n.
Legge, Heneage, 29
Levack, Brian P., 20n.
Levin, Harry, 65n., 77n.
Levine, George, 17n., 65n., 181n.
Lidz, Theodore, 128n.
Life as a trial, 44–46, 54–55, 62, 91–93,
  169–70, 174, 199–200, 211
Locke, John, 12, 90–91, 103, 149; *Essay
  Concerning Human Understanding*, 13
Lonoff, Sue, 217n.
Lubbock, Percy, 236
Lukács, Georg, 77n.
Lyell, Charles, 181; *Principles of Geology*,
  155, 179–80, 183–84, 187, 193
Lyttleton, George, 56n.

Macaulay, Thomas Babington, 156n.
Mackensie, George, 21–22
McKeon, Michael, 54n., 77n.
McKillop, Alan Dugald, 96n.
Maine, Henry Sumner, 156
Maitland, Frederic William, 175n.
Malthus, Thomas, 182
Mansel, Henry, 216n.
Mansfield, William Murray, Lord, 21
Marx, Karl, 150
Mattes, Eleanor B., 190n.
Matthew, 20n.
Matthiessen, F. O., 240n., 251n., 253n.
Mayr, Ernst, 183n.
Mill, John Stuart, 36; *System of Logic*,
  158, 160, 177
Miller, D. A., 40n., 220n., 222n., 229n.,
  234n., 245n.
Miller, J. Hillis, 255n.
Millgate, Jane, 77n.
Modernism, 198–201, 254
Morgann, Maurice, 106–7, 129–30, 138,
  145, 179, 210, 240; *Essay on . . .
  Falstaff*, 104, 106–21, 122; *Plan for the
  Abolition of Slavery*, 106
Morris, Corbyn, 107
Motives, 6, 39, 75–76, 87, 137, 139–140,

205, 211; unconscious, 134–35, 142–43,
  145, 223–27, 231
Murder, 25, 147–48, 152–54, 159–65,
  170–74, 175, 177–78, 190–91, 201–2,
  213–14, 244–45

Nadel, Ira Bruce, 223n.
Natural history, 174, 179, 181–82
Natural religion, 13–14, 35, 40–41, 154,
  165–71, 172–74, 176–78, 181–82, 186–
  87, 188–90, 195
Natural selection, 41, 167, 181, 182
Nelson, William, 24n.
Newman, John Henry, 213n.
Newsom, Robert, 12n.
Novak, Maximillian E., 41
Novels, 6, 11, 17, 41–42, 48–49, 62–63,
  76, 126; of circumstances, 48, 88, 97,
  98–99; detective, 152, 174, 218–23;
  didactic, 93–94, 237; displacement in,
  94–98; historical, 77–78, 183; marriage
  plot, 250–52; property convention,
  200, 215, 231–36; proposal scenes,
  230–31; sensation, 215–16, 244
Nussbaum, Martha Craven, 246n.
Nuttall, A. D., 113

Oedipus complex, 137, 143, 145, 147–48,
  150
Omychund v. Barker, 33n.

Paleontology, 179–81
Paley, William, 24, 41; *Evidences of
  Christianity*, 166; *Horae Paulinae*, 166;
  *Principles of Moral and Political
  Philosophy*, 15–17
Pateman, Carole, 149n.
Patey, Douglas Lane, 12n., 55n., 70n.
Patriarchy, 90–93, 148–50
Pattison, Mark, 166
Paul, 7
Paulson, Ronald, 75n.
Pearson, Gabriel, 247n.
Peters, Edward, 10n.
Phillips, Samuel March, *Theory of
  Presumptive Proof*, 27–28
Playfair, John, 183n.
Pocock, J.G.A., 20n.
Point of view, 198, 201, 223, 236, 238,
  240, 245

260

Index

Index

Designed by Glen Burris
Set in Bembo by Capitol Communication Systems, Inc.
Printed on 50-lb. Glatfelter Supple Offset and bound in Holliston Aqualite cloth
by Princeton University Press